The Laws of Yesterday's Wars 3

International Humanitarian Law Series

VOLUME 67

The International Humanitarian Law Series is a series of monograhs and edited volumes which aims to promote scholarly analysis and discussion of both the theory and practice of the international legal regulation of armed conflict.

The series explores substantive issues of International Humanitarian Law, including:

- Protection for victims of armed conflict and regulation of the means and method of warfare
- Questions of application of the various legal regimes for the conduct of armed conflict
- Issues relating to the implementation of International Humanitarian Law obligations
- National and international approaches to the enforcement of the law and
- The interactions between International Humanitarian Law and other related areas of international law such as Human Rights, Refugee Law, Arms Control and Disarmament Law, and Intenational Criminal Law.

The titles published in this series are listed at *brill.com/ihul*

The Laws of Yesterday's Wars 3

From the Highlands of Papua New Guinea to the Island of Malta

Edited by

Samuel White

BRILL | NIJHOFF

LEIDEN | BOSTON

Cover illustration: Dani tribe men perform a mock tribal war in Walesi district in Wamena, Papua Province on August 8, 2016. The performances at the 27th Baliem valley festival, featuring highland tribes of Dani, Yali and Lani in their mock battles as symbol of high spirit and power that have been practised for generations, is held in Wamena on August 8–10. ADEK BERRY/AFP

Library of Congress Cataloging-in-Publication Data

Names: White, Samuel C. Duckett, editor.
Title: The laws of yesterday's wars 3 : from the highlands of Papua New Guinea to the Island of Malta / edited by Samuel C. Duckett White.
Other titles: Laws of yesterday's wars three
Description: Leiden ; Boston : Brill/Nijhoff, 2024. | Series: International humanitarian law series, 1389-6776 ; volume 67 | Includes index.
Identifiers: LCCN 2024006170 (print) | LCCN 2024006171 (ebook) | ISBN 9789004512559 (hardback) | ISBN 9789004512566 (ebook)
Subjects: LCSH: War (International law)–History. | War–History. | Humanitarian law. | Human rights.
Classification: LCC KZ6385 .L39 2024 (print) | LCC KZ6385 (ebook) | DDC 341.6–dc23/eng/20240209
LC record available at https://lccn.loc.gov/2024006170
LC ebook record available at https://lccn.loc.gov/2024006171

Typeface for the Latin, Greek, and Cyrillic scripts: "Brill". See and download: brill.com/brill-typeface.

ISSN 1389-6776
ISBN 978-90-04-51255-9 (hardback)
ISBN 978-90-04-51256-6 (e-book)
DOI 10.1163/9789004512566

Contents

Foreword

The unrelenting advance of technology, paired with unprecedented opportunities for exchanges between and clashes of cultures over the finite resources of a shrinking world sadly promise a dynamic, enduring, and destructive character for future warfare. Preventing and limiting the effects of war have never been more urgent humanitarian imperatives.

It is unsurprising, and perhaps even a little encouraging, that a flurry of efforts to regulate conflict more effectively has emerged from so many quarters. As much as, or perhaps more than, any preceding period, the present features a frenzy of forecasts and legal diagnoses for regulating future warfare. Military, diplomatic, academic, and humanitarian communities have all dedicated impressive human and financial resources to further control the conduct of hostilities. Military and diplomatic legal circles have worked to update legal doctrine to account for predictions of increasingly remote and pervasive warfare. Meanwhile, academic and humanitarian communities have probed existing doctrine for interpretive possibilities that lend greater protections to the civilians who will inevitably be swept up in it and will suffer most. Where these respective communities' predictions and prescriptions find common ground will no doubt influence and form the future laws of war.

While envisioning the future of warfare and generating palatable and effective regulations for it are commendable, whether ongoing efforts adequately account for past experience is also worth considering. The challenge of balancing military imperatives with humanitarian ideals has been at the heart of the law of war project since its earliest days. The past offers us instructive successes and failures at using law to regulate warfare. Across time, space, culture and religion, valuable lessons await those with the opportunity, patience, and skill to discern them.

In this third volume of the series *The Laws of Yesterday's Wars*, Dr Samuel White and his contributors expertly tackle precisely this task. Together with its preceding volumes, this volume offers an unrivalled survey of military, legal, and cultural experience with regulating the conduct of hostilities. Its chapters are highly informative of how an exceptionally wide range of cultures has (and has not) regulated warfare through law. They will certainly stand as lasting contributions in this respect, or as White has termed them a "wider dataset," in our shared field.

But these chapters are also highly relevant to sorting deeper and enduring assumptions behind the regulation of war. Readers will find themselves asking whether a truly universal war convention has ever been attainable in any wartime context. The similarities of restraints adopted by geographically and culturally distinct civilizations are striking. That so many different societies have formed somewhat similar war conventions lends the laws of war both a logical and intuitive appeal that surely strengthens its compliance pull. But even when regulatory parallels between otherwise disparate cultures can be found or when agreement between them has been secured, have these restraints on the conduct of hostilities actually survived the bitter test of human combat? What do frequent and even endorsed departures from ostensibly foundational restraints like the requirement to distinguish combatants from civilians portend for their alleged universality? Related, but perhaps on a deeper level, are such purportedly shared notions of humanity during war truly as universal as assumed? How should outlying war conventions register in a catalog of the world's war convention? Can a law of war project be conceived short of universality? Less drastically, though no less importantly, to what extent can culturally bound concepts like honor, spirituality, or loyalty be permitted to inform or even temper law of war obligations. And by what measures can international laws of war be judged fit for purpose if they are not actually or entirely international?

Conceptions of the law of war as an essentially international project have seemed to ripen in step with conceptions of an international community itself. When we speak of laws of war today, or perhaps more so of "international humanitarian law," we now mean to refer not to a municipal, local or parochial ruleset or code. We increasingly mean to convey notions of restraint that are shared as fundamental and universal to their agreed context, an essentially universalist convention. But, as White asks, how international is this most codified branch of international law and how international can it ever really be?

As well or better than any preceding text, this volume present readers, and it is hoped international legislators in whatever form the future finds them, new and valuable grist for this legal mill. We at the Lieber Institute for Law and Warfare and the U.S. Military Academy at West are grateful to White and his contributors for this ground-breaking study. It has been our distinct pleasure to feature its preceding volumes on our electronic publication *Articles of War*. We wish the best of luck to Dr White and his contributors in hoping that the laws of yesterday's wars and of the various cultures that developed them can produce a more effective law of tomorrow's wars.

Professor Sean Watts

Tool on African Traditions and the Preservation of Humanity during War

Sarah Mabeza and Tamalin Bolus

A critique often held is that international law and, in this case, specifically International Humanitarian Law (IHL) is based on western philosophies.[1] One could argue that given the universal nature of the principles enshrined in the Geneva Conventions, it encompasses ideals of traditions and customs which transcend borders. However, a more nuanced understanding of the development of IHL in Africa presents compelling reasons as to why this criticism is well founded. Reflecting on the negotiations of the Geneva Conventions and the lack of African state participation, provides one such reason as to why there is a lack of ownership over this important body of law.[2] Moreover as the status of African states in the international legal order changed alongside the development of contemporary IHL, many African states who had not benefitted from IHL during the fight for independence were now obligated to adhere to the same rules.[3]

As a means of better explaining the relevance and authority of IHL, the ICRC undertook to examine the historical relationship between Africa and IHL, as reflected in traditional customs. With the objective that the resulting research could contribute to current debates on the relevance of IHL to Africa and thereby increase the understanding and acceptance of IHL rules on the African continent. From the research conducted it became evident that established norms that regulated the conduct of hostilities existed in many African tribes and cultures. In addition, it became clear that these norms or practices had broad connections with the general rules of modern-day IHL. This could

1 Mutoy Mubiala, "International Humanitarian Law in the African Context", in Monica Kathina Juma and Astri Suhrke (eds), Eroding Local Capacity: International Humanitarian Action in Africa, Nordiska Afrikainstitutet, Upsala, 2002, p. 48.

2 To illustrate, all of the 12 countries that signed the 1864 Geneva Convention at the conclusion of its negotiation were European. See https://ihldatabases.icrc.org/applic/ihl/ihl.nsf/States.xsp?xp_viewStates=XPages_NORMStatesParties&xp_treatySelected=120 (accessed 09.01.2022). *For a more in depth discussion see* Gus Waschefort. "Africa and international humanitarian law: The more things change, the more they stay the same" above note 1, p. 593–624.

3 Gus Waschefort. "Africa and international humanitarian law: The more things change, the more they stay the same", above note 5, p.602–603.

be due to the fact that both IHL as well as African traditions have a basis in humanity – the principle of humanity underlies the body of IHL, and the principle of Ubuntu, which focuses on solidarity and interdependence, underlies African traditions.[4] This broad link identified by the research between African practices and IHL rules applicable today clarifies and confirms that the rules contained in modern IHL are not foreign concepts in Africa.

As the research provided some clarity into the norms of traditional African customs in war, it became important to conceptualize a means of showing the link between culture and law that would effectively contribute to current debates on relevance of IHL to Africa and to and increase understanding and acceptance of IHL rules on the African continent. The outcome was the production of the "Tool on African Traditions and the Preservation of Humanity during War", a resource with which to engage various audiences on the relationship between Africa and IHL.[5] The tool consists of 11 cards, highlighting firstly the African traditional custom in question, secondly the African tribes or cultures who have a history of practicing that traditional custom, and thirdly the related rule under modern-day IHL. The cards are available in various formats, including as playing cards, which can easily be shared with armed actors manning check points, for example. They are also available as post cards, which are useful in a pedagogical context, and finally in a poster format, so they can be showcased as part of a photo exhibit. The tool has also been adapted into additional formats which it is hoped will be beneficial in operational settings - these include a short video that can be used on social media but also shown by humanitarian actors to armed actors on a mobile device, as well as the inclusion of the Tool in a recently produced ICRC notebook for armed actors in the field. Additionally, the Tool has been translated into French and Portuguese, with the intention to translate into further languages in the future. Additional research has been conducted and the Tool will be updated with further examples in 2024.

The Tool by no means reflects a different set of IHL norms to be respected. It is clear that contemporary IHL, both treaty and customary, is the definitive set of rules applicable today. Indeed, the hope is that by providing these examples and exploring the development of IHL on the Africa continent, the Tool will rather illustrate how IHL is relevant, and perhaps garner greater respect for the law, thereby contributing towards the reduction of suffering during times

4 Mutoy Mubiala, "International Humanitarian Law in the African Context", above note 4, p. 37–39; Gus Waschefort, "Africa and international humanitarian law: The more things change, the more they stay the same" above note 5, p. 597.

5 https://www.icrc.org/en/document/african-customs-tool-traditional-customs-and-ihl.

of armed conflict, which remains the ICRC's ultimate goal. The ICRC believes there to be a clear correlation between IHL and African practices and norms, and therefore hopes that it has produced a useful and helpful Tool. It must however be noted that there are a number of questions related to the research that remain unanswered, and that will hopefully be addressed as the research continues. Some of these questions are as follows:

- Is it sufficiently convincing that by merely demonstrating the links between culture and law is an effective means of generating increased respect for the law? Does knowledge of such traditional norms actually contribute towards achieving the objectives of IHL? Does respect and implementation of IHL rules depend on such a clear correlation between the applicable rule and local customs?
- Will the outcomes of this research actually contribute to mainstreaming IHL in Africa?
- What do these examples illustrate on how wars were fought in pre-colonial Africa? Is there a link with how Africa engages in IHL today?

We hope to address some of these questions and offer reflections on the use of the Tool in the upcoming Volume 4 of *The Laws of Yesterday's Wars*.

Acknowledgements

Like anything, these works do not just occur in isolation; thanks are required to the multiple individuals and teams that worked on the project.

To the contributors who saw the goal of the project, and who saw it through – thank you.

To Professor Tim McCormack and the Brill team, who assisted with the entire publishing process, and to Ms Helen Jeffcoat, who compiled the index – thank you.

To the University of Adelaide, that has financially sponsored Volume 3 through a Postdoctoral Research Fellowship – thank you.

Finally, and most importantly, to my wife & daughters (one of whom arrived during the gap between Volume 2 and 3!) thank you for making it all worth it.

Maps

Contributors

Editor

Samuel White
is a Postdoctoral Research Fellow at the University of Adelaide, Adjunct Associate Professor at the University of New England, and Visiting Fellow at the Australian Defence Force Academy. Samuel has served as both a Royal Australian Infantry Corps and an Australian Army Legal Corps officer in a variety of tactical, operational and strategic level postings, working across a range grey zone, intelligence and cyber operations. In 2018, he served as Associate to the Honourable Justice John Logan of the Federal Court of Australia, Supreme & National Courts of Papua New Guinea, and President of the Defence Force Discipline Appeals Tribunal. From this experience, Samuel has had a distinct focus on comparative legal history and post-colonial legal experiences. He is admitted to practice as a Solicitor in the State of Queensland and before the High Court of Australia; as well as a Barrister and Solicitor in New Zealand.

Contributors

Shadeen Ali
holds a Bachelor of Laws and a Bachelor of Health and Medical Sciences from the University of Adelaide. She has a keen interest in international law and the Law of Armed Conflict, working as a Research Assistant addressing Eurocentricity within international law, as well as at a legal aid office in South Africa, regarding refugee and immigration law, policy and practice. She is of Eritrean background and has applied some of her own translations to her work.

Justin Monyping Ater
is a law lecturer at the School of Law, University of Juba and an Advocate before all courts of law in South Sudan. He is the founding Managing Partner of Advanced Attorneys & Legal Consultants, a premier legal firm based in South Sudan. He holds an LLM from the Centre for Human Rights, Faculty of Law, University of Pretoria and LLB (Hons) from the School of Law University of Juba. His research interests are in the areas of human rights law and international humanitarian law. While a student, Justin participated in various International Humanitarian Law Competitions. He participated in the first South Sudan national moot competition where he was the best national oralist. He further

participated in the All-Africa IHL moot court competition in Arusha where he was also nominated among top three best oralists. Additionally, Justin had the best country paper in the 2019 Eastern Africa IHL competition. he could be reached on monypingjustin@gmail.com/+211928117812.

Marco Chol Ayat
is South Sudanese lawyer, a legal advisor at the International Committee of the Red Cross at South Sudan delegation. He hold a master degree in international Humanitarian Affairs from the University of York, UK; a Human Rights and IHL Post-Graduate from the University of Khartoum, and a Bachelor of Laws from University of Khartoum. Marco has a significant transactional experience in law career, ranging from law practice as an advocate in both Sudan and South Sudan, shifting to international law with focus on IHL. As a legal advisor at ICRC, Marco has extensive experience in the national implementation of IHL. For almost a decade, Marco is closely in charge of organizing and conducting the following IHL activities; thematic discussion, public lecture, teachers training, students moot court, essay competition, providing expert opinion and blogs writing. As an ICRC legal advisor, Marco has experience of conducting IHL activities in South Sudan and in different African contexts.

Samara J. Cassar
is an Australian qualified solicitor and a member of the International Arbitration practice at White & Case in Singapore. Prior to her move to Singapore, Samara worked at an international law firm in Brisbane, Australia. Samara has completed a Secondment with the Public Interest Advocacy Centre, and sat on the Board for the Australian Conservation Foundation, as the representative for Queensland. Samara has a keen interest in international law and social justice. She holds a Bachelor of Laws (with First Class Honours) and a Bachelor of International Relations and Peace & Conflict Studies from the University of Queensland. Samara has co-authored several publications, and served as the Assistant Editor for the Australian Journal of International Law and the Journal of International Humanitarian Legal Studies.

Emily Defina
is a Legal Officer at the Office of International Law, Attorney-General's Department. She is a former Legal Adviser for the International Committee of the Red Cross Regional Delegation in the Pacific, based in the Canberra Mission. Emily attained a Bachelor of Laws (Hons I) and a Bachelor of Arts (Distinction) from the University of New South Wales, where she completed her honours thesis in International Humanitarian Law.

Angeline Lewis
is a Senior Legal Officer in the Australian Defence Force. She has completed doctoral research in law and history, focussing on different themes concerning the relationship between ideas of security, power, legitimacy and the rule of law. Her history thesis, titled "Rajah Brooke and the 'Pirates' of Borneo: A Nineteenth Century Public Debate on Sea Power" was awarded the University of New South Wales Dean's Prize for outstanding PhD research, and the Ria de Groot Prize for best results for a female postgraduate student, in 2019. Her publications also include work on individual conscience in international law; air power in the rules-based global order; law of the sea; emerging technologies in the law of armed conflict; and women, peace and security. Dr Lewis previously taught international and security law part-time at the Australian National University College of Law, and was the inaugural Minister for Defence Fellow in Women, Peace and Security at the University of New South Wales (2018–19).

Sanoj Rajan
is currently serving as a Distinguished Professor of Law at Zhejiang Gongshang University in Hangzhou, China. Professor Rajan maintains additional affiliations with several esteemed institutions. He serves as a Visiting Professor at the Indian Society of International Law, Al-Farabi Kazakh National University in Almaty, and the International Christian University in Kinshasa, Congo. With a broad range of publications to his name, Professor Rajan's contributions span books, research articles in peer-reviewed journals, book reviews, and op-eds. His latest book, titled "International Humanitarian Law in India: A Handbook", is published by Thomson Reuters, Asia Pacific, and is a comprehensive resource with 2190 pages (ISBN 978-93-90529-04-9). In addition to his contributions as an author, Professor Rajan is a member of the Editorial Board of the Indian Society of International Law's Yearbook of International Humanitarian Law and Refugee Law. He also peer reviews the ICRC Commentaries to the Geneva Convention and the Statelessness and Citizenship Review, which is published by Melbourne University. A recipient of the Commonwealth Scholarship, Professor Rajan's academic qualifications includes a PhD, an LLM in International Law, and an MSt. in Human Rights from Oxford University.

Sheena Sivadasan
is an experienced history academic, focusing predominantly on Indian history, with a particular emphasis on Kerala history. Currently, she teaches history at LVHS Pothencode, India. She has earned both her Bachelor's and Master's degrees in History from the University of Kerala. Her academic pursuits have led her to explore the intricate interplay of cultural, political, and social aspects

of Indian history. Beyond the classroom, Sheena is actively engaged with the broader academic community. She regularly partakes in interdisciplinary scholarly endeavours and collaborates with fellow scholars. Her research and writings centre predominantly on the history of Kerala. She exhibits a keen interest in examining the impacts of historical milestones on ancient and contemporary Kerala society.

Tatiana Tairova-Yakovleva
is the Gerda Henkel Stiftung Fellow and an Independent Researcher. During 2004–2022 she was the Director of the Center for the Ukrainian Studies in St. Petersburg State University and Professor of Ukrainian History at St. Petersburg State University. Her main focus in the history of the Ukraine and Polish-Lithuanian Commonwealth in the Early Modern period (16–18 centuries). Particularly she is dealing with different aspects of the Cossack`s Hetmanate, including military events, politics and culture, as well as Ukrainian-Russian relations. She is the author of 16 monographs and over 150 articles. She is also involved in the academic publications of the archival sources.

Ruben S P Valfredo
is a former lecturer at the School of Law, University of Juba in South Sudan. He holds a Master of Laws Degree in Public International Law from the University of Leicester in the United Kingdom; and a Bachelor of Laws Degree (Honours) from the University of Khartoum in the Sudan. During his tenure as a lecturer at the School of Law, University of Juba, he taught International Humanitarian Law, and facilitated the internal rounds of the School's International Humanitarian Law Moot Court Competition and coached and mentored the School's team which participated at the All Africa International Humanitarian Law Moot Court Competition in Arusha, Tanzania. He was also engaged by the International Committee of the Red Cross Delegation in South Sudan, as an independent consultant for the collection and study of national practice of International Humanitarian Law in South Sudan. He also attended and participated in trainings and conferences for lectures and researchers of International Humanitarian Law in the East Africa region held in Nairobi, Kenya and Addis Ababa, Ethiopia. The views and opinions expressed in this chapter are entirely personal and private and do not reflect the views of the entities mentioned herein.

Introduction

These Volumes find their origin in a rather odd place. On one rather unexceptional evening, I was watching the HBO show, *Vikings*. The eponymously named show follows the mythic origins of Scandinavian raiders, who as they expand to find new land and new resources, come up against 'civilised' European society. For the most part, these Scandinavian men and women maintain their culture of warbands, raiding and looting. Yet, some do not – Rollo becomes a Francophile, adopting the culture and the warfighting of the Franks in return for land and titles. This is all to say that after a few seasons of slowly less and less violence, by the time we come across a scene where a warband of Vikings defile and destroy a small French homestead, we are reminded of the brutality of the times. Outraged that these raiders would do such a thing to some innocent peasants, I said to myself 'surely that was a war crime even under Viking law.'

This book started in trying to address that question – which I did not even answer (Andrew Butler did).[1] Yet it catalysed a wider research question of: how international is international humanitarian law? The answer can be found in *The Laws of Yesterday's Wars: From Indigenous Australians to the American Civil War*[2] and *The Laws of Yesterday's Wars: Ancient India to East Africa.*[3] The question remains the same with this Volume, and successive works to follow. Whilst in many ways whist the primary question remains the same, secondary research questions have begun to evolve.

Evidently, the concept of 'law' will change from culture to culture. In some cultures, it was codified; in others, it is found only in certain usages, customs, traditions, and the like. In this Volume, Dr Angeline Lewis makes this point repeatedly in her work on *adat,* highlighting the risk in trying to find equivalents with 'law' when writing on the Iban (being a concept that 'is considerably broader and spiritually deeper than its traditional translation as customary law').[4] So too do Dr Sanoj Rajan and Sheena Sivadasan highlight how the martial art of *kalarippayattu* cannot simply be viewed as law. It is an

1 Andrew Butler, 'Viking Laws of War' in Samuel White (ed.) *The Laws of Yesterday's Wars* (Brill Nijhoff, 2021) 150–171.

2 (Brill Nijhoff, 2021).

3 (Brill Nijhoff, 2022).

4 Angeline Lewis, 'Iban Laws of War' in Samuel White (ed.) *The Laws of Yesterday's Wars: Volume III* (Brill Nijhoff, 2024).

 | DOI:10.1163/9789004512566_002

> old martial art embodying Kerala's cultural, myth-historic heritage, a traditional psycho-physiological discipline cultivating mental, physical, and spiritual benefits, practical fighting art a system of physical training beneficial to athletes, dancers, and actors.[5]

So when we say 'law' here, the concept is much more nuanced. Equally, the concept of 'war' is a culturally unique – the Mongols had no words for peace or war, only of domination and submission to the Empire-in-the-Making. First Nation Australians had a similar spectrum of competition, and developed similar checks-and-balances. There is just one slight difference: the Mongols killed all that were not useful, whilst First Nation Australians had a complete taboo on blood in formal battles.

These Volumes have also highlighted that the terminology of war is perhaps misleading. War, as a concept, is difficult to define. Perhaps it cannot be. Any complex idea such as war has multiple pasts, and it is the role of the legal historian to show the paths taken to our modern understandings. Friedrich Nietzsche originated this form of conceptual genealogy in his *On the Genealogy of Morality,* where he held that:

> anything in existence, having somehow come about, is continually interpreted anew, requisitioned anew, transformed and redirected to a new purpose by a power superior to it.[6]

More simply, only something which has *no* history can possibly be defined. War, being a fundamentally political concept, must be seen within its historical construct. Shadeen Ali highlights this through her expert and nuanced analysis of the Ottoman approach to the world – based on Mongol-Turkic *yasa* (the so-called ancient customs *adet-i qadime*), refined by Islamic law. It is due to its historical basis that its employment successfully constitutes a generative metaphor.[7]

That logical starting point for war's intellectual genealogical journey is Rome – not simply because the laws of war have within international law a Latin etymology (*jus in bello; jus ad bellum*) but because the binary nature of

5 Ian McDonald, 'Bodily Practice, Performance Art, Competitive Sports: A Critique of Kalarippayattu, the Martial Art of Kerala,' *Contribution to Indian Sociology* 41, no. 2 (May 2007), 143–168.

6 (1887, republished Penguin 2007) 44.

7 Julia Slupska, 'War, Health & Ecosystem: Generative Metaphors' (2020) 42(1) *Philosophy & Technology* 27–57.

the international legal paradigms of war and peace have Roman foundations. Augustus Caesar boasted that on three occasions during his reign he closed the doors of the Temple of Janus, God of Two Faces.[8] Closing the doors demonstrated that there were no declared wars within the Empire, against recognised enemies.[9] This concept of declared war flowed into 'just war' theory in the Medieval and Renaissance periods before shaping modern conceptions of international humanitarian law. Jean-Jacques Rousseau, in his *Social Contract,* perhaps offers the best example of this school of thought:

> War is … not a relationship between one man and another, but a relation between one State and another … any State can only have other States, and not men, as enemies.[10]

This definition somehow sweepingly omits the idea of private war – either within Japan,[11] or Medieval Europe.[12] Rousseau's narrow European approach was narrowed further by Lassa Oppenheim, with respect to which organ of the State conducted war:

> War is a contention between two or more States *through their armed forces*, for the purpose of overpowering each other and imposing such conditions as the victor pleases.[13]

Very Clausewitzian. The flaws with these arguments jump out at any reader – war can be fought outside of armed forces (in the nomadic culture of the Mongols, there was no such concept of a warrior – all were able to fight); and exist outside the framework of a State. Cultures and nation states engaged in many levels of armed conflict throughout the millennia which did not meet the thresholds of European war: such as the wars for resource control in

---

8 Samuel White, 'Roman Laws of War' in Samuel White (ed.) *Laws of Yesterday's Wars Volume 2* (Brill Nijhoff, 2022) 110–126.

9 Ibid – this went to the core of the concept of *hostius juris* – of which pirates were not included. See Andrew Read, 'Pirates and Privateers' in Samuel White (ed.) *Laws of Yesterday's Wars Volume* (Brill Nijhoff, 2021) 171–187.

10 *The Social Contract* (1762, Penguin Publishing 1998) 22.

11 Anna Kretowicz, 'Japanese Laws of War' in Samuel White (ed.) *The Laws of Yesterday's Wars Volume II* (Brill Nijhoff, 2022) 183–214.

12 Samuel White 'The Late Middle Ages' in Samuel White (ed.) *Laws of Yesterday's Wars* (Brill Nijhoff, 2021) 101–127.

13 *International Law: A treaties II* (Longman, Green & CO, 1906) 56; emphasis added.

pre-colonial Australia,[14] the silent wars of ancient India,[15] the covert wars of Sun Tzu,[16] the Flowery Wars of the Mexica,[17] the private warfare of Japan,[18] or the blood wars of North-Eastern Native Americans.[19] This Volume introduces the head-hunting of the Iban; the Keralite tradition of *ankam* (duel) by trained professionals; the inter-communal violence of Highland Papua New Guinea; and the 'domestic' peacekeeping operations of an ever-expanded Mongol Empire. All are expressions of imposing one's will on an enemy; all are the continuation of politics by other means. All fall under the ambit of the laws of war, even if they do not constitute 'war' in the Roman sense or 'law' in a Eurocentric meaning.

This is all to say that the scope of this series is one that is simplified when it is labelled the *Laws of Yesterday's Wars.* In many ways, to be accurate, the series should be:

> The Laws, Usages, Customs and Traditions of Warfare Prior to the Geneva Conventions relating to cultural understandings of conflict resolution and violence mitigation

It doesn't have the same punchiness, so for now we stick with *The Laws of Yesterday's Wars.* Rest assured, however, it is done in a culturally safe manner and through the lens of ensuring respect.

It is an important concept to expand on. Common Article 1 (CA1) of the *Geneva Conventions* reads:

> The High Contracting Parties undertake to respect and to ensure respect for the present Convention in all circumstances.

This provision was reiterated in Article 1(4) of Additional Protocol I. As such, the obligation to respect and ensure respect applies to international conflicts

14 Ray Kerkhove & Samuel White, 'Indigenous Australian Laws of War' in Samuel White (ed.) *The Laws of Yesterday's Wars* 3–44.

15 Zuzana Spicova, 'Ancient Indian Laws of War' in Samuel White (ed.) *The Laws of Yesterday's Wars Volume 2* (Brill Nijhoff, 2022) 5–45.

16 Sun Tzu, *The Art of War* (Penguin, 2008).

17 Samuel White & Ray Kerkhove, 'The Aztecs' in Samuel White (ed.) *Laws of Yesterday's Wars Volume* (Brill Nijhoff, 2021) 69–101.

18 Anna Kretowicz, 'Japanese Laws of War' in Samuel White (ed.) *The Laws of Yesterday's Wars Volume II* (Brill Nijhoff, 2022) 183–214.

19 Wayne E. Lee, 'Eastern Native American Laws of War' in Samuel White (ed.) *The Laws of Yesterday's Wars Volume II* (Brill Nijhoff, 2022) 146–183.

and, indeed, to non-international conflicts to the extent that the latter are covered by Common Article 3. While conflicts of a non-international character as defined by Additional Protocol II are not explicitly covered by the obligation to respect and to ensure respect, they can nonetheless be considered as indirectly falling within the purview of the provision, insofar as Protocol II is merely an elaboration of Common Article 3 of the four Geneva Conventions, a fact stated in its Article 1(1).

It is a rather vexing concept: does CA1 have a purely internal role? Most likely not.[20] Does it have an element of externality? Logically so, but remains a questioned proposition. To what extent does CA1 provide a legal authority for State action? It is uncertain but likely not to the extent of authorising force.[21] Are non-State actors bound by it? To the extent that the *Geneva Conventions* and their Additional Protocols apply to non-State actors.[22] Should individuals ensure respect for IHL? A basic *Vienna Convention on the Law of Treaties* analysis highlights that the obligations apply only to States; that is, High Contracting Parties. At first instance then, lawyers neither have a duty nor obligation as individuals to try promulgate and ensure respect for the laws of war.

Yet it is widely accepted that the single most important challenge to the laws of war is a lack of respect for it.[23] As practitioners of international law, I believe that there is a moral (if not strict legal) duty to ensure respect. In *Nicaragua*, the International Court of Justice held that the duty to respect and ensure respect did not derive only from the Geneva Conventions, but "from the general principles of humanitarian law to which the Conventions merely give specific expression".[24] Again, the Trial Chamber of the International Criminal Tribunal for the former Yugoslavia stated in its judgments in *Furundžija*[25] and *Kupreškić*[26] that the norms of the laws of war were norms *erga omnes*. All States therefore had a "legal interest" in their observance and consequently a legal entitlement to demand their respect.[27]

20 Eve Massingham and Annabel McConnachie, 'Common Article 1 – An Introduction' in Eve Massingham and Annabel McConnachie (eds) *Ensuring Respect for International Humanitarian Law* (Routledge, 2020) 3.

21 Ibid, 7.

22 Catherine Drummond, 'Ensuring respect for IHL by, and in relation to the conduct of, private actors' in Eve Massingham and Annabel McConnachie (eds) *Ensuring Respect for International Humanitarian Law* (Routledge, 2020) 51.

23 International Committee of the Red Cross, *Challenges Report* (2019) 55.

24 *Military and Paramilitary Activities in and Against Nicaragua* (*Nicaragua v United States of America*) (Merits) (1986) ICJ Rep 14.

25 (IT-95-17/1).

26 (IT-95-16).

27 *Furundžija* (n 25), Judgment (*ibid.*, § 47) and *Kupreškić* (n 26), Judgment (*ibid.*, § 48).

The concept of ensuring respect has been analogous to 'a ripening fruit that has emerged from a tiny seed'[28] and I see no reason why it cannot be expanded to the organs of a State – which include its lawyers – as being bound by the need to ensure respect. To that end, seeking to understand the golden thread that runs between cultures – separated geographically and temporally – in their customs and laws of war that seek to control the violence of war goes to the heart of ensuring respect.

If a logical *expansion* of the duty to ensure respect is viewed as weak however, there is clearer *lex lata* support in the *Rome Statute*. Amongst the jurisdictional limbs of the International Criminal Court lies that of war crimes.[29] Article 8 of the *Rome Statute* outlines four categories of war crimes:

a) Grave breaches of the *Geneva Conventions*
b) Other serious violations of the *laws of war and customs* applicable in international armed conflict
c) Serious violations of Common Article 3
d) Other serious violations of the *laws and customs* applicable in armed conflict not of an international character.

Whilst the Rome Statute provides useful examples within the above limbs, it is not a definitive list. As Volume 1 demonstrated with respect to the colloquially called 'Lieber Code',[30] the partial codification of the laws of war (being the Laws of Geneva and the Laws of the Hague) and customs of war has placed a particular importance on the undefined latter.[31] Customary international law relies upon State practice (*usus*) and a believe that such a practice is required, prohibited or allowed as a matter of law (*opinio juris*). The approach taken in this study to determine whether a rule of general customary international law exists is a classic one, set out by the International Court of Justice in a number of cases, in particular in the *North Sea Continental Shelf*.[32]

28 Frits Kalshoven, 'The Undertaking to Respect and Ensure Respect in All Circumstances: From Tiny Seed to Ripening Fruit' (1999) 2 *Yearbook of International Humanitarian Law*, 2, 3–61.
29 Article 5 (c).
30 Christopher Bailey, 'Code of Necessity – Lawfare During the United States Civil War' in Samuel White (ed.) *The Laws of Yesterday's Wars* (Brill Njihoff, 2021) 187–209.
31 The divide being one of Jean Pictet, "Humanitarian Ideas Shared by Different Schools of Thought and Cultural Traditions", in Jean Pictet (ed.) *International Dimensions of Humanitarian Law* (Henry Dunant Institute, M. Nijhoff, 1988) 3, 4; see further Knut Dörmann, *Elements of War Crimes under the Rome Statute of the International Criminal Court: Sources and Commentary* (Cambridge University Press, 2003).
32 ICJ, *Continental Shelf case (Libyan Arab Jamahiriya v. Malta)*, Judgment, 3 June 1985, *ICJ Reports* 1985, pp. 29–30, § 27.

The use of the 'customs of war' provides a gate through which non-codified laws of war are incorporated. Yet no study exists that definitively outlines these customs throughout history: the ICRC's work only looks to modern warfare (being from the 1970s-2000s).[33] It is therefore limited and bound by international treaties, which have shaped and reflected Eurocentric concepts of just war and non-combatant status. It does not go to the heart of human societies, isolated geographically and temporally. This Volume introduces two extensive, qualitative studies in the Highlands of Papua New Guinea, and across the communities of South Sudan. Further studies are required in order to distil them, in order to ensuring respect for international humanitarian law. There are additional Volumes of this work that are planned for the near future, and it is hoped that each Volume adds to the breadth and depth of analysis that can occur in this field.

Finally, lest it be unsaid and notwithstanding that this is a work of legal history rather than legal analysis, contribution reflect individual views and perspectives. Indeed, the difference between writing on legal history, rather than a legal brief, is that one actually looks forward to having errors pointed out.

Samuel Camden Duckett White

33 Jean-Marie Henckaerts & Louise Doswald-Beck, *Customary International Humanitarian Law Study* (International Committee of the Red Cross, 2003).

CHAPTER 1

Highland Papua New Guinea Laws of War

Emily Defina

1 Introduction

In July 2019, tribal fighters killed at least ten women, including two who were pregnant, and six children in Karida, Hela province. In late January 2021, a land dispute between two relatives in Papua New Guinea's Hela province turned deadly. Twenty-one were reported to be killed, including two teenage girls and their mother. Some of the victims were beheaded and had their limbs hacked off.

Such massacres are a disturbing recurrence in the highlands of Papua New Guinea. Whilst violent disputes in the highlands are by no means a recent phenomenon, concern is being expressed over the seemingly new tactics of targeting of women, children, medical personnel, aid posts and schools.[1] Yet such warfare is not new; it is an old form of conflict resolution that has corresponding cultural parameters. However, with colonisation and globalisation impacting on traditional life, "our traditional law has been forgotten and now we kill women and children like wild pigs," one man told staff from the International Committee of the Red Cross (ICRC) in a village in Hela's Komo district.[2]

This Chapter seeks to address the understudied area of Highland Papua New Guinean laws of war. It first touches upon the means and methods of warfare in the Highlands, in order to place cultural restrictions within cultural contexts. The Chapter then turns to addressing the key cultural prohibitions on Highland warfare during times of communal fighting, in both the recent era and according to accounts of past practice. Three sets of data will be used. The sources chosen span both more historic custom and modern day practice. Firstly, custom collected from the Papua New Guinea highlands by University of the South Pacific students for an ICRC-led project to map traditional

---

1 Jonathan Pineault, 'Bring Highland Killers in Papua New Guinea to Justice: Provincial, National Authorities Have a Responsibility to Protect Public' *Human Rights Watch* (7 March 2021) <https://www.hrw.org/news/2021/03/07/bring-highland-killers-papua-new-guinea-justice>.

2 ICRC, 'The Old Ways are Gone: Papua New Guinea's Tribal Wars Become More Destructive' *Humanitarian Law & Policy Blog* via *Medium* (22 June 2017).

 | DOI:10.1163/9789004512566_003

pre-colonial warfare practices in the Pacific and their possible similarities with contemporary principles of humanitarian law.[3] Secondly, academic research focussing on case studies of tribal fighting in the highlands, some relating to the pre-colonial era and some to the contemporary post-colonial period. Thirdly, the backbone of the data is provided by a set of interview responses to questions posed by ICRC field staff to 16 communities in the highlands with recent involvement in tribal fighting. The communities were located in the three bordering provinces of Hela, Enga and the Southern Highlands. Where possible, both sides of a conflict were surveyed in these interviews. Separate focus group discussions were carried out with different sections of the community, typically one with leaders and older men, one with fighters and another with women. In some cases, children or church leaders were also interviewed. Open questions were used and rephrased as necessary in the interviews. This accommodated the discursive conversational style of community members and allowed for unanticipated responses. In total, 17 days of group interviews were held with 158 male and 92 female participants between June 2019 and February 2020. The names of the villages, tribes and clans have been removed in this paper to preserve confidentiality.

2 Means & Methods

Papua New Guinea is arguably the most socially and linguistically diverse country in the world, with over 800 languages – not dialects – spoken.[4] With such a rich diversity and distinctive cultures, it is unsurprising perhaps that, for many people, allegiance to tribes, clans and sub-clans remains significantly stronger than loyalty to abstract concepts of nation and citizenship.[5] Any analysis of culture in Papua New Guinea must therefore be caveated with the acknowledgement that as a heterogeneous collection of many cultures, generalisations cannot capture the breadth and depth of custom and practice. Some recurring characteristics will be highlighted in this paper, however practices may well differ from one community to its neighbour, as well as over time.

3 ICRC, *Under the Protection of the Palm: Wars of Dignity in the Pacific* (ICRC, 2009).

4 Prime Minister Michael Somare, (State at the World Leaders Forum, Colombia University, New York, 21 September 2006).

5 Sinclair Dinnen and Edwina Thompson, 'Gender and Small Arms Violence in Papua New Guinea' (2004) 8 *State, Society and Governance in Melanesia Project,* Australian National University discussion paper 1.

This also makes addressing particular means and methods of warfare difficult. In 2021, the ICRC estimated that approximately 30,000 people were displaced by communal violence in Papua New Guinea's Enga, Hela and Southern highlands provinces.[6] Intercommunal fighting has a long tradition in the highlands, however the nature of the fighting has changed and become increasingly lethal over the past several decades.[7] Young men, rather than elders, appear to be increasingly making unilateral decisions to initiate fights, without broader community input, and the introduction of modern weaponry and mobile phones has changed the battlefield.[8]

Traditional spears, bows and arrows are less lethal than today's weaponry. Modern firearms are often provided by influential "big men"[9] and have become available on the internal black market, when not stolen or leaked from the police and defence force.[10] The range of weapons now used includes automatic and semi-automatic rifles such as M16s, AR15s, and SLRs (Self-Loading Rifles), grenades, as well as steel machetes.[11] Whereas previously communication on the battlefield was primarily verbal, or through bodily gestures and smoke signals, the spread of mobile phones has become a tool to organise fighters more effectively.[12] This has added to causalities and geographically broadened the battlefield area, making it easier to set up ambushes and facilitating fighter mobility.[13] This includes taking the fight to neutral grounds such as Port Moresby or other urban centres in the country.

At the peak of fighting across Hela, Enga and the Southern Highlands in 2021, an estimated 30,000 people were displaced and taking refuge in neighbouring

---

6 Andrew Kobylinski, 'Forgotten Conflicts 2022: Tribal Violence in Papua New Guinea', *Australian Institute of International Affairs* (14 March 2022) <https://www.internationalaffairs.org.au/australianoutlook/forgotten-conflicts-tribal-violence-papua-new-guinea/>.

7 Ibid, see also Dinnen and Thompson, above n 15, and Fraser Macdonald and Jonathan Kirami, 'Women, Mobile phones, and M16s: Contemporary New Guinea Highlands Warfare' (2017) 28(1) *The Australian Journal of Anthropology* 104.

8 Macdonald and Kirami, above n 17.

9 A big man is a highly influential individual who may not have formal tribal or other authority, but can maintain recognition through skilled persuasion and wisdom. The big man has a large group of followers, who can be both from his clan and from other clans. He provides his followers with protection and economic assistance, in return receiving support which he uses to increase his status.

10 Macdonald and Kirami, above n 17, 109.

11 Ibid.

12 Ibid, 107. "Once the fighting is underway, text messages and calls continue to be made back and forth between these allied groups, relaying information concerning ammunition supplies, injuries, enemy positions, required support, and so forth" 113.

13 Ibid.

villages and in the forest.[14] Furthermore, intensity of the violence can also indicated by the ubiquitous use of high powered weapons such as semi-automatic firearms, and including in 2021, the reported use of a hand grenade to kill seven people in Kainantu Town in Eastern Highlands Province.[15]

On the other hand, the number of fighters and casualties involved in the fighting is on the comparatively low end of the scale. Casualties in the highlands are difficult to estimate due to lack of data. As noted, fatalities do include a series of gruesome massacres such as the 19 dead in the Hela Province in 2021 and the notorious 2019 Karida massacre of 24 people, both of which included women and children.[16] However, even these numbers are lower relative to those seen in armed conflicts taking place in other parts of the world. Although numbers of fighters are similarly difficult to estimate, by most accounts they are on a relatively small scale that would not indicate satisfaction of the intensity threshold. For example, several of the communities interviewed by ICRC in 2019–2020 estimated that they had between 30 and 60 fighters in their recent fights and the highest estimate given by one community reported 150 fighters in their 2018 fight.

Probably the crucial factor weighing against an organised armed group in the highlands is the lack of an ability to speak with one voice.[17] The various fights are conducted by different people, for different motives. Some violence is sparked by land disputes or by disagreements over women or resources, others are more political in nature, including election violence. There is no one common cause. They are all individual disputes for very localised reasons. The recent ICRC interviews showed that the various groups generally demonstrated an ability to negotiate and conclude peace agreements and compensation arrangements. Initial smaller *bel kol* compensation payments can be used to symbolically conclude fighting and larger payments, gathered over the course of years restore the relationships between communities and are intended to compensate for deaths.[18] However, such arrangements are usually made with the assistance of the wider community which is not involved and does not necessarily support the fighting, detracting from the degree of cohesion of the

14 Rebecca Kuku, 'Tribal conflict worsens in Papua New Guinea as firearms rewrite the rules' *The Guardian* (27 February 2021).

15 Kobylinski, above n 16; Rebecca Kuku, 'Police warn of 'all-out war' as tribal violence in Papua New Guinea kills 19' *The Guardian* (12 April 2021).

16 Leanne Jorari, 'PNG: Mistaking Massacres for Tradition' *The Interpreter* (9 February 2021).

17 *Prosecutor v Boškoski & Tarčulovski (Judgement)* (International Criminal Tribunal for the Former Yugoslavia, Trial Chamber II, Case No IT-04-82-T, 10 July 2008, [203].

18 Responses to 2019–2020 interviews with ICRC.

fighters from an 'organisation' perspective. Furthermore, whilst smaller groups may be able to 'speak with one voice', there is no suggestion of a highlands-wide group all fighting for one cause.

Most fights in the highlands do show the exercise of a commanding hierarchy, even though this is not always formalised – unsurprisingly for community-based groups. Disputes in the highlands often have an "owner of the fight" with whom the grievance or source of conflict is identified. However, this person is not necessarily the leader of fighters. In the survey by the ICRC in 2019–2021, of the sixteen communities surveyed, eleven described their fighters being led by either a 'commander' or 'planner', another three identified a group of 'team leaders' and the remaining two gave unclear answers. In most cases commanders were chosen spontaneously by fighters once the conflict began, based on their experience, their skill in fighting, the number of people they had killed or for their charisma.

The most common organisational structure for a fight involves a commander, sometimes supported by one or more deputies or advisors, overseeing a group of three to five team leaders. The commander sometimes, but not always, goes to the battlefield. He is typically responsible for deciding what targets to attack, when and how, and the allocations of weapons and manpower. The team leaders serving under him, also chosen for their experience, typically lead groups of up to 20 fighters. The team leaders are armed with factory-made guns, where available, and may be supported by one or more similarly armed fighters. Behind them come fighters with home-made guns or bows and arrows, and then spears and bush-knives. Fighters move up these ranks as they become more experienced.

Discussions on strategy, tactics and targets typically take place in meetings of fighters. These can be held in the *hausman*,[19] spontaneously in the open or at night in the camp where fighters often sleep together in the bush. Some of these meetings have active participation from all fighters, in others the commander and team leaders discuss while the rest listen, and some are more like briefings in which the commander simply gives instructions.

Aside from command structure, the systems described above demonstrate a level of logistics which falls short of the threshold of organisation. Factors associated with this aspect of organisation include the ability to recruit new members and to provide military training, the supply of weapons, the supply and use of uniforms, and the existence of communications equipment for

19 A *hausman* is a men's house. In traditional highland societies, men and boys usually slept in the *hausman*.

linking headquarters with units or between units.[20] Fighting knowledge in the highlands appears to be gained through experience rather than training. Recruitment is also limited, as is weapons supply. On the other hand, mobile phones are increasingly playing an important role in communications. The lack of uniforms would appear to be a less relevant indicia given that tribal face painting plays a prominent role in Papua New Guinea culture, with each tribe having their own unique way of painting their faces and body. The tradition of face painting is also used before, during and after tribal fights to communicate the situation to those around.[21]

Discipline is another factor informing the assessment of the organisation of an armed group.[22] Eight of the sixteen communities surveyed used allied fighters in their recent fights. It was unclear whether three communities also used hired fighters. Hired fighters are a phenomenon that has been reported since the adoption of guns in the highlands. In 2010, Wiessner observed the emergence of a new class of fighter called the "hireman" or "Rambo" – experts in wielding high-powered weapons, hired by clans in exchange for money, pigs and sexual access to women.[23] Both allied and hired fighters are part-time fighters. Allied fighters support clans based on kinship or other close personal links and usually come from the same district as the clans they support, or from neighbouring districts. Conversely, Rambos are hired because of their reputation in handling weapons or because of their possession of high-powered weapons which can influence the outcome of a fight.[24] According to allied fighters, and to those from host communities, outside fighters generally respect the authority of the commanders of the communities they support, and the rules and targets that they choose.[25] This is not necessarily true of hired fighters. Some hired fighters do not respect the commanders or leaders of the fight and do as they please as they "work for money" and have no real

20 *Prosecutor v Boškoski & Tarčulovski (Judgement)* (International Criminal Tribunal for the Former Yugoslavia, Trial Chamber II, Case No IT-04-82-T, 10 July 2008) [201].

21 Ahmad Hallak, 'In the Fight: The Challenge of Tribal Conflict in Papua New Guinea' *Australian Institute of International Affairs* (29 October 2019) <https://www.internationalaffairs.org.au/australianoutlook/in-the-fight-the-challenge-of-tribal-conflict-in-papua-new-guinea/>.

22 *Prosecutor v Boškoski & Tarčulovski (Judgement)* (International Criminal Tribunal for the Former Yugoslavia, Trial Chamber II, Case No IT-04-82-T, 10 July 2008) [202].

23 Wiessner, 'above n 4, 11.

24 Ibid, 11–12.

25 Responses to 2019–2020 interviews with ICRC.

affiliations or obligations to respect the commanders. It is not easy to discipline fighters who sometimes overpower or dictate to the actual conflicting parties.[26]

The ability to exercise control not only over one's own fighters, but also over allied fighters, suggests a level of discipline. Although this concept of discipline is critically undermined by both the conduct of some hired fighters and the fact that widespread responses in the 2019–2020 interviews reflected that, to preserve unity within the group, there are generally no consequences imposed for rule-breaking fighters. There was broad agreement that killing 'innocent' people would lead to death or defeat in battle, either through the bad luck generated or being targeted by the spirit of the deceased.[27] The lack of a single group-wide discipline system may reflect not only social imbalances of power in favour of youth with weapons and drugs[28] but also the lack of identity as a cohesive group as discussed under organisational characteristics.

An analysis of the general characteristics of the highlands communal fighting suggests individual fights will likely not approach the legal threshold for a NIAC. The spontaneity, brevity and relatively small number of fighters are unlikely to meet the intensity threshold. Whilst fighters in the highlands demonstrate some features that are indicative of organisation, overall the threshold is not met. The separate groups and motives lack a common cause, added to the lack of discipline systems or the ability to carry out concerted and sustained large-scale military operations, and the limitations on logistics capacity amongst fighters, all fall short of the organisation requirements for an armed group in a NIAC. Therefore, the communal fighting in the highlands is more accurately qualified as a situation of violence to which IHL does not apply. The question is not completely closed to debate, as underscored by similarities to Central American gang violence which has divided academic views on whether "drug wars" can be classified as armed conflict.

Nevertheless, in a context where historic traditions of warfare persist and a largely absent state renders the law enforcement paradigm diminishingly relevant,[29] the fighting raises customs and practices around warfare – whether these be traditions and limits which are respected or breaches of past customs of restraint. Simply put, regardless of whether it meets the legal threshold for armed conflict, tribal fighting is a form of warfare in the sociological sense.

---

26 Weissner, above n 4, 1; Jacka, above n 29, 11–12.

27 Responses to 2019–2020 interviews with ICRC.

28 Weissner, above n 4.

29 Schwoerer, above n 34.

The underlying cultural values are a relevant comparator to the principles that underpin concepts regulating armed conflict under IHL.

3 Prohibitions

In a study of 350 years of warfare amongst the Enga, in the province neighbouring Hela, Weissner observes that warfare has fluctuated between periods of relatively unrestrained violence and periods of rules and restraint.[30] During a century-long cycle of relative peace and prosperity from circa 1850, clansman agreed on a set of rules recorded by Weissner as follows:[31]

- Do not kill a person on the land of another clan.
- Do not deface corpses.
- Do not kill women and children.
- Do not pursue and kill a wounded man.
- Avoid killing leaders, for they have the wealth and skills to make peace.
- Fight wars on one front.

Rules were backed by proverbs, such as:

- The blood of a man does not wash off easily.
- You live long if you plan the death of a pig, but not if you plan the death of a person.

The data collected and collated by this study, however, identified six categories of practice. The first three case studies will focus on the protection of people: women, children and neutral clans. The fourth will consider the topic of reprisals, the fifth protection of community property, and the last will focus on respect for the dead killed in the fighting in the highlands. Practice and custom in the highlands will be mapped against concepts of protection of people, property and respect for the dead under IHL to assess the commonality of underlying principles.

3.1 *Prohibition on Targeting Women*

A complex image emerges of the protection and role of women during precolonial era fraternal conflicts in the Papua New Guinean highlands. In traditional wars between patrilineally related clans, due to a practice of delivering warnings, communities were often able to prepare for the outbreak of fighting

30 Wiessner, Polly, 'Youth, Elders, and the Wages of War in Enga Province, Papua New Guinea' (2010) 3 *State, Society and Governance in Melanesia Project,* Australian National University Discussion paper 1.

31 Ibid, 8.

and all wards of the belligerent villages were evacuated once battle began.[32] Women, children, pigs and valuables could be relocated away from border territory to safer positions inside the clan domain or sometimes were allowed refuge with friendly neighbours.[33] Warriors were not supposed to seek out the evacuees according to the tenet that "A decent man should not try to kill the wives and children of the 'brothers' who oppose them; in particular, they should not set fire to women's houses in order to incinerate the occupants."[34] A woman was customarily regarded as neutral by her natal group when warring with her conjugal group and therefore she should not be targeted, although this taboo was not always followed.[35]

The rules and customs discussed above appear to be predicated on the assumption that women are non-combatants. Indeed, as Macdonald and Kirami explain, warfare has historical been seen throughout the highlands as a strictly male domain.[36] Wars were "men's affairs" and a woman's place was to ensure that warriors were fed and the domestic sphere was maintained.[37] As a category of non-combatants, the protection of women in the highlands bears essential similarities to concept of distinction under IHL, which has been called the cardinal principal of IHL.[38] The principle of distinction determines who and what may be targeted, following the underlying tenet that the only acceptable action in an armed conflict is to weaken the *military* capacity of an adversary.[39] Therefore, a distinction must be made between those who are combatants[40] – or directly participating in the hostilities – and those who are not or are no longer participating, as well as and between objects which are military objectives and those which are not. The latter in each category cannot be targeted. As a general rule, under IHL, combatants who are not *hors de*

32 *Under the Protection of the Palm,* above n 13, 32, referencing Mervyn Meggitt, *Blood is Their Argument: Warfare Among the Mae Enga Tribesmen of the New Guinea Highlands* (Mayfield Publishing Co, 1977) 30.

33 *Under the Protection of the Palm,* above n 13, 18–19.

34 Meggitt, above n 71, 31.

35 Ibid, 265.

36 Macdonald and Kirami, above n 17, 107.

37 Ibid, 108.

38 *Legality of the Threat or Use of Nuclear Weapons (Advisory Opinion)* (International Court of Justice, 8 July 1996) [78].

39 ICRC, 'Principle of Distinction: Introductory text' *How does law protect in law? ICRC casebook online* <https://casebook.icrc.org/law/principle-distinction>.

40 Combatants exist as a category only in international armed conflicts between States, whereas in a NIAC the terminology and complexity of categorisation differs, although the underlying principle of targeting fighters and protecting those who are not or are no longer participating in the hostilities remains consistent.

combat can be targeted whereas civilians are protected from intentional attack unless and for such time as they directly participate in the hostilities.[41] On the face of it, the general taboo on attacks on women, small children, the elderly and the disabled reflects the essence of the distinction of fighters from non-fighters under IHL.

When we look deeper, the rationale underpinning the protection of women in tradition patrilineal warfare in the highlands departs from the principle of distinction, to the extent that it does not necessarily appear to be related to her character as a non-combatant, nor to considerations due to her sex. Rather, whether or not a woman could be considered a legitimate target depended on consideration as to whether injury to her would be advantageous or disadvantageous to the group as a whole, in terms of the retribution it would attract. Indeed, Koch notes that women tended to be at greater risk where fighting occurred between unrelated tribes, as the need to maintain relations was a less important factor.[42] This is in contrast to principle of distinction in IHL, where the lawful targeting of a person is directly related to one's combatant status or participation in hostilities.

More recent scholarship and reports of activities in the highlands diverges from the archetype of women as strictly non-fighters. Macdonald and Kirami document a recent shift amongst the Aiya of the Southern Highlands, where women are taking a more active role in the fighting. They document women and girls information gathering and acting as distractions or decoys on or close to the battlefield, for example by walking past naked. According to their research, the disturbing occurrences of battlefield corpse mutilation are mainly performed by women armed with machetes and bush knives amongst the Aiya. Some women are taking up arms and fighting in tribal conflicts themselves: "We call the ladies our brothers because they do almost everything men do."[43] Weissner conducted extensive interviews with a group of twelve rambos, one of whom was a woman.[44]

---

41 The term "combatant" in this paper is used in its generic meaning, indicating persons who do not enjoy the protection against attack accorded to civilians. The use of the term combatant in this paper does not imply a right to combatant status or prisoner-of-war status and the author acknowledges the differences in the legal frameworks applying to international and non-international armed conflicts Derived from Article 3(1) common to the Geneva Conventions, the notion of taking a direct or active part in hostilities is found in many provisions of IHL.

42 *Under the Protection of the Palm*, above n 13, 18–19; Klaus-Friedrich Koch, *War and Peace in Jalemo: The Management of Conflict in Highland New Guinea* (Harvard University Press, 1974) 77.

43 Ibid, Koch, 115.

44 Wiessner, above n 4, 11.

Dinnen and Thompson describe contemporary attacks against women in tribal conflicts in the context of older beliefs the remain deeply ingrained in today's social institutions. "Women have long been viewed as subordinate to men and in some areas relations between the sexes continue to be marked by deep-seated antagonism."[45] The most comprehensive survey to date by United Nations Interregional Crime and Justice Research Institute (UNICRI) was published in the 1990s, and it found that family violence occurred in more than two-thirds of households.[46] Gender-based and sexual violence remains prevalent. In a 2013 study in one region of Papua New Guinea that endured a 10 year armed conflict, 80 percent of men reported that they had perpetrated physical and/or sexual violence against a partner.[47] Macdonald and Kirami conclude that, consistently with domestic dynamics, women in some communities may now "share with men the right to act violently and the pride attached to victory in battle, but their inclusion in warfare is on perilous and subordinate terms."[48]

Whilst in some areas, some women are taking more active roles in contemporary fighting as spies, decoys and even fighters,[49] the participants in the 2019–2020 interviews with ICRC spoke about women who are not actively involved and were considered non-fighters. These responses supported the custom that some categories of people are considered 'innocent' even when they belong to warring parties. Most communities interviewed reported that attacks on women and children are not allowed, and some added the elderly and disabled to this category. There were, however, numerous exceptions. The most common two exceptions reported were firstly, that women and children could be targeted if they were on the battlefield or secondly, they could be attacked on the basis of payback for the killing of women and children on one's own side.

A quarter of the communities surveyed reported that women and children could be killed if they were on the battlefield. Most communities consider killing anyone outside the battlefield taboo and their expectation was that women and children would run away as soon as fighting starts. Two communities gave examples of women who had been killed due to their presence on the battlefield. The leaders of one community acknowledged that a woman from the

45 Dinnen and Thompson, above n 15.

46 Ugljesa Zvekic and Donald James Weatherburn, 'Papua New Guinea Crime and Criminal Justice Information' 1994 Report, *UN Interregional Crime and Justice Research Institute*.

47 Medical Council of South Africa, 'Family, Health and Safety Study: Bouganville, Papua New Guinea Quantitative Summary Report, May 2015.

48 Macdonald and Kirami, above n 17, 116.

49 See for example, Macdonald and Kirami, above n 17.

opposing side had been killed by their fighters. They thought she may have gone to the battlefield to feed fighters, which in their eyes made her a legitimate target. In the second community, fighters stated that killing women was forbidden, but acknowledged killing a woman by 'accident' when she surprised them coming out of a house on the battlefield. They partially excused themselves on the basis that she had taunted them, telling them they were not fit to be fighters.

Other communities had a clear payback mentality, which will be discussed further in the following section on reprisals. The only other mention of women and children being specifically targeted was in one community, which reported that it was important to kill women to stop them giving birth to children who would seek revenge, although this had not happened in their recent fight.

Other customs related to women during times of fighting also suggest that restrictions in the highlands are strongly linked to beliefs in supernatural effects on a group's fighters, rather than to the protection of non-combatants *per se*. Half of the communities surveyed mentioned a taboo on sex during fighting, including with one's wife. Sex is believed to lead to defeat and appears to underlay the rationale for prohibiting rape, rather than a concern for the victim's wellbeing. Interestingly, women also had a distinct set of beliefs and practices about the work and activities they could undertake during times of fighting. For example, sitting with crossed legs, twisting rope or making *bilums* (string bags) during a fight, were commonly tabooed since they would cause male relatives' legs to twist and make them fall. Such beliefs demonstrate the potency and plurality of supernatural beliefs in the highlands, and underline the importance of better understanding the nuance and complexity of customs and beliefs. In the case of these restrictions, whilst the outcomes can superficially look like distinction, the deeper motivation is not necessarily in fact aligned with IHL-like considerations.

The highlands concept of a geographic restriction on the scope of legitimate targeting delineated by the battlefield, arguably does bear parallels with the concept of distinction under IHL. Since non-fighters are expected to flee when fighting begins, people on the battlefield could logically be expected to have a role in the combat. IHL also contains obligations to locate military objectives away from densely populated civilian areas and to take feasible precautions to protect the civilian population and civilian objects from the effects of attacks.[50] These principles appear to correlate with the rationale of the

50 API Article 58(b)-(c). According to Rules 22 23 of the ICRC's Customary Law Study, State practice establishes these rules as norms of customary international law applicable in international armed conflicts, and arguably also in NIACs: Jean-Marie Henckaerts

limited battlefield scope in the highlands. Although, notably under IHL the intermingling of civilian and military personnel and objects does not relieve the attacker of their obligation to refrain from intentional attacks against non-combatants.[51] Highlands practice departs from the rationale of IHL in this respect, since many communities apparently saw direct attacks on non-fighters as justifiable according to their presence on the battlefield alone. The example of the killing of a woman thought to be bringing food to fighters also diverges from lawful targeting principles under IHL.[52] Under IHL, non-combatants performing support services, such as food preparation and delivery to combatants, that do not cause direct harm to the adversary, maintain their protection from intentional attack.[53]

3.2 *Prohibition on Targeting Children*

Some similarities in the protection of women can be observed in the protection of children in highlands fighting. In traditional warfare in the highlands, as described in *Under the Protection of the Palm,* mutual limitations governed warfare between kin, while warfare with unrelated tribes was less likely to be limited. Where conflict took the form of a raid into enemy country, casualties were kept to a minimum, though no distinction was drawn between civilians and fighters. The goal was to capture or kill one or more enemies in retaliation for a prior killing, and it was of little consequence whether the victims were men, women or children.[54] In the 2019–2020 interviews, leaders of a single community described a historical tradition of impaling enemy children on spikes, to stop them seeking revenge as adults. This was mostly done to male babies or children and the custom is no longer practised. In contrast, other historic practice amongst kin – as opposed to unrelated tribes – prohibited the killing of children. This prohibition is demonstrated by the rules developed amongst the Enga in circa 1850.[55] "Traditional" historic rules show a

and Louise Doswald-Beck, *Customary International Humanitarian Law: Volume 1 Rules* (Cambridge University Press, 2005) 68, Rules 22 and 23.

51 See for example, Henckaerts et al, above n 89, Rule 22.

52 ICRC data from 2019–2020 interviews.

53 For example, the ICRC's *Interpretive Guidance on the Notion of Direct Participation in Hostilities under International Humanitarian Law* notes "although the delivery or preparation of food for combatant forces may occur in the same place and at the same time as the fighting, the causal link between such support activities and the causation of the required threshold of harm to the opposing party to a conflict remains indirect": Nils Melzer, *Interpretive Guidance on the Notion of Direct Participation in Hostilities under International Humanitarian Law* (2009) ICRC 55.

54 Under the Protection 12.

55 Weissner, above n 4, 1.

tendency to bifurcate based on the relationship between fighting groups. The less restricted warfare between unrelated groups evidently diverges from the principles of distinction under IHL. However, rules governing conflict between more closely related groups tend to correspond with IHL norms which protect children not participating in hostilities from direct attack.

Boys are often involved directly in the fighting. Where participation in fighting is optional, especially amongst younger boys, they are generally considered to be off-limits to attack unless they take on an active role. Under the IHL principle of distinction, civilians are protected unless and for such time as they directly participate in hostilities.[56] In this way, for younger boys, contemporary highlands practice appears to correlate with the targeting principles underlying IHL. Whereas, the picture is quite different once boys are older in the highlands. They lose their protection from attack and are more likely to be targeted regardless of their participation. Communities reported that they were liable to be attacked due to their age alone. In this way, attacks on older boys diverge from the participation-in-hostilities-based-approach under IHL. Neither age nor sex affect the prohibition on attacking civilians under IHL and indeed under customary IHL, adverse distinction in the application of IHL based on race, sex, birth or any similar status is prohibited.[57]

Norms have also developed around when children participate in fighting. Examples of contemporary practice emphasise the different levels of protection and expectations of boy children, and to boys of different ages. In the recent interviews with ICRC field staff, all the surveyed communities considered it normal for boys to participate in tribal fights as soon as they are able. Most reported them acting as spies, scouts or look-outs, or carrying food and water to the battlefield, from the age of 10 or 12.[58] At this age participation is generally considered optional, described as for the 'brave' boys, while the rest run to safety with their mothers. A primary school pupil from one community was interviewed and described performing a lookout role going ahead of fighters to check whether their route was safe. He said that if he had been caught by the enemy he would have been beaten, but not killed. From the ages of 14 to 16 more boys participate in fights, reportedly out of a sense of duty to defend their land and communities. The women of a different community added that from this age boys will be targeted by the enemy as potential fighters, which adds to their motivation. Boys in this age bracket usually participate in a support

56 See Additional Protocol I Article 51(3).

57 Henckaerts et al, above n 89, Rule 33. This is a customary rule in both international armed conflict and NIAC.

58 Most people in rural highlands communities do not know their age, so ages are estimates.

role with bush-knives and spears before graduating to bows and arrows and guns as they become older. This was described as an important opportunity for them to learn from more experienced fighters, suggesting that their role in the fighting may be limited more due to inexperience and weapon availability as opposed to concern for welfare.

At its bare minimum IHL requires that, when feasible, children under the age of 15 years should not take direct part in hostilities and that, when recruiting young people, priority should be given to the oldest.[59] This is a minimum age and the vast majority of States support a higher age limit of 18 set by the Optional Protocol to the Convention on the Rights of the Child on the involvement of children in armed conflict.[60] Whilst, it is undeniable that practice in the highlands does not reflect this rule, the principle of priority being given to the oldest is reflected in the responses given by communities. The less lethal consequences of being caught reported by one young spy could also reflect a status-based distinction made between seasoned fighters and younger children – even those who have an active role in the hostilities. The age of participation in violence the highlands is clearly at odds with the standards set by IHL, however on the face of it there appears to be some shared norms of prioritisation by age. Like the rationales underpinning the protection of women, the motivations underlying this practice are more complex and perhaps less close to IHL concepts than they could appear. To the degree that boys' participation is correlated with gaining experience and not with a concern for not involving children in fighting, any commonality with IHL ends.

3.3 *Prohibition on Breaching the Neutrality of Clans*

The law of neutrality,[61] rather than IHL, appears to have the most parallels with the conduct and treatment of neutral clans in the highlands. The law of neutrality is beyond scope of this paper but it would be interesting to consider similarities and differences with that body of law. In essence, the principal right of a neutral state is that of inviolability and its principal duties are those of abstention and impartiality.[62] For example, neutrality law prevents belligerents from using neutral territory to launch attacks or to transport troops or munitions.[63] The parallels to traditional warfare in the highlands are clear.

---

59 API Article 77(2).

60 As at September 2022, Papua New Guinea was one of 17 UN Member States who have not signed or ratified the Optional Protocol. A further 8 States have signed but not ratified.

61 (Which only applies in situations of international armed conflict).

62 AR Thomas and James C Duncan (eds), Chapter 7 'The Law of Neutrality' 365 in *Annotated Supplement to the Law of Naval Operations* (Naval War College, 1999) 367.

63 Ibid.

Traditionally, battlefields were clearly demarcated and fighting took place strictly on the battlefields. For one clan to pass through the lands of a neutral clan to launch an attack on the enemy was strictly prohibited unless they had permission from neutral clans to pass through, which was rare as neutral clans did not want to be dragged into the fight for allowing one party to cross their land.[64]

The protection of neutral clans in the highlands also shares strong commonalities with IHL principles. The prohibition against killing on the land of another clan was the first stricture listed by Weissner amongst the rules adopted by the Enga between circa 1850 and 1950.[65] In the 2019–2020 interviews with ICRC staff, the most widely reported restriction, mentioned by nine communities, was that fighting can only take place and enemies can only be attacked in the battlefield, meaning the land of the clans involved in the fight. In two fights, neutral clans reportedly marked the boundaries of their land so that fighters would not enter. This seems to be generally respected, although the principle was broken in two fights where displaced communities were attacked on the land of neutral hosting clans. This was particularly abhorrent and was referred to by the by the affected community as 'stealing lives'.

The modern development of urban centres has added a possible exception to the neutral ground rule. Two communities mentioned that killing in cities and towns is permissible since these are public places. In general, people who do not belong to warring parties are not targeted. However, consistent with the approach taken to women and children from fighting communities, the expectation is that they will leave the battlefield. Interestingly, the property of an outsider may be afforded more protection than their own person, because while a person can leave the battlefield their possessions sometimes cannot. The leaders of one community emphasised that the premises of a timber and plumbing business next to the battlefield of their 2018 fight was not touched by either side. This was partly a pragmatic decision, as damaging the property could have led to conflict with the owner's clan.[66] Similarly, the neutral status of other clans also contributed to protecting some community services, because attacking shared facilities would risk conflict with the neutral party. A tribe from the Southern Highlands province described how a neutral clan set up barriers of logs and branches to protect schools and churches close to the battlefield.

64 Helen Walters Amnol.

65 Weissner, above n 4, 1.

66 Responses to interviews with ICRC staff in 2019–2020.

Highlands practice around the protection of neutral clans appears to more closely accord with the status-based system of distinction per IHL, than does the protection of women or children for example. In most cases, presence of neutral parties on the battlefield would be seen as a signal to stop fighting and collect the dead or to start negotiating for peace, depending on the status of the neutral party being present on the battlefield. In rare cases neutral parties may be attacked on a battlefield for mistaken identity or a honest mistake but usually, all precautions are taken not to kill or injure neutral people.[67] The protection afforded to the property of neutral parties further supports this status-based concept. The distinction drawn between fighting "parties" and neutral non-combatants in the highlands finds common ground with belligerency in IHL. Combatants belonging to parties to a conflict are legitimate targets whereas IHL does not permit the military operations against third parties who are not participating in hostilities. The primacy of relations with other communities is highlighted in highlands custom, whereby the limitations on the use of force have traditionally formed an integral part of maintaining relationships between people and groups, a rationale behind conduct of hostilities rules which is not a feature of IHL. IHL on the other hand is premised on considerations of individual dignity, rather than communal relationships.

The protection of neutral clans to prevent escalation of fighting and the protection of displaced communities on neutral territory, including specific demarcation of neutral areas, also resembles the concept of a demilitarised zone in IHL.[68] Article 60(3) of Additional Protocol I embodies the concept of a demilitarised zone, which is generally understand to be a mutually agreed area which cannot be occupied or used for military purposes by the belligerent parties. The breach of the prohibition on attacks against demilitarised zones is a grave breach of Additional Protocol I,[69] similarly to the particular abhorrence of attacks in neutral territory.

3.4 *Prohibition on Reprisals*

Some of the communities interviewed in 2019–2020 had a clear payback mentality. Older men from the village whose fighters killed eighteen women and children in neighbouring Karida, explained that traditionally women and children could not be targeted. The fighters justified their actions as revenge for six women and children that their enemy had killed, reporting that their

67 Helen Amnol Walters.

68 Demilitarised zones are a feature of international armed conflicts and do not exist in the law of NIAC.

69 Additional Protocol I Article 85(3)(d).

commander had specifically authorised the action on this basis. Similarly, two other communities involved in a fight explained that women and children were not usually targeted, and none had been killed in their recent fights, but that in principle they could be in retaliation.

Other examples of property destruction further reiterate the theme of payback. One community explained that they burned an aid post because its building was donated by a councillor linked to the other side in the fight, and therefore it was not truly neutral and therefore not entitled to protection as neutral property. Fighters from an Enga community justified their burning of an elementary school and a church on the basis that their enemy had burned two churches in a previous fight.

Reprisal attacks in the highlands have a deeper history than recent cases of payback. Concepts of retribution (and restorative justice) have deep roots in broader Melanesian culture, including in Papua New Guinea. The *Under the Protection of the Palm* study notes that traditional dispute resolution was hyper-aware of the dangers of conflict escalation and generally limited payback between interdependent groups to facilitate cooperation.[70] Dinnen and Thomspon draw attention to the perceptions and practices of justice reflected in the social and political organisation of the small, essentially 'stateless', societies of 'traditional' Melanesia. Rather than being centralised in a single entity, authority was typically dispersed throughout the social body in pre-colonial Papua New Guinea. In the contemporary period in the highlands, with its continued social pluralism and the absence of a formal welfare state, the extended family and wantok[71] system still provides a critical informal safety net for many citizens, reinforcing the importance of kinship ties.[72]

The retributive justifications invoked by some communities for the killing of women and children do not find parallel in modern IHL. IHL specifically rejects as a basis reciprocity for restrictions on violence and has therefore increasingly constricted the space in which lawful reprisals may occur as it has developed. The law of belligerent reprisals now specifically excludes reprisals against persons protected by the Geneva Conventions, including civilians,[73] and many States also increasingly recognise that they are ineffective

70 *Under the Protection of the Palm*, above n 13; Dinnen and Thomspon, above n 15.

71 'The pidgin term wantok connotes one who speaks the same language (literally, 'one talk') and, in popular usage, describes the relations of obligations binding together relatives, and members of the same clan or tribal grouping': Dinnen and Thomspon, above n 15, 16 endnotes.

72 Ibid, 2.

73 For example, GCI Article 46; GCII Article 47; GCIII Article 13(3); GCIV Article 33(3).

as a means of enforcement since they "carry a danger of escalation through repeated reprisals and counter reprisals."[74] Traditional limitations on reprisals in Melanesia between related groups mirror this trend in the develop of IHL, recognising the need to set limits to avoid conflict escalation. The lack of such limits between unrelated groups however is contrary to the spirit of IHL, which sets universal standards for the treatment of adversaries.

3.5 *Prohibition on Attacking Property*

Like IHL, past practice collected in the *Under the Protection of the Palm* study, demonstrates examples of customs protecting sources of livelihood and cultural property from attack. For instance, temporary ceasefires often happened in order to harvest food[75] and it was regarded as wrong to destroy the cult-houses or the great old trees.[76]

Schools, health centres and churches did not exist in the pre-colonial era when such traditional beliefs developed. The data gathered by the 2019–2020 ICRC interviews shows that opinions as to whether they can be attacked were sometime divided within communities, but the majority opinion was that they are protected as neutral services that benefit the whole community. As with custom surrounding the protection of neutral clans, this majority view correlates with the principle of distinction under IHL.

The interviews showed that churches are considered neutral even by some who consider schools and health centres to be legitimate targets. In some fights this principle is rigorously upheld. According to the fighters from a Hela community, their commander emphasised the neutrality and inviolability of schools and health centres even as he planned the retributive mass killing of women and children. Another Hela community was similarly clear that these structures should not be attacked, a rule they followed in their recent fight.

A minority of respondents – leaders and fighters from two communities – reported that no justification is needed to attack schools, health care centres and churches. In another community, a teacher and owner of the fight was a rare dissenter in his community when he said that schools can legitimately be attacked so that the enemy's children grow up illiterate. He explained that it did not happen in their recent fight because the two communities live side by side and know each other well, but that it would have happened if they had been fighting a more distant enemy. This view was not shared by other interviewees

74 Kenya, *Law of Armed Conflict, Military Basic Course* (ORS), 4 Precis, The School of Military Police, 1997, 4, cited in Henckaerts and Doswald-Beck, above n 89, Rule 145.

75 *Under the Protection of the Palm*, above n 13, 27.

76 Ibid, 28.

but does reflect the more stringent historic limitations imposed on fights with more closely related kin as opposed to strangers.[77] Even under this aberrant view, schools would be protected in fights between kin in principle.

In general, the people that work in these institutions have less protection than the buildings themselves, repeating the pattern of presence on the battlefield legitimating attack. Teachers or health workers from neutral clans are not usually targeted, but they are expected to leave the battlefield when fighting begins. If they are from the enemy's community, they can be attacked like any other member of that clan; just two communities said they would give them a warning and the opportunity to leave before attacking them. Pastors and priests have a more protected position, with most communities agreeing that they cannot be attacked. As already discussed in the case studies above, whilst the lack of absolute protection departs from the rationale of the IHL concept of distinction, the prohibition on attacks outside the battlefield bears similarities to the principle underlying the concept.

Under IHL, schools and churches are protected from attack on account of their civilian character.[78] In cases of doubt, there is a presumption that buildings which are normally dedicated to civilian purposes remain so. When such buildings, including places of worship and schools, are used for a military purpose they become open to attack.[79] Amongst the highlands communities who believed that these institutions should be protected, the rationale behind the protection of such buildings appeared to share the same principle as the IHL protection. That is – that they should be protected according to their nature as a civilian building unrelated to the fighting. Protection was also bolstered in the highlands by the neutral status of these buildings in some circumstances.

The division in opinions as to the protection of religious, medical and civilian infrastructure among highlands communities may reflect the relative newness of these institutions, which have not necessarily been subject to the same historical development of customary protection as neutral clans for example. Therefore, the protection or lack thereof afforded to these buildings and their occupants appears to be more *ad hoc* as suggested by the example of the dissenting teacher. The rationale given by the teacher is also contrary to the limitations on reprisals in IHL, as previously discussed. The restraint showed in that case also shows the importance placed on neighbourly relations in highlands culture and a concomitant recognition of reciprocity of more stringent

---

77 Ibid, 18–19; Klaus-Friedrich Koch, *War and Peace in Jalemo: The Management of Conflict in Highland New Guinea* (Harvard University Press, 1974) 77.

78 For example, Additional Protocol I Article 52.

79 Ibid, Article 52(3). And subject to obligations to take precautions.

limitations amongst kin. In contrast, IHL has moved away from the principle of reciprocity and respect for the rules is not dependent on the conduct of one's adversary.[80]

Attacks on schools and churches that are being used as bases for fighters is comparable to the protection of civilian objects under IHL, which is also not absolute. For such time as these buildings are used for a military purpose they correspondingly lose their protected status under IHL.[81] Medical personnel and buildings can also lose their protection under a similar rationale. Medical personnel exclusively assigned to medical duties must be respected and protected, however, they lose their protection if they commit, outside their humanitarian function, acts harmful to the enemy.[82] Similarly, buildings with a medical purpose and which are recognised as such, such as aid posts, are protected by virtue of their *function* under IHL.[83] This runs contrary to the justification given for the burning of an aid post, which was reportedly associated with a political figure from the opposing side.

3.6 *Prohibition on Disrespecting Corpses*

Papua New Guinea is amongst the regions of the Pacific which in the past practiced ritual cannibalism in some areas. The custom during these times that "people whose face is known should not be eaten"[84] appears to follow the same rationale as other cultural and social restrictions on means and methods of warfare with kin and related groups. This was a limited rule applying to the treatment of the dead, ensuring respect amongst related communities.

Such practices can be contrasted with the old rule amongst the Enga not to deface corpses[85] and traditions amongst the Aiya in the Southern Highlands recorded by Macdonald and Kirami. They note that killing an adversary in battle was surrounded by many ritual prohibitions. "The body of the fallen warrior was not moved or in any way harmed by the enemy, instead being left for kinsmen to come and collect at nightfall. Should the corpse be disrespected in any way, then it was believed the warrior's spirit would cause illness and

80 See Henckaerts and Doswald-Beck, above n 89, Rule 140.

81 See Additional Protocol I Article 52(2) for the definition of a military objective. As previously noted, military objectives are the only lawful target under IHL.

82 See Additional Protocol I Article 15.

83 See Henckaerts and Doswald-Beck, above n 89, Rule 30 stating that State practice demonstrates that the use of a distinctive emblem of the Geneva Conventions does not confer protection as such. Protection is attached to the recognition of the medical function.

84 *Under the Protection of the Palm*, above n 13, 25.

85 Weissner, above n 4, 1.

misfortune. Treating the body ethically would promote victory in future warfare."[86] Respect for one's own dead, both recently and long departed, was considered essential to success in battle. Success in battle also hinged crucially on maintaining good relationships with one's own dead relatives, both recently and long departed. This manifested through appeals to one's ancestors and to relatives killed in recent battle. Indeed, this respect extended in some cases to sleeping next to the fallen warrior's corpse as a demonstration of affinity, in addition to appealing to the dead man's spirit.[87]

Writing in 2017, MacDonald and Kirami record a significant transformation within the conduct of warfare amongst the Aiya. They argue that the treatment of fallen enemies exemplifies the erosion of ritualised codes of deference and respect within fighting mentioned earlier. Writing about instances of gruesome dismemberment, they observe that combatants now not only mutilate the dead bodies of their enemies, but there is a tendency to make these attacks as horrific as possible.[88]

There is evidence that these new practices have continued in other areas of the highlands. A recent example of beheading and hacking off of limbs of slain adversaries is the notorious Karida massacre. In the ICRC's interviews in 2019–2020, treatment of the dead was raised by one Enga community. The fighters stated that they cannot cross a dead body, and that after killing one or two enemies they must pull back and perform a ritual to cleanse themselves of ghosts.

The treatment of the dead during armed conflict has always been a subject of cultural and religious concern. IHL, too, has a long history in this regard. In particular, IHL requires that the remains of those who have died during armed conflict be properly managed and their dignity protected.[89] The core obligations enshrining respect for the dead in IHL treaties are mirrored in customary IHL.[90] These range from norms around the search for, collection and evacuation of the dead and the identification and return of human remains and personal effects of the dead. For example, the ICRC's study of customary IHL found that state practice had established as a norm in both international and non-international armed conflicts, an obligation on parties to a conflict to

86 Macdonald and Kirami, above n 17, 108.

87 Ibid, 108.

88 Ibid, 110.

89 Per numerous rules in the Geneva Conventions and their Additional Protocols pertain to treatment of the dead. For example, parties to an armed conflict must take all possible measures to prevent despoilment of the dead (GCI, Article 15(1); GCII, Article 18(1); GCIV, Article 16(2); API, Article 34(1); APII, Article 8; ill-treatment and mutilation of dead bodies is prohibited (GCIV, Article 3(1)(c); AP II, Article 4(2)(a).

90 Henckaerts and Doswald-Beck, above n 89, Rule 113.

take all possible measures to prevent the dead from being despoiled and a corresponding prohibition on the mutilation of dead bodies.[91] Traditional rules amongst the Enga and the Aiya reflect the same regard for the dead which underpins the treatment of the dead under IHL. Needless to say, contemporary practices of humiliation and degradation, as MacDonald and Kirami describe them,[92] are in direct conflict with the principles reflected by both IHL and past custom in parts of the highlands.

4 Conclusion

The comparison of local traditions and practice with IHL is an interesting exercise in the context of discussions on influencing behaviour and restraint, however, it is clear that caution must be exercised. As discussed, there is a risk of blurring the legal paradigms by applying this sort of comparative exercise to a situation that is not an armed conflict. Comparisons in this case should be careful not to suggest that IHL is applicable to the situation in the highlands and especially must not imply that violence is legitimate whether directed against non-fighters or fighters. Furthermore, some practices diverge dramatically from IHL. These practices would be violations of IHL if committed during an armed conflict, and constitute criminal conduct under the domestic law. The cases studies also demonstrate that custom is not fixed but is changeable over time and variable amongst different communities living in neighbouring regions. The transmutability of custom confirms that value of law. IHL presents consistent and universal standards that develop predictably and slowly with the adoption of new treaties and retains basic fundamental principles. Where they converge, IHL and local traditions can be mutually reinforcing. Yet, the highlands case studies also show that where there are apparent convergences, the underlying rationales for rules may differ and it is important to understand more about these philosophies to engage in a meaningful exchange.

As Mr Fredrick Tamarua of the Papua New Guinea Department of Justice and Attorney-General illuminated, while there is a wide diversity of traditional practices in Papua New Guinea – and while such practices might not all mirror modern IHL – they nevertheless can encourage discussion about what IHL means in particular cultural contexts and help to reinforce the universality of

91 Ibid.

92 Macdonald and Kirami, above n 17, 110.

the notion that even wars have limits.[93] Convergences between tradition and IHL demonstrate that these are not foreign concepts.

In an era where humanitarian organisations and IHL practitioners are increasingly becoming conscious of problematic colonial legacy and the importance of active anti-racism, starting discussions on the richness of local traditions and how they intersect and diverge from IHL is one way of embracing diversity and inviting different perspectives. Such discussions have the potential to increase ownership of humanitarian principles and strengthen the mandate of governments, including in the Pacific, to engage in developing IHL at the international level and at home. Even where practice differs, value can be added, for example by the one could foresee the contribution of the Melanesian notion of viewing harm done during conflict through the lens of later compensation and as a mechanism for restraint and future relationships. Thinkers from Papua New Guinea would be well placed to engage in the discourse on neutrality and to apply their perspectives to new domains such as cyberspace or outer space. Bringing IHL home, could look like recognising the universality of humanitarian principles in domestic custom and contributing to its universalisation in treaty law through the ratification of fundamental IHL treaties, including the Additional Protocols.

Some recent practices of humiliation and degradation in the highlands appear to be departures from past norms and violations of agreed custom amongst communities. In these cases, young men with access to firearms often appear to be writing their own rules of engagement and in some cases ignoring traditions of restraint.[94] Some see these aspects of contemporary violence as an erosion of principles. Weissner argues that the bigger historical picture in the highlands shows us that violence has followed a pattern of swinging between a pendulum of unrestrained violence and periods of stricter adherence to custom, which promotes stability and prosperity.[95] To the extent that these customs are being violated in the highlands, it is hoped that discussion around traditional practice be one aspect of the effort to foreground restraint and embed these principles in the identities of the young male fighters. As the *Roots of Restraint* research found, rules are more tenacious when they are

93 Foreign, Commonwealth & Development Office, British Red Cross and ICRC, *'Partnership, Persistence and a Sense of Possibility: National IHL Committees and the Commonwealth'* (Report of the Fifth Meeting of Representatives of National IHL Committees of Commonwealth Countries, 26–30 April 2021) 4.

94 Weissner, above n 4, 1.

95 Ibid.

part of the identity of a group – "this is who we are" – and not just abstract legal concepts (whether they be IHL or criminal law). Value and identity-based restraints are even more relevant community embedded groups where the influence of a hierarchy is diminished.[96]

Some traditions in the highlands draw different limits to IHL, yet overall they do share the basic premise that even wars have limits. Whilst practice departs from IHL principles distinctly, it is also striking that the essence of some customs developed completely in isolation from modern IHL share a common spirit. Speaking about Islam and IHL, Dr Farah Ibrahim said he found a "similarity of intent, objective, approach and consequence".[97] Although there are many difference between practice and tradition in the highlands and modern IHL, he could have been speaking of the underlying commonalities of principle that also exist in the treatment of neutral clans in the highlands or the rules agreed by the Enga in the 1800s. These congruences pay tribute to Pictet's sentiment, in which:

> the uniformity of human psychological make-up and the universality of standards governing the behaviours of nations are recognised, and no longer is there belief in the supremacy of any one civilization: indeed the plurality of cultures and the need to take an interest in them and study them in depth is recognised.

Acknowledgements and Disclaimer

The author is grateful for the work of ICRC staff in Papua New Guinea and the Suva Delegation who collected and collated data from 16 communities in the highlands from 2019–2020 and to the ICRC for the use of this data for the purposes of this paper. The views expressed in this paper are that of the author's and do not represent the views of the ICRC.

---

96 *Roots of Restraint,* above n 68, 65.

97 Foreign, Commonwealth & Development Office, British Red Cross and ICRC, *'Partnership, persistence and a Sense of Possibility: National IHL Committees and the Commonwealth'* (Report of the Fifth Meeting of Representatives of National IHL Committees of Commonwealth Countries, 26–30 April 2021) 4.

CHAPTER 2

Mongol Laws of War

Samuel White

1 Introduction

History is not always written by the winning side. The steppe nomads – warriors from the vast belt of open grassland stretching from the Carpathain mountains in eastern Europe to the Pacific Ocean – are seen through the eyes of their victims. Mongol history is largely written by the settled, nomadic people they defeated; and their legacy is that of the destroyer of cities; the ruiners of agriculture; the exterminators of entire people. Only dedicated academic work can allow for the reputation of the 'Mongol Hordes' to be stripped backed and analysed – in particular with respect to their customs and laws of war. On this niche aspect of Mongol culture, history does not favour a positive outlook. Christopher Marlowe's play, *Tamburlaine the Great** reflects Western notions of the Mongols, through the mouth of the 'Soldan of Egypt'

> Merciless villain, peasant, ignorant
> Of lawful arms, of martial discipline!
> Pillage and murder are his usual trades:
> The slave usurps the glorious name of war

As will be seen, the Mongols were not ignorant of lawful arms or martial discipline. Quite the opposite.

Although the Mongols had confederated over a hundred years prior to Temujin – who would later go on to become Genghis Khan[1] – the Mongghols

---

* Many thanks to Dr Battogtokh Javzandolgor - Professor at the National University of Mongolia for her helpful comments and guidance on earlier drafts of this paper. The spelling of Mongol names varies according to the cultural perspective it has been translated through. In Mongol, Tamerlane's name was spelt *Timur-I Lenk* – Timur being his name, Lenk meaning lame. For the most part, this Chapter seeks to use the original Mongol spelling. The prime example of this is Genghis, Chingis or Chinggis Khan. The spelling varies, depending on Persian and Arabic transliterations. There is no accepted national, let alone international norm. For ease of preference, Genghis is used when discussing a European source, and Chingis is used when referencing a Mongol source.

1 I.IV.i.

 | DOI:10.1163/9789004512566_004

(which they called themselves, and from which Mongol derives) were not a linguistic or ethnological group but simply the dominant tribe of one tribal confederation that inhabited the steppe north and south of the Gobi desert. The *Secret History of the Mongols* ('*The Secret History*') speaks of people with 'nine tongues' – presumably dialects and languages.[2] Amongst this confederation were the Tatar (Tartar in English), the Naiman, the Kereyid, Uriats, Merkits and Jalair. All were in constant competition over finite, and seasonally varied, grassland for their horses.[3] There was no concept of 'peace' or 'war' but a constantly evolving mosaic of personal and family ties which supported ever-shifting goals and desires. Equally, the distinction between soldier and herdsman did not exist. Raiding and vengeance (*os*) were to the glory of the tribe and the nation.[4] This Chapter, whilst using the concept of 'laws of war', is necessarily focused upon the customs of battle and prohibited conduct in battle.

To facilitate such a discussion, timeframes and sources are particularly important. The Chapter focuses specifically on the customs of four Khans: Chingis; Ogedi; Kublai & Tamerlane; so from 1162 to 1405 AD. Within this three-hundred-year period however Mongol culture adapted and evolved in accordance with the cultures they became sedentary in. Genghis was the last truly nomadic Khan; Ogedi had an administrative capital built; Kublai founded the Yuan dynasty and settled (and demonstrated a particularly Sinofied approach to warfare[5]) whilst Tamerlane, although sedentary in his deposit of loot at Samarkand, maintained the Mongol tradition of mobile raids and destruction as a method of warfare. He is therefore included in this discussion, and Kublai primarily excluded.[6]

There are very limited primary sources to rely upon: Imperial Edicts and Letters from the Mongols to vassal states are some; eyewitnesses are the other. The earlier are the only written Mongol records; the latter are through the perspective of their victims. Of course, not all opinions of the Mongols are negative. Some European sources seem odd considering latter European bemoaning of the Mongol Hordes (sometimes referred to as Tartars) after the European raids of Batu in 1245 AD. Columbus justified his exploration of the

---

2 (trans. Paul Kahn, Cheng & Tsui, 2005) 178 ('*The Secret History*').

3 Similar to Indigenous Australians – see Samuel White, 'Digital Payback: Indigenous Laws of War for Cyberspace' (2022) 4(2) *Journal of Defence and Strategic Studies* 235–258.

4 Joseph Fletcher, 'The Mongols: Ecological and Social Perspectives' (1986) 46(1) *Harvard Journal of Asiatic Studies* 11, 14.

5 David Nicolle, *The Mongol Warlords* (Firebird Books, 1998) 63 ('*Mongol Warlords*').

6 Burma campaign – took a city without killing anyone to demonstrate to his Chinese advisor it could be done – see *Mongol Warlords* (n 5) 58.

Atlantic on the basis that the Spanish could re-establish sea contact with the Court of the Great Khan.[7] Geoffrey Chaucer wrote that:

> His fame reached as far as England
> This noble king was called Genghis Khan
> Who in his time was of so great renown
> That there was nowhere in no region
> So excellent a Lord in all things.[8]

Yet the very word 'Mongol' has a negative connotation: to be 'Mongoloid' is an old fashion term to be disabled. Dr Francis Crookshank captured popular opinion when giving medical advice that Jewish persons were of lower genetic quality because of breeding with the Khazans of the Steppe.[9] European sources – after the shattering of Eastern European forces in Poland, Austria and the Balkans in 1241/1242 – led to the idea of Mongols being 'the devil's horsemen from a mysterious quarter of the Earth, pagans who lacked a recognized law and indulged in unusual, even bizarre, customs'.[10] To counter this source bias, it is useful to look either at European sources prior to 1240 free from apocalyptic speculations. (such as the records of Papal embassies to the Khan's court) alongside non-European sources.

The Secret History of the Mongols also is a logical source to use, if not with the regular historical care. Written after the death of Ogedi, but prior to the appointment of the next Khan, *The Secret History* describes the life of a hero but with personal details less flattering to its subject – Temujin who murders his half-brother Bekter; Ogedi's deathbed confession of his four failings as a Khan.[11] It is a resource focused on the noble class – concerned with who fought, who won, and what conflicts arose amongst the Mongols themselves. Sequence of actual campaigns are wrong or greatly abbreviated.[12] As Paul Kahn notes in the foreword to his translation and adaption *The Secret History*:

> The political situation that preceded Temujin's birth was centred on competition and conflict between the Mongol and Tatar tribes. The Mongol had been organised under a central leadership for several generations [by

7 Jack Weatherford, *Genghis Khan and the Making of the Modern World* (Crown, 2004) 254.
8 'The Squire's Tale' in *The Canterbury Tales* (Penguin, 2007).
9 Francis G. Crookshank, *The Mongol In Our Midst* (Kegan Paul, Tench & Trubner, 1924).
10 Johannes Gibauf, 'A Programme of Terror and Cruelty' (2007) *Chronica* 85, 88.
11 *Mongol Warlords* (n 5) 9.
12 *The Secret History*, XXIII.

> Ambaghai Khan] … behind the scenes, however, is the long Chinese tradition of using one 'barbarian' people to weaken another.[13]

Temujin's success, in many ways, was both the destruction of his neighbours with Qin support and surviving the subsequent attempts to fragment the Mongol coalition. *The Secret History* does not reflect customary practices that were common place to the audience. It is, moreover,

> an intriguing and frustrating creation. Because it claims to explain Mongol origins, it invites comparison with other great foundational works – the Bible, the Iliad, the Norse sagas, the Mahabharata. But it lacks their scale … and lacks both epic grandeur and historical rigour.[14]

Yet it captures a moment on Mongol history inaccessible through other sources; prior to generational exaggeration through the mode of an epic; and can be used to show some customs of battle that applied.

2 Means and Method

2.1 *Society*

In order to understand the two central pillars of Mongol laws of war – 'the great principle' (*yeke*) and protecting religious buildings – it is necessary to canvass some key social rules. Religion was of utmost importance to the Mongols, and to Genghis Khan in particular. Tengri (Tenggeri, Tngr) was the universal victory-granting sky god who migrated with the Aryans, and who also had cultural taboos around exposure of the dead (expanded upon below). Success in battle demonstrated favour from Tengri (which differed slightly from the concept of divine right in Europe which applied even if you lost).

The tribe was the basic unit of society with 'its own traditions, institutions, customs, beliefs and myths of common ancestry … all members of the tribe were, by tradition, considered descendants of a single ancestor'.[15] Each member of the tribe had to be self sufficient. Tengri connected all these individuals, and supported a flexible approach to tribal structure. If a leader was successful in battle, Tengri would allow for tribes to grow or decay. If a leader was unsuccessful – and therefore abandoned by Tengri – then religion and custom

13 *The Secret History*, XVII.

14 John Man, *Genghis Khan: Life, Death and Resurrection* (Bantam, 2005) 33.

15 Fletcher (n 4) 16.

allowed for the tribe to move on. Underpinning success was the generation of wealth.

Battle brought wealth; the role of the Khan then was to obtain and distribute wealth – the ultimate aim of the tribe.[16] After a battle, supporters of rival candidates, being proclaimed rebels by the *khuriltai* (executive body) would be legitimately despoiled and their goods distributed

What was wealth to the Mongols? When appointing Temujin to be Chenggis Khan, his nobles pledge:

> We'll search through the spoils
> For beautiful women and virgins
> For the great palace tents
> For the young virgins and loveliest women,
> For the finest geldings and mares
> We will gather all these and bring them to you.[17]

Or as Rashid al-Din defined, citing Temujin, wealth was the freedom:

> to cut my enemies to pieces, to witness the tears of those who are dear to them, to drive them before me, to seize their possessions, to ride their horses and their wives.[18]

Wealth generation of course could drive escalation in conflict. The stealing of a bride is part of the opening scene of *The Secret History.* Temujin's father – Yusegi – observes a marriage cart being drawn by an Merkit (an enemy tribe). Yusegi steals Holgen with the aid of his tribe; the Merkit escapes.[19] A generation later, the Merkit return to revenge the debt by taking Temujin's wife;

> The men who pursued Temujin were the chiefs of the three Merkid clans,
> Toghtoga, Dayir Usun and Khagatai Darmala
> These three had come to get their revenge, saying
> "Long ago Mother Hogelun was stolen from our brother Chiledu"
> When they couldn't catch Temujin they said to each other:

16 Fletcher (n 4) 23.

17 *The Secret History,* 44.

18 *Compendium of Chronicles* (Sheila Balir, Nour Foundations in association with Oxford University Press, 1995) 1.V.32.

19 *The Secret History,* 13.

> "We've got our revenge.
> We've taken their wives from them"

For this, in turn, Temujin pledges to Tengri that he would

> We'll fight until their wives and their sons are all dead,
> Striking his door-frame, where his guardian spirit lives,
> We will break it to pieces.
> We will fight until this people are completely destroyed,
> Until in their place there is nothing but emptiness.[20]

Tribes logically confederated in order to defend themselves, and have a higher chance of success in battle. Accordingly, after raising a confederacy, Temujin achieves his oath –validating his rhetorical question of 'Aren't the Mongol a people whose word is sacred?'[21] The three hundred Merkit leaders are executed, along with the

> Seed of their seed,
> So that they were extinguished like a fire, and their ashes blown away in the wind.
> From their women who remained he took as wives those fit to be wives.
> From the rest he took as his slaves those fit to be slaves.[22]

In turn, if any Merkit survived, the conflict continues all in the bid to generate wealth. For the Mongols, this never happened. Once consolidation of a supra-tribal confederation occurred, then the generation of troops often followed, as:

> A leader who won battles won followers. A leader who lost battles lost followers. Everyone wanted to be on the winning side. Everyone wanted a share of the spoils.[23]

With internal stability secured after his appointment as Genghis, external operations followed.

---

20 *The Secret History*, 34.
21 *The Secret History*, 36.
22 *The Secret History*, 39.
23 Fletcher (n 4) 29.

2.2 *Wealth Generation Tactics*

Being easier to be given goods, rather than take thenm, maximising wealth required maximising fear – and so the Mongol reputation for brutality arose. This is in part propaganda spread by the Mongols;[24] and in part truth. Brutal tactics were used against *mo balya* (bad cities which resisted).[25] Thomas of Spalato, a canon of Spalato (Split) writes in 1240 AD of a massacre in the East, from the testimony of survivors:

> Gathering [men, women, boys and girls] together like a flock of sheep he made his executioners behead them all ... All captives were cut down and like sheaves in a cornfield, their corpses were strewn on the plain. But the Tartars did not plunder the dead, to make clear they had not slaughtered them because of lust for booty.[26]

On another occasion, Thomas of Spalato reports that to instil fear, the Mongols rode along the Danube with the corpses of children impaled on lances, 'like fish on a spear'.[27]

Others were more matter-of-fact with describing Mongol tactics. John of Piano Carpini is a particularly useful source. He was dispatched in 1245 AD, alongside a Polish companion, by Pope Innocent IV as papal envoy to the Mongol court.[28] They were the first European traveller of the thirteenth century to enter the core of the Mongol Empire. John compiled a detailed dossier of his account in *Historia Mongalorum* which provides a surprisingly candid and unbiased account of Mongol tactics, weaponry and strategy. He states:

> When the Tartars are going to make war, they send ahead an advance guard and these carry nothing with them but their tents, horses and arms.

24 The Mongols, with an incredibly limited number of troops due to the sparsely populated steppes, relied upon spies to plant rumours of their 'huge numbers, stupidity and ferocity' among enemy populations to lower morale and frighten the enemy before an attack: Paul MA Linebarger, *Psychological Warfare* (Duell, Sloan & Pearce, 2nd ed, 1948) 15.

25 See Juvaini *History of the World Conqueror* (trans. J.A. Boyle, Harvard University Press, 1958) Vol 1, 79–80 ('*History*').

26 Thomas, *Historia* XXXIX, 174; I.R. Sweeney, "Thomas of Spalato and the Mongols: A thirteenth-century Dalmatian view of Mongol customs," (1982) 4 *Florilegium*, 156–183.

27 Ibid, XXXVI, 163.

28 The two letters of Pope Innocent IV (5 March 1245, *Dei patris immensa,* and 13 March 1245, *Cum non solum*).

> They seize no plunder, burn no houses, slaughter no animals; they only wound and kill men or, if they can do nothing else, put them to flight.[29]

This was to generate a reputation and instil fear in the target population, so that when an order came to surrender they would. So too does Giovanni recount:

> They send a detachment of captives and men of other nationalities who are fighting with them to meet the enemy head-on, and some Tartars may perhaps accompany them [...] Moreover, when it pleases the masters they take all the young men with their wives and children and compel them to follow them with all their household; from henceforth they are counted as Tartars, or rather as captives, for although they are numbered among the Tartars, they are never shown the respect that these enjoy but are treated as slaves and are sent into every kind of danger like other prisoners; they are first in battle and if a swamp or a dangerous river has to be crossed, they have to try the passage first.[30]

Particularly difficult campaigns would result in increasingly brutal strategies – all in the aim of minimising Mongol casualties, and maximising profit.

They could produce a terror so stupefying that, as Ibn al-Atir records, a single Mongol horseman could enter a Persian village and begin killing people while no one dared to raise a hand to stop him.[31] Ibn recorded as well that he had heard a Mongol to take a man captive, but had no weapon with which to kill him. He told his prisoner to lie with his head on the ground without moving.[32] The terror-stricken man did so, and remained there until the Mongol returned from fetching his sword and cut his head off.[33]

It is obvious that Ibn al-Atir exaggerated the details. This does not mean that al-Atir's work is of little value. It holds importance in capturing the clearly visible effect of Mongol strategy. One credible eye-witness to these tactics was

29 Giovanni Carpini, *Historia,* cap. VI, 11: 103 – recorded inEnglish translation: *The Mongol Mission. Narratives and Letters of the Franciscan Missionaries in Mongolia and China in the thirteenth and fourteenth centuries* (trans. Anon, ed. C. Dawson, 1955) 35 ('Carpini, *Historia*').

30 Carpini, *Historia,* VI, 14:103; VII, 11:107.

31 I follow the French translation of the Persian text from M.C. d' Ohsson, *Histoire des Mongols depuis Tchinguiz-Khan jusqu'à Timour Bey ou Tamerlan,* Vol. 3, The Hague and Amsterdam 1834–1835, 69.

32 Ibid, 69.

33 Ibid.

Roger of Torre Maggiore, who survived as a hostage until the sudden withdrawal of Mongols in 1242:

> Soon rumour spread that the Tartars had occupied the German village of Thomasbrucke where they slaughtered everyone not fit for slavery. Hearing such news my hair stood on end with fright, my whole body started trembling and my tongue refused its duty because of the unavoidable and terrible death which awaited me. In my mind's eye I saw the slaughterers and the cold sweat of death made the blood freeze in my veins. I saw people in fear of death, unable to control their hands and weapons, unable to raise their arms or legs only staring into space. And what more? I laid my eyes on people half-dead from panic.[34]

Roger's testimony is corroborated by others,[35] and is there is nothing to discredit the details of which he was an eye witness.[36]

The common denominator of the above, however, is the realisation of the authors that Mongol success relied upon weakening and demoralising the foe by means of cruelty. Because of the brutal success of the Mongols, their enemies were often in a state of terror and, in effect, were already defeated psychologically before they were even engaged in battle. Therefore the Mongols fostered their terrible image to fool their victims into thinking that they were super-human, mounted demons appearing out of nowhere to destroy utterly the known world, in order to make wealth generation more efficient. Similar conclusions were drawn by Vernadsky-Karpovich, who states:

> Chingiz's principle seems to have been much the same as President Truman's over Hiroshima and Nagasaki. The apparent rationale was that if the population of one city was subjected to a frightful massacre, the next city would be more likely to surrender without resistance, thus avoiding unnecessary Mongol casualties. The morality of this approach to warfare is no doubt open to discussion, but there can be no disputing that it worked.[37]

34 *Epistola magistri Rogerii in Miserabile Carmen super destructione regni Hungarie per Tartaros facta* ed. L. luhâsz, in *Scriptores rerum Hungaricarum tempore ducum regumque stirpis Ar-padianae gestarum,* Vol. 2. Budapest 1938, cap. 34, 579.

35 For such massacres in the realm of the Chorezm-Shah, see Juvaini, *History* (n 25) 121, 131, 145.

36 GieBauf (n 10) 89.

37 *The Mongols,* 116; Bezzola, *Die Mongolen,* 88; Göckenjan-Sweeney, *Der Mongolensturm,* 52–54,.

2.3 *Mongol Law*

After confederation, the legal landscape changed. The appointment of Genghis Khan saw a consolidation of multiple family groups into formal bodies of public and military order. So too did the legal landscape change – away from customary, oral history to written, codified laws.

This was aided by a new series of laws – formally proclaimed and later recorded as the *Yassa* (*jasagh, yasa, yassaq*). The *Yassa* regulated combat, inheritance, and overall public law. The *Yassa* had three aims: to create a legal duty and enforcement mechanism to demand obedience to Genghis Khan; to bind together nomad clans and wider members of the Empire, and the creation of a criminal code. The *Yassa* was particularly novel in assuring Mongols that dying without an heir did not result in property going to the Khan – which had been previous practice. Wealth generation was now inter-generational, and secured by law. There was incentive for the confederation to remain together.

Although no original, completed version survives there is no doubt that the *yasa* as a written document existed as it has been recorded and referred to by several reliable chroniclers.[38] Persian historian and official of the Mongol State, Ala-Ad-Din Atâ-Malek Juvayni, wrote an account of the Mongol Empire and describes the *yasa* as 'a rule for every occasion and a regulation for every circumstance; while for every crime he fixed a penalty.'[39] Juvayni stated that these *yasas* and ordinances were ordered to be written down on rolls which were then preserved in the treasury of each of the descendants of Chinggis Khan.[40] Similarly, renowned traveller Ibn Batuta has stated that Chinggis Khan composed a book of laws called *al-Yasak*.[41] The first khan of the Golden Horde, Rashīd ad-Dīn Fażlallāh Hamadānī, has mentioned the existence of the *yasa* and has quoted its laws and regulations. Medieval Egyptian historian of the Mamluk era, al-Maqrīzī, has also referenced a copy of the *Yassa* in Baghdad.[42]

Recent scholars of the 20th century have two different views of the *Yassa*: some consider it to be a codification of the ancient Turkic and Mongol legal systems, whereas others theorise that it was new imperial legislation. However, there is an agreement amongst them that the *yasa* was a codified legal

38 Pochekaev, R. Yu, 'Chinggis Khan's Great Yasa in the Mongol Empire and Chinggisid States of the 13th–14th centuries: Legal Code or Ideal "Law and Order"?' (2016) 4(4) *Golden Horde Review* 724, 725.

39 Juvaini, *History* (n 25) 25. See also George Vernadsky, 'The Scope and Contents of Chingis Khan's Yasa' (Pt Harvard-Yenching Institute) (1938) 3(4) *Harvard Journal of Asiatic Studies* 338.

40 Juvaini, *History* (n 25) 25.

41 Vernadsky (n 38) 338.

42 Ibid.

act.[43] A minority of scholars have disputed the belief that the *yasa* was a legal code, noting the polysemy of the term "*yasa*" and the secondary character of most sources.[44] Additionally, a controversial view is offered by D Morgan: he reasons that the mentions of *yasa* in 13th-14th century Mongol and Persian sources do not give reason to regard it as a legal code but it should instead be seen as separate acts.[45] Agreeing with Morgan and Ayalon, Pochekaev also does not see reason to view the *yasa* as a codified legal act, however has disagreed with their statements to only regard it as "law and order."[46] It seems to have been focused upon regulating Mongols, rather than their subjects, on the maxim that:

> People conquered on different sides of the lake should be ruled by different sides of the lake.[47]

It is a useful source, particularly as it focuses upon the Mongol experience of legal pluralism. Pochekaev suggests that the *yasa* can be treated either as a series of Chinggis Khan and his successors' laws and official acts or that law and order existed due to the observance of these regulations.[48]

In addition to the *Yasa,* the Khan used to make suggestions or comments on different occasions – known as *Bilik* (knowledge). Some significant work by George Verndasky has collated both the *Yassa* and *Bilik*. For the purposes of this Chapter, some rules are particularly relevant

> *Rule 1* – It is ordered to believe that there is only one God, creator of heaven and earth, who alone gives life and death, riches and poverty as pleases Him – and who has over everything an absolute power.
>
> *Rule 5* – It is forbidden to ever make peace with a monarch, a prince or a people who have not submitted.
>
> *Rule 8* – It is forbidden, under the death penalty, to pillage the enemy before the general commanding gives permission; but after this permission is given the soldier must have the same opportunity as the

---

43 Pochekaev, R. Yu, 'Chinggis Khan's Great Yasa in the Mongol Empire and Chinggisid States of the 13th–14th centuries: Legal Code or Ideal "Law and Order"?' (2016) 4(4) *Golden Horde Review* 724, 725.

44 David Ayalon, 'The Great Yāsa of Chingiz Khān. A Re-examination (Part A)' (1971) 33 *Studia Islamica* 99, 105, 135.

45 David Morgan., 'The 'Great Yāsā of Chingiz Khān' and Mongol law in the ĪLkhānate' (1986) 49(1) *Bulletin of the School of Oriental and African Studies* 164.

46 Pochekaev (n 41) 727.

47 Weatherford (n 7) 125.

48 Ibid.

> officer, and must be allowed to keep what he has carried off, provided he has paid his share to the receiver for the emperor.

In addition, regulations were enacted to enforce discipline within the troops. Michael Prawdin states:

> At a later date, when Temuchin had become lord 'of all the peoples dwelling in felt tents' whom he had united into one armed nation, he gave this obligation of comradeship in extremity the force of law. The smallest unit of his armies, consisting of nine men with a tenth in command, was composed of persons bound together for life or for death. They must allow themselves to be cut to pieces rather than abandon one of them who was wounded. He who forsook a comrade would ruthlessly be put to death.[49]

Giovanni Carpiniarp also held that soldiers were collectively punished if a comrade fled; or if a comrade was captured and a rescue raid wasn't organised.[50] David Nicolle opined:

> Commanders who betrayed cowardice, or a lack of resolution, were humiliated by having their beards shaved and their faces painted with women's make-up and being forced to run barefoot through the streets.[51]

The introspective family group, with shifting loyalties thus became an externally-faced, imperial administration dedicated to the Khan. In an attempt to be efficient, wealth generation from sedentary cultures began to be formalised through the aforementioned Imperial Letters and Edicts. These "legal instruments reveal[ed] essential features of Mongol public law and public ideas".[52] They identify carefully what in Mongol opinion was due process of law – part formal instruments of information, and part commentary on fundamental rules of constitutional law of the Empire. Indeed, as Juvayni noted:

> When (the Mongols) have need to write any letter to rebels, and they must send an envoy, let them not threaten with the great size of their army and their numbers, but let them say only, If ye will submit yourselves

49 *The Mongol Empire* (Routledge, 2017) 69.

50 Carpini, *Historia,* VI, 14:103.

51 *The Secret History,* 173.

52 Eric Voegelin, 'The Mongol Orders of Submission to European Powers – 1245–1255' (1940) 15 *Byzantion* 378–413.

> obediently ye shall find good treatment and rest, but if ye resist – as for us what do we know? But the everlasting God knoweth what will happen to you.[53]

They would precede any request for vassalhood, and tribute. The formula are the same:

> In Heaven there is God, The One, Eternal, Immortal, Most High
> On Earth Genghis Khan is the only and Supreme Lord

The true essence of world order is in a state of potential, but true. It materialises upon contact with outside groups – not as sovereign nations to be bargained with but uneducated vassals to be incorporated.

3 Prohibited Conduct

The Mongol Empire, by its own interpretation, was a World-Empire-In-The-Making. Territories, rules and people may be *de facto* beyond control, but *de jure* members of the Empire. There is therefore no concept of peace or war; but only of submission or rebellion. There therefore can technically be no concept of war crimes, as all operations were domestic law enforcement or punitive expeditions. Enemies were 'rebels' because of universal declaration of Mongol jurisdiction.

There is a divide that comes through the *Secret History* that relates to how the laws of war are approached and their consequences. This is between matters of the steppe (being on campaign) and matters of the tent.[54]

When the original Mongol confederacy combines, oaths are given that

> If we disobey your command during battle,
> Take away our possessions, our children, and wives
> Leave us behind in the dust
> Cutting off our heads where we stand and letting them fall to the ground.[55]

Yet, the same oath holds a nuance:

53 Juvaini, *History* (n 25) 41.
54 *The Secret History*, 172.
55 *The Secret History*, 45.

> If we disobey your counsel in the tent,
> Take away our tents and our goods, our wives and our children
> Leave us behind when you move,
> Abandoned in the desert without a protector.[56]

The below discussion then is through the lens of 'matters of the steppe'. It primarly relies upon observations made in *The Secret History,* and

3.1 *The Great Principle*

The *Yassa* required a proper declaration of war with the promise to spare the enemy population in case of voluntary submission. Mongke, the new Khan after Guyuk, held a *quriltay* (or gathering of leaders) in 1251 AD. He instructed his younger brother Hulegu to the chaotic province of Iran, instructing him to:

> Establish the usages, customs and laws of Genghiz Khan from the banks of the Amu Darya river to the ends of the lands of Egypt. Treat with kindness and good will every man who submits and is obedient to your orders. Whoever resists you, plunge him into humiliation.[57]

The Edicts created a legal framework for declaring *mo balya*: bad cities which resisted and were obliged to be plunged into humiliation.[58] These cities breached "the great principle" – one of the two pillars of Mongol laws of war, as established by Genghis. The great principle was concerned with maintaining one's word (such as Temujin's treatment of the Merkit) and upholding Tengri. As Genghis, after his appointment, notes:

> If you change at noon what you said in the morning,
> If you change the next morning what you said at midday
> Such a man's word wont be believed.
> I've already given you my word.
> All right.
> Let it stay that way.[59]

---

56 *The Secret History,* 45.

57 As quoted in *Mongol Warlords* (n 5) 103.

58 Juvaini, *History* (n 25) 121, 131, 145. J. Masson Smith, "Demographic considerations in Mongol siege warfare," *Archivum Ottomanicum* 13 (1993/94), 329–334.

59 *The Secret History,* 145.

The great principle permeates throughout *The Secret History.* The opening scene of *The Secret History* shows Ambaghai Khan poisoned by the Tatars whilst enjoying their hospitality. On his deathbed, he commands his sons to not

> forget that I was betrayed by the Tatar,
> You must try to avenge me with all the strength you can find,
> Till the ails of your fingers wear off,
> Till your fingers themselves wear away from your hands![60]

This fate befalls Temujin's father, Yesgui, five generations later.[61] All Mongols are reminded, and empowered, generationally to maintain the great principle. *The Secret History* is full of instances – and punishment – relating to the great principle. Tokhuchar – a senior general – plunders allies without permission. Chiggis decrees:

> As for you,
> You've wilfully disobeyed me and attacked cities on the frontier.
> This caused Amin al-Mulk to join forces with Jalal al-Din against us,
> For having done that I'll have your head cut off.
> But instead he lectured him,
> And removed him from command of the army.[62]

The Secret History informs us multiple times that the great principle is to be enforced, regardless of personal friendships or shared history. After a split in the confederacy, Temujin captures nobles who had pledged to fight for him but did not.

> Sacha Beki and Taichu said,
> "We have not kept our promise"
> Remembering the oath that they'd sworn when they'd elected him Khan,
> They stretched out their necks to him.
> And Chingis made them honour their oath,
> Executing them on the spot where they stood.[63]

60 *The Secret History,* 11.
61 *The Secret History,* 16.
62 *The Secret History,* 158.
63 *The Secret History,* 52.

So too after the contest for control of the Mongols by Temujin and his *anda* (blood brother) Jamugha does the great principle need to be upheld. In this respect, however, there are some material differences. Jamugha is betrayed and captured by his servants, who expect a reward from Chingis for bringing his enemy to him. Chingis, in turn, executes them in front of Jamugha for their lack of loyalty.[64] What, then, to do about Jamugha?

Temujin the man grapples with the friction of laws – *anda* are to be respected and protected, but the great principle is to be enforced. Chingis Khan, the leader, offers him an alliance once again, holding their enemies had brought them apart. Jamugha responds:

> And now my anda, the Khan, wants to favour me,
> And says to me, 'lets be allies'
> When I should have been his ally I deserted him
> Now, my anda, you've pacified every nation
> You've united all.
> The Great Khan's seat is yours.
> What good would I be as your ally?
> I'd only invade your thoughts,
> Like a louse on your collar,
> Like a thorn under your shirt
> I went wrong when I strove to be a better man than my anda,
> It is I whose reached the end of his days.
> When you have me killed, my anda,
> See it is done without shedding my blood,
> And my bones are buried high on a cliff.[65]

And so Chingis Khan did, enforcing the great principle. It was fundamental to the operations undertaken by the Mongols against the Tatars by Genghis. Before the battle with the four Tatar clans, the Khan

> spoke with his soldiers and set down these rules
> "if we overcome their solders, no one will stop to gather their spolits.
> When they're beaten and the fighting is over,
> Then there will be time for that.
> We'll divide their possessions equally amongst us."[66]

64 *The Secret History*, 110.
65 *The Secret History*, 111, 112.
66 *The Secret History*, 65.

The battle is successful, and Chingis Khan holds a council to decide the fate of the Tatars. It is recited that

> Since the old days,
> The Tatars have fought our fathers and grandfathers.
> Now to get out revenge for all the defeats,
> To get satisfication for their deaths,
> We will kill every Tatar man taller than the linchpin on the wheel of a cart.
> We'll kill them until they're destroyed as a tribe.
> The rest we will make into slaves and disperse them among us.[67]

There are some significant points of difference with the treatment of the Tatars and others (such as the Merkits). Not just nobles are killed – all men are. Indeed, not just men, but young men and boys as well.

The same fate befell the Sultanate of Khwarezm. Genghis Khan started campaign against Korezm Shah Mohammed in 1219 on the basis of the killing 'of the hundred ambassadors led by Ukhuna'.[68] Juvayni's account, written a generation after the event, offers the details:

> Now amongst the merchants was an Indian who had been aquainted with the governor [of Khwarezm] in former times. He now addressed the governor by name, not title, and being rendered proud by reason of the power and might of his own Khan [Chingis] he did not stand aloof from him. On account of this the Governor became annoyed and embarrassed and placed them under arrest. They were killed and deemed the seizure of their goods to be lawful ... *For every drop of their blood there flowed a whole Oxus; in retribution for every hair on their heads it seemed that a hundred thousand heads rolled in the dust at every crossroad; and in exchange for every dinar a thousand khintars of gold were exacted.*[69]

All males who stood higher than the butt of a whip were killed.[70] Giovanni of Caprini remarked, on the topic more generally:

---

67 *The Secret History*, 65.
68 *The Secret History*, 152.
69 Juvaini, *History* (n 25) 79–80. Italics authors own.
70 Man (n 14) 172 (quoting Juvanli).

> The third reason was that we feared lest they be put to death, as our people for the most part are arrogant and hasty: thus it was that when the servants who were with us at the request of the Cardinal Legate in Germany were going back to him in Tartar dress, they came near being stoned by the Germans on the road, and were forced to leave off that dress. *And it is the custom of the Tartars never to make peace with those who have killed their envoys till they have wreaked vengeance upon them.*[71]

A review of *The Secret History* shows the Xi Xia were entirely exterminated after breaking their faith of vassalhood;[72] and the Merkid (who had been severely humiliated by Temujin ten years earlier) were utterly destroyed after successive uprisings in the Great Camp.[73]

Enforcing the great principle could be achieved through deception. The Assassins were granted safety if they exited their castles; they were then summarily executed.[74] Merv – a vassal city which had commited successive instances of insubordination and perfidy – was assured of safe treatment if they surrendered. After four days of occupying the city, the Mongols executed all citizens (including women and children). Juvayni estimated approximately 1.2 million were killed in a week;[75] John Man, through articulate calculations, agrees but says this death toll was over two years (not 4 days) and multiple attacks on the city after it rebelled.[76]

3.2 *Protection of Places of Worship*

Beverly May Carl, citing Weatherford, made a claim that:

> He [Chengis] decreed complete and total religious freedom for everyone – Buddhists, Manichaenists, Muslims, Christians and Hindus (at a time when dissidents in Europe were being tortured and burned). He forbade the killing of priests, monks, nuns, mullahs, and other holy people.[77]

71 Carpini, *Historia*, 30.

72 *The Secret History*, 101.

73 *The Secret History*, 107. Only one exception appears from the sources, and is an outlier to the near-four hundred years of consistent execution of the great principle. The son of a rebel vassal, who had Mongolised, and risen through the ranks interceded to save his former home (Tsagaan was his name, see John Man, p 212–213).

74 *Mongol Warlords* (n 5) 106.

75 Juvaini, *History* (n 25) 82.

76 Man (n 14) 244.

77 'The Laws of Genghis Khan' (2012) 18(2) *Law and Business Review of the Americas* 147, 161.

No sources are given for the sweeping proposition except Rossabi. A closer analysis of that citation shows Rossabi wrote:

> The Mongol khans appointed Muslims from Central Asia and Iran to be fiscal administators, and in one case governor of a province, Tibetans to supervise the Buddhist monasteries, and a Nepalese to serve as a manager of all the artisans in China.[78]

There is nothing in the secondary sources that support the proposition of that 'holy people' were sacrosanct. Yet it is an interesting concept to explore.

The second pillar of Mongol laws of war relates to the extreme religious tolerance across the Empire. Noting Mongolia's geographic location as a crossroads of faith, it is unsurprising but still merits exploration. Tengri was based upon a shamanistic approach to religion, but other models existed and were tolerated: Buddhism, Christianity, Confucianism and Islam all were preached across the steppe. As the Mongols expanded, so too did their understanding of Tengri – Tengri as manifested in Allah; Tengri as Deus; Tengri as Enlightenment. Gibbon notes it best when he held:

> But it is the religion of Zingis [Genghis] that best deserves our wonder and applause. The Catholic inquisitors of Europe, who defended nonsense by cruelty, might have been confounded by the example of a Barbarian, who anticipated the lessons of philosophy, and established by his laws a system of pure theism and perfect toleration. His first and only article of faith was the existence of one God, the Author of all good; who fills by his presence the heavens and earth, which he has created by his power. The Tartars and Moguls were addicted to the idols of their peculiar tribes; and many of them had been converted by the foreign missionaries to the religions of Moses, of Mahomet, and of Christ. These various systems in freedom and concord were taught and practised within the precincts of the same camp; and the Bonze, the Imam, the Rabbi, the Nestorian, and the Latin priest, enjoyed the same honorable exemption from service and tribute: in the mosque of Bochara, the insolent victor might trample the Koran under his horse's feet, but the calm legislator respected the prophets and pontiffs of the most hostile sects.[79]

---

78 Michael Rossabi, "The Mongols and Their Legacy," in *Legacy of Genghis Khan – Courtly Art 1256–1353* (Michael Rossabi ed., Metropolitan Museum of Art, 2002) 20.

79 Edward Gibbon, *Decline and Fall of the Roman Empire* (Christian Classics Ethereal Library, 2023) 656–6.

This was a both a matter of religious tolerance, and religious in-difference. *The Secret History* makes no comment as to foreign religions – exemptions in the form of *tarkan jarlips* (tax exemptions) for religious sects only occur after the Empire is built. Atwood suggests this to be a matter of religious indifference, so long as they supported the Mongols' world claim.[80] Yet there seems to be some grounds to the idea of religious tolerance. As Genghis sought to conscript able-bodied men in 1219 in preparation for his campaign against Khwarezm, Buddhists were exempted so they would not breach their custom on killing.[81] So too were Muslims allowed to practice with tax exemptions.[82]

Overshadowed by the brutal nature of Mongol wealth extorsion from sedentary cultures is the oft-recited fact that they preserved places of worship. In Hulgeu's Syrian campaign, Christians were spared and Christian buildings protected.[83] Indeed, the burning down of the Great Mosque in Aleppo appears to have been against orders and was committed by auxiliary troops – Armenian Christians to be precise.[84]

Shamanistic taboos however were enforced across the Empire. As foreshadowed, Aryan taboos on blood and exposed bodies were strictly enforced. This manifested in two ways. First, royal blood was not to be shed. A clear example of this is how Prince Mstislav Romanovich of Kiev and others were bound, placed on flat ground where they became the foundation for a heavy wooden platform on which Mongol generals feasted whilst they suffocated slowly beneath them.[85] So too was Jamugha insistent that

> When you have me killed, my anda,
> See it is done without shedding my blood,
> And my bones are buried high on a cliff.[86]

The taboo manifested in particular practices of Christians to worship the body parts of saints. Fighting in the Levant, Carl writes that Christian priests 'paraded the bones of their saints before the Mongol army.'[87] Accordingly, 'Mongols retaliated by killing the clerics and burning their churches, priests

80 Christopher Atwood, 'The Date of the Secret History Reconsidered' (2007) 37 *Journal of Song-Yuan Studies* 1–48.
81 Ibid, 45.
82 Ibid.
83 Man (n 14) 188.
84 *Mongol Warlords* (n 5) 112.
85 Man (n 14) 190.
86 *The Secret History*, 111, 112.
87 Carl (n 77) 153.

and relics to purify themselves' going on to suggest that 'European knighthood never recovered from losing nearly 100,00 men'.[88]

Overall, notwithstanding the poor citations of Carl, it would seem that there was some level of religious tolerance and protections of places of worship, even within *mo balya.*

3.3 *Law of Plunder*

A final custom of armed conflict – both captured in practice, and codified in the *Yassa* – was to do with the division of wealth. In the 3rd century BCE, the Hsiung-nu (an East Asian steppe confederacy) had established that in warfare each person kept whatever plunder they seized.[89] This individualist approach to plunder had slowly been centralised by the respective confederacy rulers. Among the Hsien-pi, who were subsequent to the Hsiung-ni in approximately 200 AD, the rule had the right to distribute booty.[90] By the time of the Mongols, Khans had a customary right to the best of the plunder, and often would jealously guard (or proactively take) the wealth of others. As noted above, this caused a cycle of conflict and escalation that the *Yassa* sought to resolve

Before the battle with the four Tatar clans, Genghis Khan

> spoke with his soldiers and set down these rules
> "if we overcome their solders, no one will stop to gather their spoils.
> When they're beaten and the fighting is over,
> Then there will be time for that.
> We'll divide their possessions equally amongst us."[91]

Yet Altan, Kuchar and Daritai – three of Chingis' generals, ignored the orders

> When Chingis Khan heard this, he said:
> "They've broken their word"
> And he sent Jebe and Khubilai to punish them.
> They took away from them everything they had gatherhed,
> And left them nothing at all.[92]

88 *The Secret History,* 152, 53.
89 Fletcher (n 4) 21.
90 Ibid.
91 *The Secret History,* 65.
92 *The Secret History,* 65.

Here we see the concept of plunder being linked to the great principle: an order was given and disobeyed. It is implied that the Khan takes into his possession Altan, Kuchar and Daritai's goods. Twenty years later, the requirement for the Khan to get an equal spoil is raised by *The Secret History*. It is a particularly illuminating section, as it relates to the Khan's three sons' in Gurganj.

> When Jochi, Chagadai and Ododei took the city of Gurganj,
> They divided the city's people three ways
> And didn't leave a part for Chingis Khan
> When these sons came to pitch their tent with him
> Chingis Khan yelled at them
> And for three days he wouldn't see them,
> For all is possession of Chingis Khan.[93]

His war council petition him, saying

> Why do you heap such abuse on your sons?
> In warfare they're only immature falcons whose feathers are gray,
> They're only learning what to do in war.[94]

He forgives them, but the custom is clear: plunder is to be shared with the Khan, and failure to do so is a breach of custom. It is particularly interesting then that the *Yassa* makes clear that wealth is to be kept by the family if one died without an heir: an apparent back-track from customary Mongol laws 'of the tent'. For reasons outlined above, it may be that this is to ensure higher morale 'on the steppe', or to reduce in-fighting amongst troops.

4 Defences

Although direct membership of the *altan urag* (Golden Clan, or direct descendants of Genghis) seems to be a mitigating factor in breaches of custom there was another legal category whose role was much more entrenched and defined: that of the *tarkhan* or *darqan*. The word means literally 'excepted' (thus used above to discuss religious exemptions) and denoted a class of individuals to whom the law did not apply.

93 *The Secret History*, 159.
94 *The Secret History*, 159.

The creation of the *tarkhan* seems a novelty of Genghis. The first mention is in *The Secret History*, where two average soldiers who saved Genghis in battle are rewarded:

> For what they have done,
> I give them Ong Khan's golden tent just as it sits here,
> With servants to carry all the basins and bowls.
> *Let these two men be allowed to wear quivers and drink holy wine,*
> And let them be free men from now on,
> Down to the seed of their seed
> *When we defeat our enemies and take our spoil,*
> *Let them take whatever they want.*[95]

The *tarkhan* thus was exempt from the laws of plunder, and were perpetually freed from servility. This was a privilege held for seven generations. The *tarkhan* system revolutionised Mongol society, moving away from appointments based on inherited position within a tribal hierarchy but on the services rendered.

The Secret History expands on the *tarkhan* system, when Genghis grants senior generals the honour. In particular, this honour and awards system entitles *tarkhan* to be liable for prosecution only of the 9th crime committed. Nothing more is said on the matter, but some legal reasoning of the above would suggest some inherent limitations on the *tarkhan*. If an *adan* could be executed for breaking the great principle then it would suggest that a *tarkhan* was liable for prosecution under one of the key pillars of Mongol society. It is likely that the *tarkhan* role allowed for certain elements of the *Yassa* to be broken (such as taking someone's slave) but not, say, murder of members of the *altan urag*.

5 Conclusion

J.J. Saunders was wrong to suggest the Mongols wreaked havoc 'out of some blind unreasoning fear and hatred of urban civilisation'.[96] As this Chapter has outlined, the Empire-In-The-Making (as a legal construct) took every step to maximise wealth generation and minimise Mongol casualties. Urban civilisations offered a wide spectrum of wealth; but equally they offered a lot of useless people. The logical strategic option, through the cultural lens of steppe

95 *The Secret History*, 91.

96 *Muslims and Mongols: Essays on Medieval Asia* (University of Canterbury Press, 1977) 48.

nomads, was the use of these individuals as slave labour; siege warfare fodder; or artisans. When no longer useful, they were executed.[97]

The great principle provided a pillar to Mongol society that bound it together, and sought to stop the cycle of competition and conflict between the tribes. It was a custom of warfare that was honoured above all else and enforced vigorously, and runs contrary to Marlowe's description of a Mongol leader as a:

> Merciless villain, peasant, ignorant
> Of lawful arms, of martial discipline!
> Pillage and murder are his usual trades:
> The slave usurps the glorious name of war.[98]

If warfare is the continuation of politics by other means, then it is clear the Mongols in a generation were able to rapidly focus and control their politics to generate wealth in the most effective means possible.

---

97 *Mongol Warlords* (n 5) 44.

98 I.IV.i.

CHAPTER 3

Cossack Laws of War

Tatiana Tairova-Yakovleva

1 Introduction

The word "Cossack" is of Turkic origin and means a brave, free person. That was how the representatives of the free military communities in Eastern Europe were called. In history, there were several main groups of "Cossacks", which, despite the similarity of name, were completely different from each other in their traditions, methods of warfare and the role they played in history. They also differed in their system of restrictions, laws and punishments. Some Cossacks belong to the history of Ukraine, others to the history of Russia. This chapter seeks to address the Ukrainian perspective of Cossack laws of war and explore their nuanced approaches to resolving conflict.

The Cossacks has emerged in the 15th – 16th centuries at the so-called "Great Cordon", i.e. steppe border of Europe. The steppe was an ideal region for the development of cattle breeding, crafts (hunting and fishing) and agriculture. Due to competition with nomads, agriculture here developed under constant external threat.

Central to this was the Wild Field: a frontier, a crossroads between East and West, as well as the religious border of the Christian and Muslim worlds.[1] Ukraine (which was part of the Grand Duchy of Lithuania in the 14th-16th centuries) and Russia (the Moscow State) inherited the so-called Wild Field from the time of the Tatar-Mongol invasion – huge fertile territories, not inhabited by people, covered with tall grass, abounding in game and fish.

The Wild Field stretched from the Crimean Khanate up to Bratslav and Poltava, creating a wide belt separating Ukraine from the Muscovite state, and the Western world from the Ottoman Empire. These vast expanses, rich and free, created extraordinary opportunities on the border of Ukraine and of the Moscow state. The desire to escape from the oppression of their landowners, to gain freedom and independence, as well as to engage in free trade and military affairs gave rise to typologically similar communities of Cossacks.

1 Brehunenko Viktor. Kozaky na stepovomu kordony Jevropy. Kyi'v, 2011. P. 26. Kappeler Andreas. Iuzhnyi i Vostochnyi forntir Rossii v XVI–XVIII veka. // Ab Imperio. 2003. № 1. P. 49.

 | DOI:10.1163/9789004512566_005

Only if the Don Cossacks were cut off from the outside world due to Ottoman control over the mouth of the Don, and were forced to rely on an alliance with the Muscovite state, the Ukrainian Cossacks were much more free in their geopolitical possibilities.

Initially, the Cossacks groups has aroused on the borderlands of the Grand Duchy of Lithuania and of the Moscow state. The first mention of the Cossacks dates back to 1492.[2] They occupied the territory of the Wild Field and lived in it according to their own laws. However, the Ukrainian Cossacks not only isolated themselves in free lands, but maintained an inextricable connection with Ukraine, where their wives and families lived. Gradually they turned into the social elite of Ukraine. The Ukrainian Cossacks managed to create their own statehood, lead the religious and spiritual struggle of Ukraine, and become bearers of national identity. The Don Cossacks remained an isolated part of the Moscow state, which did not seek to incorporate. This Chapter addresses the means and methods, traditions and prohibited conduct of three different classifications of Cossacks: the Free Cossacks and the Registered Cossacks of Ukraine, and the Don Cossacks of Russia. It does so to highlight the nuanced differences in the laws of war between the three, and to dispel popular imaginations of lawless, cruel horsemen.

2 Ukrainian Cossacks

The Cossacks that arose in Ukraine are divided into two main types: Zaporozhian (free) and Registered, urban (in the service of the king or tsar). The Zaporozhian Cossacks lived as a separate group in *Zaporizhzhia* (Lower Dnipro). The Registered Cossacks were located in the main cities and provinces of Ukraine. Both of these types of Cossacks had different military tactics, laws and traditions. However, the origins of the emergence of these Cossack groups were common.

The first Ukrainian Cossacks were called "*Ukhodniki*" (those who leave). The Wild Field, with its abundance of game and fish, attracted people from border villages, who initially went there for animal hunting and fishing. They usually left their homes in the spring, spend all summer in the Wild Field, huddling in dugouts or huts made of brushwood. They dried and salted meat and fish, and tanned skins. They set up berms and apiaries in the steppes. And by winter they returned to their families, to their villages, to sell what they had earned.

2 Hrushevsky Michailo. History of Ukraine-Rus. v. 7. Edmonton-Toronto, 1999. P. 61.

This type of business provided the leavers with an enviable income, but was extremely unsafe. The Tatars roamed the Wild Field, and often attacked the leavers, robbed, killed them or captives. They had to take up arms, defend themself, or hide skillfully. The leavers often united into hordes and attacked the Tatars. Such brave men began to be called Cossacks, and their campaigns and way of life – *Cossackovanie*.

The rapid development of the Ukrainian Cossacks was explained by its broad social base, which was constantly updated and developed. This was one of the main differences from the Don and other types of Russian Cossacks. Over the years, hundreds of thousands of representatives of various social groups of the Ukrainian society, including the gentry, peasants and townspeople, gained the Cossack experience in Ukraine.[3]

Over time, dashing Cossack escapades became more and more popular not only among the youth of the gentry, but also among magnates who were thirsted for "knightly glory." By the end of the 16th century, many representatives of the Ukrainian noble families chose the Cossacks life as their path. Most of them became Cossack officers – "*starshyna*". Majority of the Cossacks were from the peasants and townsfolk of the free frontier.

Such inclusion in the ranks of the Ukrainian Cossacks of the gentry, educated and ambitious people, contributed to the fact that in the middle of the 17th century precisely the Ukrainian Cossacks, as a social group, became the creators of national statehood, going far beyond the scope of Cossack interests. The Cossack officers became the co-authors of the brilliant culture of the Ukrainian Baroque.

The Zaporozhian Cossacks were liquidated by Catherine II in 1775, and the Registered Cossacks, together with the autonomy of Ukraine, were liquidated in 1783.

2.1 *Means and Methods of Zaporozhian Cossacks*

Any Christian man could come to Zaporozhian Host. No one cared about their social status, but the Cossacks were strictly forbidden to bring women to Zaporizhzhia. The Cossacks were distinguished by their piety, they observed Orthodox fasts and rituals. Already in the 17th century there was a church in Zaporozhian Host. They also had priests among themselves.

All the most important matters among the Cossacks were decided by the *Rada* (i.e., the general meeting), in which all Cossacks (who wanted) took part. The Rada, in particular, elected the *Kosh Ataman*, who had absolute power

3 Tairova-Yakovleva T. Istoriia Ukrainy. Sankt-Peterburg, 2015. P. 108–111.

both during military campaigns and in the internal affairs of the Zaporozhian Host. Every year there was a change of the ataman.[4] Zaporozhian Cossacks also had *Pysar* (a clerk), an *Osaul* (responsible for order in the army), a Oboznyj (responsible for the camp and artillery) and a Judge.

The Rada also judged Cossacks for misdeeds, drew up agreements with foreign states, and discussed plans for military campaigns. Voting was carried out by shouting, with the majority often forcing the minority to submit.

The Cossacks ran a joint household that provided everyone with food, clothing, weapons and other necessities. Receiving rich booty during their campaigns, many Zaporozhian Cossacks became wealthy people. However, among the Cossacks there were many "*golytba*" ("*siromahi*" – from "gray" clothes). These were unmarried people, who had not yet acquired their own farm, could not or did not want to run it. Some of them has drank away and lost everything in the cities and returned to Zaporozhian Host in the hope of new loot. Unlike the *Siroma*, the rest of the Cossacks had families in Ukraine.

The main opponents of the Zaporozhian Cossacks were the Tatars and Turks. Tatar detachments penetrated into the Wild Field and attacked the borderlands of the Polish-Lithuanian Commonwealth and of the Moscow State. Also, the Cossacks were opposed by Turkish troops in their campaigns. This determined the weapons and basic methods used by the Zaporozhian Cossacks in the war. Unlike the Western European tradition, they used as bladed weapons not swords and rapiers, but sabers. Pistols, shotguns and muskets were widely used as firearms. When controlling horses, the Cossacks used whips rather than spurs.

It should be noted that horses were the most valuable commodity in the Wild Field. The Cossacks stole the horses from the Tatars.[5] The Zaporozhian Cossacks went on ground campaigns by fast detachments, in which each Cossack had two horses, in order to be able to make lightning-fast transitions and attacks.

If they encountered large detachments of Tatars, which many times outnumbered them, the Cossacks avoid the fight by using tricks: they divided into several groups and dispersed in different directions. Large detachments rode in the way of the goose, small detachments – by 3–4 horsemen in a row, trying to trample as much grass as possible in order to give the Tatars a false idea of the size of each party. In order to carry out the pursuit, the Tatars also had to devide. And after some time the Cossacks gathered at a pre-agreed place

4 Javornyc'kyj D. Istorija zaporoz'kyh kozakiv. Kyi'v, 1990. P. 210.

5 Iavornits'kii D. Zaporozh'e v ostatkakh stariny i predaniiakh naroda. Sankt-Peterburg, 1888. 11. 26–27.

and defeated the devided Tatar`s detachments. Often the Cossacks drove into small steppe rivers, and, throwing off the pursuit, drove along the bottom for some time.

They also used another technique: they cut out long last year's dry reeds, blew them through, took all their goods and lowered them into the water. They placed thorns under the horses' sweatshirts and struck them with a whip, causing them to run away into the steppe. And the Cossacks themselves took a reed in their mouths and plunged into the water between the reeds and sedges. After some time, when the pursuit was away, the horses returned to their owners.[6]

The Zaporozhian Cossacks were well oriented in the steppe by the stars, could cry like an eagle owl ("pugu-pugu", this cry even often served as a conventional sign), and knew many animal and bird cries.

In addition to small raids against the Tatar detachments, the Zaporozhian Cossacks also carried out long-distance ground campaigns. Severeal times with large detachments they attacked the outskirts of Ochakov (on Dnipro).[7] In the steppe they always marched against the Tatars in a *tabor* (a convoy or a camp formed by horse-drawn wagons), with infantry inside and cavalry outside. They moved slowly, often at night, stopping during the day along deep ravines and ravines with bushes. During their ground compaigns they observed strict precautions – they did not light fires, did not smoke, did not allow horses to neigh, tying scarves around their muzzles. And even spoke in whispers among themselves. They navigated by the stars and used the Nuremberg quadrant.

The Zaporozhian Cossacks became famous in particular for their participation and significant contribution to the liberation of Vienna from the Turkish siege in 1683. But most of all the Zaporozhian Cossacks were known for their sea campaigns. The Cossacks carried them out on ships called *Chajka* ("seagull"). They were 18 meters long, had from 10 to 15 oars on each side, and one sail.[8] The Zaporozhian Cossacks carried out campaign with a flotilla of up to 80–100 ships, 50–70 people on each, armed with sabers and muskets. Their ships also had 4–6 falconets each.[9] In less than two days Cossacks reached the coast of the Black World along the Dnipro, trying to use the effect of surprise. To achieve this, the Cossacks set out on a dark night, shortly before the new moon, staying hidden in the reeds, where the Turkish galleys that protected the mouth of the Dnipro into the Black Sea did not dare to enter.

---

6 A. Kuz'min. Zaporozhskaia Sech': istoricheskii i bytovoi ocherk. Moskva, 1902. P. 32–34.

7 Korolev V.N. Bosforskaia voina. Rostov-na-Donu, 2002. P. 174–181.

8 Boplan Giiom Lavasser. Opisanie Ukrainy. Moskva, 2004. P. 259.

9 Boplan Giiom Lavasser. Opisanie Ukrainy. Moskva, 2004. P. 261.

However, the Zaporozhian Cossacks sometimes attacked even Turkish galleys which were many times more powerful than them. Having noticed the enemy, the Cossacks removed the mast and rowed, trying to stay in the position that the sun was shining at their backs. An hour before sunset, they quickened their pace and around midnight reached the galleys, which they then boarded.

The Zaporozhian Cossacks carried out military raids on the Turkish coast of the Black Sea, plundering and destroying cities and fortresses. On the way back, avoiding pursuit by Turkish squadrons, they often resorted to the following trick: they dragged their ships, reaching the Dnieper in two or three days by land and returned home by river.[10]

Successful campaigns across the Black Sea, carried out under the leadership of Petro Sahaidachnyi, brought European glory to the Zaporozhian Cossacks already in the beginning of the 17th century. In 1614, led by 2000 Cossacks, Sahaidachnyi launched a campaign against Sinop. His pilots were former slaves freed from Turkish captivity, who knew all the approaches to the coastal Turkish cities, the features of their fortifications, the typography of the area, etc. The Cossacks sailed into the Black Sea on 40 ships (*Chajki*), crossed the Sea, reached Asia Minor and unexpectedly landed at Sinop – a beautifully fortified, populous and fabulously rich harbor. It was like a bolt from the blue, because none of the enemies had reached Sinop for more than 250 years – "since the Turks took possession of Asia, there has never been anxiety or danger there." In addition, Sinop was guarded by an impregnable fortress built of stone, with iron double-leaf gates, which had 6,100 loopholes, and a citadel with several towers. Sinop was a powerful Turkish naval base and the largest Black Sea shipyard.[11]

The attack on Sinop was planned and carried out brilliantly. It was at night and came as a complete surprise to the Turks. With the sudden appearance of the Sahaidachnyi soldiers of the local garrison, the crews of the ships and the population were seized by panic. Using ladders, the Cossacks broke into the fortress, captured the citadel, the shipyard, the galleys and the city, destroyed the Sinop castle and burned its workshop, causing a huge material loss to the Turks. They also burned several mosques and private houses. The garrison was almost completely killed, large stocks of weapons and ships were captured, and numerous Christian slaves were freed, the joy of which was beyond description. According to contemporaries, the Cossacks' booty reached 40 million

10 Boplan Giiom Lavasser. Opisanie Ukrainy. Moskva, 2004. P. 265–267.

11 Hrushevsky Michail. History of Ukraine-Rus. V. 7. Edmonton-Toronto, 1999. P. 270–291.

golden ducats. Having loaded booty and the freed prisoners onto ships, the Cossacks left the Sinop`s harbor and disappeared from sight.[12]

The Turks overtook them, in a fierce battle killed about 200 Cossacks and captured 20. The rest, having thrown part of the loot into the water, still managed to and sail away with the most valuable goods. Having learned his lesson, Sahaidachnyi attacked Constantinople at the beginning of 1615 with 80 ships. His Cossacks burned the harbors of Mizevna and Arkhyuk, devastated the area and left, frightening the Sultan himself. The Turkish fleet chased the Cossacks, caught up with them near the mouth of the Danube, but the Cossacks, under the cover of darkness, rushed to attack and, in the best traditions of real pirates, boarded the galleys. A fierce and bloody hand-to-hand battle ensued. But from the moment the Cossacks burst onto the decks of the Turkish ships, their victory was predetermined. Some of the Turkish ships were sunk. The Cossacks took the other galleys to Ochakov and sneery burned them in front of the Turkish garrison (it was not possible to take them to Zaporozhian Host). During the battle near the Danube, the commander of the Turkish fleet was captured. The winners returned safely to Zaporozhian Host with rich booty and glory.

After this, the Cossacks of Sahaidachnyi attacked and burned Kafa, one of the largest slave markets in the Black Sea region, freeing thousands of Christian captives.

The campaigns of 1615 were an insane audacity carried out almost under the very nose of the Sultan himself. But everything was executed so delicately and professionally that their success was more of a pattern than simple luck.

2.2 *Traditions of Zaporozhian Cossacks*

The Zaporozhian Cossacks represented a special group of the Ukrainian Cossacks. We are talking about those Cossacks who settled up in the territory on the lower of the Dnipro River, beyond the Dnipro rapids. This territory was called "*Niz*" (Lower) or "Zaporizhzhia". Among the countless branches of the Dnipro and small islands, the Cossacks found a safe refuge. The access there was difficult, and it was not easy to find the Cossacks. There were lots of game on the islands and lots of fish in the rivers, which provided them with everything they needed.

Peasants and townspeople fled to the Zaporozhian Host from the Polish-Lithuanian Commonwealth, fleeing from the hard corvee (forced labor for landlords). The Zaporozhian Host existed until the end of the 18th century, and

12 Korolev V.N. Bosforskaia voina. Rostov-na-Donu, 2002. P. 167–169.

only Catherine II considered it impossible to have a free region in the empire. It was the Cossacks who played a key role in the wars with the Ottoman Empire during the 16th-18th centuries, as well as in the conquest of the Crimea.

The creation of winter huts and forts became the starting point for the formation of the Zaporozhye Sich (Sich – from the word "*zaseki*", defensive constructions that the Cossacks built against enemies). The first Tomakovska Host (located on the island of the same name) appeared in the 80s of the 16th century. By that time, Zaporozhian Host was already a unique form of a republic, which many compared to a medieval monastic order, since the presence of women there was strictly prohibited. And this ban was in effect until the end of the existence of the Zaporozhian Host (unlike the Don Cossacks).

One of the founders of the Zaporozhian Host was the Volyn magnate Dmitry Wiśniowiecki, who was the richest landowners of the Polish-Lithuanian Commonwealth, but devoted himself to the Cossacks fate and the fight against the Tatars. In 1553, Wiśniowiecki, founded the Zaporozhian Host on the island of Malaya Khortytsia. He devoted many years of his life to the fight against the Ottoman Empire. When he was captured by the Turks, by order of Sultan Suleiman II, he was given a painful execution in Constantinople, hanging by his rib on a hook at a tower. The Wiśniowiecki suffered for three days, but did not stop cursing the Muslim faith and at the end, by order of the Sultan, he was killed with an arrow. In people's memory, Dmitry Vishnevetsky remained under the nickname Baida, i.e. "carefree person" in Tatar language.

2.3 *Prohibitions and Punishments in the Zaporozhian Host*

The Zaporozhian Host had strictly enforced laws. Usually in their lives the Zaporozhian Cossacks followed the established tradition,[13] but there also existed laws adopted by the *Rada* (General meeting).

The judgement of the committed offenses or crimes was carried out publicly. The offender and the offended presented their case in front of the judges. It is important that the Zaporozhian Cossacks were never tortured during the investigation, thus equating them to the knightly, gentry class of Polish-Lithuanian Commonwealth (which was exempt from torture). The main crimes that were considered the most serious were:

- the murder of a comrade by a Cossack,
- theft from a comrade (for large ones they were executed by death),
- offending a woman,
- violence in Christian villages,

13 Javornyc'kyj D. Istorija zaporoz'kyh kozakiv. Kyi'v, 1990. P. 231.

- drunkenness during a campaign,[14]
- the offence of the Ataman (major officer),
- the disrespect of the Host customs,
- and the flight from the battlefield.[15]

The Koshevoy Ataman was the highest judge. For minor crimes (such as theft or gambling debt) Cossacks were chained by the neck to a cannon. The person punished remained in this position until he compensated for the loss (or someone did it for him).[16] There were also death penalties for serious sins. During sea voyages, it was strictly forbidden to drink and for drunkenness Cossacks were thrown out of the ship.

The worst punishment was for the murder of a comrade – the culprit was buried alive (the murderer was placed in a coffin with the murdered man). Among other types of death penalty, Zaporozhian Cossacks practiced beating with *kij* (oak sticks like a whip) at a pillory. Also was practiced the gallows (traditional) or on an iron hook (which was threaded through the ribs). In both cases, the executed were left on the highway as a warning to others. During the procedure of the traditional gallows the criminal was put on a horse, brought under the gallows, a noose was thrown on the neck and the horse was driven away.[17] It is interesting that a Cossack, sentenced to death, could be saved by a woman – therefore the executions were carried out in the steppe, not in the Zaporozhian Host. A single woman could announce that she would take the condemned as her husband – thereby saving his life. In case of consent of the person sentenced to execution, he was released from punishment. According to legend, there were cases when the Zaporozhian Cossacks, who did not like the woman who was his savior, preferred the death to marriage.

As for the prisoners, there was a clear difference in the attitude of the Zapoirozhian Cossacks towards Christian prisoners and towards Muslim prisoners. Considering themselves defenders of the Christian world, the Zapoirozhian Cossacks always released all Christian captives. For example, this is what Petro Sahaidachnyi did when he captured Kafa (and we were talking about several thousand Christian captives). The similar episodes has happened during the fights with the Tatars in the Wild Field. If the Cossacks managed to recapture Christian Yasir, they released them or even escorted them to the nearest safe place (for example, to the Svyatogorsk Monastery).

14 Javornyc'kyj D. Istorija zaporoz'kyh kozakiv. Kyi'v, 1990. P. 232; Boplan Giiom Lavasser. Opisanie Ukrainy. Moskva, 2004. P. 261.

15 Apostolov, A. Zaporozh'e: Strana i narod. Khar'kov, 1903 . P. 70–75.

16 Javornyc'kyj D. Istorija zaporoz'kyh kozakiv. Kyi'v, 1990. P. 233.

17 Javornyc'kyj D. Istorija zaporoz'kyh kozakiv. Kyi'v, 1990. P. 235.

There was a case when the famous Zaporozhian ataman Ivan Sirko brought 13 thousand prisoners from Crimea in 1675. Sirko released all Christian captives who wished to return to their homeland, after feeding them. Those who wanted to return to Crimea Cossacks considered traitors to Christ and killed them. As for the captured Tatars, some were sent to Moscow, and the other were left in the Host. Tatars were usually taken captive as the information prisoner, that is, wanting to obtain from them important information. Some of Tatars were then sent to the king or czar in order to receive a reward. For the rest, they demanded a ransom from the Crimea, especially if we were talking about noble Tatars.[18] And for a large number of ordinary Tatar prisoners, they also could demand a ransom. But it happened that ordinary Tatars were killed after interrogation so that they would burden the campaign. During the wars with Poland, Ukrainian Cossacks demanded a ransom for Polish prisoners and kept them until they received it. In 1648 Cossacks has captured a huge number of noble Polish prisoners during the first famous victories over the Polish army. All of them were later ransomed and returned home. A ransom could also be demanded for a Registered Cossack – during periods when the Zaporozhian Cossacks were at enmity with them. The famous case of the capture of Ivan Mazepa by the Cossacks, whom they then transferred to Moscow.[19]

3 Registered Cossacks of Ukraine

Along with the free Cossacks, who lived in Zaporozhian Host, in the second half of the 16th century has appeared another category of Ukrainian Cossacks. That was so called Registered Cossacks, received monetary compensation from the state for their service. By this time, the Cossacks had already become famous for their courage and skill, so the idea of using them to protect the borderland of the Polish-Lithuanian Commonwealth from the Ottoman Empire was quite justified.

In the Polish government has appeared a plan to use the Ukrainian Cossacks for the state service. The charters of King Sigismund II (1572) and of Stefan Batory (1682) completely exempted the registered Cossacks from the judicial jurisdiction of the state and of the landlords, as well as from paying taxes. They were under the solo jurisdiction of the chief commander of the Registered Cossacks, who got the title *Hetman* (borrowing, probably from the German

18 Velichko Samojlo, Litopys. Kiïv, 2020. pp. 488–490.

19 Tairova-Yakovleva. Ivan Mazepa and Russian Empire. McGill-Queen. 2020. p. 13–14.

Hauptmann – captain). Also the Registered Cossacks got a clerk (*Pysar*), who run the "register", i.e. a list of the Cossacks, who were included in the detachment and received a salary (hence the name – registered). The Registered regiment received its insignia – *kleynods*: horsetail, seal, cannons, trumpets, kettledrums and a banner.[20]

The Registered Cossacks has formed as a separate social group with their own rights and privileges, and soon turned into the Ukrainian political elite. From that moment on, the Registered Cossacks were constantly in the service of the Polish-Lithuanian Commonwealth, until they have created their own Ukrainian state – Hetamanate. The number of the Registered Cossacks was in different years reached up to the 100 000.

3.1 *Means and Methods of Registered Cossacks*

The Registered Cossacks of the Ukraine were famous primarily for their infantry. The basis of the technique, in which Cossacks were close to perfection, was the use of the *tabor*. The Cossacks placed their wagons in two or more rows, staying themselves in the middle with guns and scythes mounted on a shaft.[21] Various forms of *tabor* were used: a quadrangular or round row of carts (*vanegburg*). The *tabor* could also be oval or crescent-shaped.[22] To strengthen the *tabor*, they locked wheel to wheel with iron chains, raised shafts upward, and placed guns in the corners.[23] Usually, the Cossacks used the *tabor* for protection when they expected the enemy to appear. But there were cases when the camp was used for active retreat or advancement among enemies.

For example, in 1628, under the protection of the *tabor*, the Ukrainian Cossacks crossed the Crimea from Perekop to Bakhchisarai.[24] In 1655, near Dzhrizhipol, the Cossacks under the leadership of Bohdan Khmel'nyts'kyi and Ivan Bohun fought off the Poles for several days. In cases when the Cossacks were forced to take up a long defense ("defensive *tabor*"), they released their horses, taking advantage of the fact that their horses knew how to walk in herds. The size of the defense *tabor* could be enormous. Thus, in the Battle of Berestechko in 1651, the camp of the Ukrainian Cossacks reached seven miles in length and width. Under the protection of such a *tabor*, even a small detachment of Registered Cossacks could withstand several thousand of the enemy.

---

20 Kohut Z. Russian Centralism and Ukrainian Autonomy. 1988. P. 45.

21 Boplan Giiom Lavasser. Opisanie Ukrainy. Moskva, 2004. P. 243.

22 Boplan Giiom Lavasser. Opisanie Ukrainy. Moskva, 2004. P. 268.

23 Javornyc'kyj D. Istorija zaporoz'kyh kozakiv. Kyi'v, 1990. P. 413.

24 Boplan Giiom Lavasser. Opisanie Ukrainy. Moskva, 2004. P. 266.

Among the techniques used by the Cossack infantry during the siege of fortresses was the construction of trenches, which they moved, approaching closer and closer to the enemy. Such techniques, for example, were used by the Registered Cossacks during the capture of Turkish fortresses Kazierman (1695) and Azov (1696).[25]

The infantry of the Registered Cossack were excellent marksmen, and their frequency of firing from muskets amazed their contemporaries.[26] The Cossacks used a multi-line formation, which allowed them to carry out such shooting.

The registered Cossacks also had cavalry. Usually it attacked by avalanche. Before the start of the actual fight, the cavalry actively participated in the duels (*Herz*).[27] The most fearless Cossacks drove up to the enemy's formation within shooting distance and challenged them to duel, showing their courage. They skillfully pranced on horses, laughed, shouted insulting curses, thus challenging brave men from the enemy camp to a duel. In some battles, the cavalry attack was launched from the flank and served as a diversionary maneuver (Battle of Batog 1652, Battle of Uman 1654). This technique, in particular, was used very successfully by famous Cossack military leader Ivan Bohun.

Unlike the Zaporozhian Cossacks, who considered their main goal to fight the enemies of the Christian world (the Crimean Khanate and the Ottoman Empire), the Registered Cossacks initially performed various military tasks that faced the Polish king. In particular, one of their opponents were Moscow troops (campaign of 1618,[28] siege of Moscow: Smolensk War of 1633).[29] Registered Cossacks played a key role in the famous Khotyn campaign of 1621 against the Ottoman Empire, and also successfully resisted the Poles in the outbreak of the Polish-Cossack wars.[30] In particular, the Ukrainian Cossacks won brilliant victories over the troops of the Polish-Lithuanian Commonwealth near Zhovti Vody, (1648), Korsun (1648), and Batoh (1652). Subsequently, the confrontation also included military actions against Moscow (the famous victory at Konotop 1659, in which almost the entire Moscow army was liquidated). In all these battles, the main methods of the Registered Cossacks was the use of military tricks and flank attacks. The leading Ukrainian Cossack commander Ivan Bohun became famous for his use of non-standard solutions and tricks (*forteli*). For example, during the defense of Vinnytsia in 1651, Bohun ordered to do patches

25 Tairova-Yakovleva. Ivan Mazepa and Russian Empire. McGill-Queen. 2020. P. 52–55, etc.
26 Boplan Giiom Lavasser. Opisanie Ukrainy. Moskva, 2004. P. 269.
27 Boplan Giiom Lavasser. Opisanie Ukrainy. Moskva, 2004. P. 268.
28 Hrushevsky Michailo. History of Ukraine-Rus. v. 7. Edmonton-Toronto, 1999. P. 292–296.
29 Hrushevski Michailo. v. VIII, Edmonton-Toronto. 2002. P. 83–102.
30 Hrushevsky Michailo. History of Ukraine-Rus. v. 7. Edmonton-Toronto, 1999. P. 360–373.

of water in the ice-covered surface of the river and to cover it with hey. He put his cavalry on ice, and then, pretending the retread, led the Polish cavalry into an ice trap, in which many famous officers drowned, and the attack was thwarted.

3.2 *Traditions of Registered Cossacks*

Almost from the times of its formation, at the end of the 16th century the Registered Cossacks were under the jurisdiction of the court of their hetman, not subordinate to any other. Subsequently, when the system of the registered army was transferred to the administrative-judicial structure of the whole of Ukraine, creating a new, Ukrainian Cossack`s statehood, the tradition of Cossack courts was preserved.

Trials were carried out by judges – centenary, regimental or general court (headed by the general judge). Foremen were also present on the courts. If the colonels were tried, then the hetman himself was certainly present at such an event. The law-suit took place orally and involved adversarial proceedings between the parties. Cossack officers (*starshyna*) and representatives of the clergy could act as defenders of the accused. Unlike the Zaporozhian Cossacks, the Registered were guided by a legal document adopted in Ukraine – the Lithuanian Statute of 1566, based on Roman law. In addition, certain provisions were supplemented or clarified by the hetmans' statements (universals).

3.3 *Prohibitions and Punishments of Registered Cossacks*

Since the time of Sahaidachnyi, who reformed the Registered Cossacks, the main offense was considered the violation of discipline. During the war, Ukrainian Cossacks were executed for this. Betrayal was also severely punished.[31]

Of particular importance was that the death penalty was imposed for violence against a woman. This was a serious difference from the traditions of the Don Cossacks. It is likely that the special treatment and rights of women in Ukrainian Cossack society was stemmed from the provisions of the Lithuanian Statute, which gave women and girls broad legal rights, including the freedom to choose husbands and dispose of their property (including inheritance and the right to make wills).

The most common type of execution for Registered Cossacks was the beheading. In special cases, shooting was used.

---

31 Krypjakevych Ivan. Istorija ukrai'ns'kogo vijs'ka. Istorija ukrai'ns'kogo vijs'ka. L'viv, 1936. P. 181.

But all other crimes, including theft from Registered Cossacks, were punished more leniently. A monetary payoff from the perpetrator was used.[32] For some other crimes, blows with *kij* (oak sticks like a whip) (up to 50 blows) or prison arrest could be imposed.

Similar to Zaporozhian Cossacks, the Registered Cossacks were not subjected to torture. This rule equated them to the gentry in the Polish Republic. This was the reason that after the incorporation of the Ukraine with Moscow Principality (the Cossacks, like the rest of Ukraine, retained the broadest autonomy, including their own special legislation), the Registered Cossacks were often taken to Moscow, where they were tortured during the trial.

4 Don Cossacks

The Don Cossacks existed until the 20th century and became widely known thanks to their participation in the wars with Napoleon and the years of the civil war in Russia (1917–1921). Despite the fact that the Don Cossacks were a very specific and autonomous group, they are often mistakenly associated with all "Cossacks", including the Ukrainian ones.

4.1 *Means and Methods of Don Cossacks*

The Cossacks appeared on the Don at the end of the 15th century, and in the 16th century there were already permanently present in the region.[33] Their numbers were very numerous at the beginning of the 17th century, up to the 20 000. Basically, the ethnically Don Cossacks (men) consisted of Russian immigrants from the Moscow state, while women until the end of the 18th century were mostly Tatars, Turkish or Circassian.

The Donets carried out military campaigns – ground and by ship. In ground campaigns, they adhered to the tactics of lightning-fast unexpected attacks. For this they used exclusively cavalry of two horses. The attacks were mainly carried out at night. If they had to defend themselves in open areas, the Don Cossacks unhorsed, stood in a square, hiding behind their horses. Another method of evading pursuit or a superior enemy wasto scatter the cavalry separately.

On sea voyages, the Don Cossacks used small vessels that could carry from 30 to 50 people. They traveled near the coast, attacked ships or plundered coastal

32 Pashuk A.J. Sud i sudochynstvo na Livoberezhnij Ukrai'ni v XVII—XVIII st. (1648—1782). L'viv, 1967. P. 147.

33 Brehunenko Viktor. Kozaky na stepovomu kordony Jevropy. Kyi'v, 2011. P. 50, 56.

regions, the coasts of the Azov, Black and Caspian seas. The Don Cossacks did not use a compass.

In ground campaigns, the Don Cossacks used the cavalry, adhering to the principle of steppe warfare. Basically, it was to burn everything in the area so that the enemy would not get anything, including horse feed.

Don Cossacks made campaigns to the Volga river, to other regions of the Moscow frontier, and even to Siberia. It was they who became the founders of the Yaitsky, Volzhsky, Siberian and a number of other Cossacks groups, similar to the Don in typology.

The most famous was the campaign of the Don Cossack 12–13 Ermak, who in 1579 or 1581 undertook a campaign into Siberia. After a series of victories over the troops of the Siberian Khanate, Ermak's detachment defeated the main forces of Khan Kuchum in a 3-day battle (October 23–25, 1582) on the banks of the Irtysh river at Cape Podchuvash. After this, Ermak's detachment occupied the capital of the Siberian Khanate – Kashlyk (17 km from Tobolsk). A few years after this, Kuchum unexpectedly attacked Ermak's detachment and liquidated it. Wounded, Ermak tried to swim across the Irtysh river. Being wounded, carrying the heavy mail he drowned.[34] However, it was Ermak's campaign that laid the foundations for the annexation of Siberia to the Moscow state.

The main types of weapons used by the Don Cossacks were cannons, arquebuses, peaks and sabers. They did not mine gunpowder and lead themselves, but received them from the Moscow state.

4.2 *Traditions of Don Cossacks*

Unlike the Ukrainian Cossacks, the Don Cossacks did not have the opportunity to freely travel to the sea. The path to the south (to the Azov and, accordingly, the Black Sea) was blocked by the Azov fortress, constructed by Turks. From the east, the territories of the Don Cossacks were pressed against various hostile tribes of the Caucasus.

Don Cossacks initially settled in towns (permanent residences) and winter settlements (temporary shelter for those who did not have homes). Cossacks left their winter quarters in the spring for fishing or for participating in the military campaigns. By the middle of the 17th century on the territory controlled by the Don people there were already 30 towns, by the end of the century it reached 125. The Don Cossacks were divided into Lower and Upper (along the Don), with the lower ones being the most influential.[35]

34 Istoriia Sibiri s drevneishikh vremen do nashikh dnei. v.2, Leningrad, 1968.

35 Istoricheskoe opisanie zemli Voiska Donskogo. T. 1. Novocherkask, 1869. P. 100 Brehunenko Viktor. Kozaky na stepovomu kordony Jevropy. Kyi'v, 2011. P. 176.

Unlike the Zaporozhian Cossacks, the Don Cossacks, although they were also located on territory isolated from the state (Ukraine or Moscow accordingly), lived a family life. Their main livelihood was hunting and fishing. Despite their family lifestyle, the Don Cossacks were not engage in grain farming (unlike the Ukrainian Registered ones, for which this was an obligation). The Don people received bread from the king or through trade exchange.

To resolve major issues and to elect a commander, a general council was used – the military *circle*. In particular, they elected the Army Ataman, who had the highest power, and the military asauls. The written affairs of the Don Army were conducted by a *Dyak* military clerk (a clear parallel with the name of an official in the historical Russian bureaucratic occupation in the Moscow state). Usually the elections of the ataman and the meeting of the *Circle* took place in the capital of the Don Cossacks – Cherkassk.[36]

4.3 *Prohibitions and Punishments of Don Cossacks*

Unlike Ukrainian Cossacks, Don Cossacks usually didn't take captives. During fight if they killed the enemy they considered their duty fulfilled and could leave the field. Don Cossacks had a tradition of robbing enemies, including the wounded ones. Cossacks took from them not only valuables, but also clothes and boots. It was also not considered shameful to cut down an unarmed enemy, even if he had already surrendered. Such a striking example is the capture of the leader of the Polish uprising 1794, General Tadeusz Kosciuszko, by the Don Cossacks. They first captured him, wounding him, then robbed him, and then gave him additional blows – not killing him by pure chance, because someone recognized him as the enemy`s commander.[37]

Among Don Cossacks, for most crimes – treason, cowardice, insult to the Army, villainous murder and theft from the Cossack – the death penalty was applied. The Don Cossacks used for this the drowning in a bag ("putting in water"). The culprit was put in a bag, sand or stones were poured into it, the bag was tied and thrown into the river. For minor crimes Don Cossacks were punished with whips or put in the chopping block. The law-suit was carried out in a Circle, under the leadership of the Ataman.[38]

The Don Cossacks, although they were Orthodox, did not have churches and priests (almost until the beginning of the 18th century). Perhaps this was due to the fact that already in the 17th century many Old Believers (opponents of

36 Istoricheskoe opisanie zemli Voiska Donskogo. T. 1. Novocherkask, 1869. P. 102.

37 Presnukhin M.A. Eshche raz o zabytom geroe. „Armii i bitvy". 2009. N 12.

38 Istoricheskoe opisanie zemli Voiska Donskogo. T. 1. Novocherkask, 1869. P. 105; Rigel'man A. Istoriia ili povestvovanie o donskikh kazakakh. Moskva, 1840. P. 10.

church reform in the Moscow state of 1651–1660, in particular the three-finger sign of the cross). The absence of a church and clergy on the Don (practically until the beginning of the 18th century) the circle took upon itself decisions on civil issues, including the regulation of marriage relations.[39]

The peculiarity of the Don Cossacks was that they allowed women into their villages (unlike the Zaporozhian Cossacks). But women were not brought from the Moscow state, but they were stolen from the Kuban, Circassians and other surrounding non-Christian peoples. Accordingly, the attitude towards women was specific, at the first stage – as to slaves.

Until the middle of the 17th century most of the Don Cossacks led a celibate life. There were often no more than two or three married Cossacks in a town. The wedding ceremony differed significantly from the Christian ceremony according to the church charter. In the early period, most Cossacks used the announcement in front of their brothers about their chosen wife when entering into marriage. To do this, the bride and groom came together to a meeting of the people in the square. Having prayed to God, they bowed on all four sides and the groom, calling the bride by name, said: "You, be my wife." The bride, bowing at his feet, also answered calling him by name: "And you, be my husband." After these words, they kissed each other and accepted congratulations from the entire meeting.

A marriage approved in this way was considered a legal one. Even after the church marriage appeared in the 19th century, the Don Cossacks first performed their ancient custom. Among the Don Cossacks there was a custom that they could refuse of their wife by publicly announcing this and offering her to anyone who wanted it. If such was not found, the woman was released or, on the contrary, accused of some offense, and drowned.

In the 18th century legends told that in the first decades of its existence, the Circle allowed the Don Cossacks to have only sons, and if girls were born, they were killed. Subsequently, this barbaric custom was overcome.

5 Conclusion

In conclusion, the Cossack history is a tale of two diverse worlds – the Ukrainian Cossacks and the Don Cossacks, each marked by distinct traditions and approaches. The Don Cossacks, in stark contrast to their Ukrainian

39 Rigel'man A. Istoriia ili povestvovanie o donskikh kazakakh. Moskva, 1840. P. 9.; Istoricheskoe opisanie zemli Voiska Donskogo. T. 1. Novocherkask, 1869. P. 110.

counterparts, exhibited unique practices in their engagements with enemies and the administration of justice.

Don Cossacks adhered to a code of conduct that, in some instances, diverged from conventional norms. They were known for their lack of captives during battles, considering their duty fulfilled upon enemy defeat. Instead, they upheld a tradition of robbing enemies, even if wounded or unarmed, shamelessly seizing valuables, clothes, and boots. Notably, the capture of General Tadeusz Kosciuszko, leader of the 1794 Polish uprising, demonstrated their unorthodox approach, as they initially wounded, robbed, and then, by chance, spared him.

Their system of justice was equally unique, with severe penalties for grave offenses such as treason, cowardice, Army insult, heinous murder, and theft. The punishment often took the form of a chilling method known as "putting in water," where the offender was placed in a bag, weighed down with sand or stones, and cast into the river. Minor transgressions incurred whippings or time in the chopping block, with legal matters deliberated in the Circle under the Ataman's guidance.

Intriguingly, the Don Cossacks, despite their Orthodox faith, refrained from having churches and priests until the early 18th century, possibly influenced by the presence of Old Believers who rejected church reforms. Instead, the Circle assumed responsibility for civil matters, including the regulation of marriage relations.

The Don Cossacks' history offers a distinctive perspective on Cossack culture, characterized by a blend of fierce individualism, unconventional ethics in warfare, and a justice system rooted in severe, even brutal, punishments. Their story, as much as the Ukrainian Cossacks', contributes to the rich tapestry of Cossack heritage, showcasing the complexity and diversity within this remarkable group

CHAPTER 4

Ottoman Laws of War

Shadeen Ali

1 Introduction

The Ottoman empire is among the great universal monarchies known in world history for the vast extent of its realm, its long duration of existence, and its unrivalled military might.[1] War played an important role in shaping Ottoman history, empowering Ottoman Sultans to transform their frontier polity into a centralised patrimonial empire.[2] The Ottomans began a new era of conquest that extended the empire's rule across and determined all political events of more than 35 modern nations. From Slovakia in the north to Eritrea in the south, from Algeria in the west to Azerbayjan in the east; The Ottoman empire represented a cultural epoch for these countries, the traces of which remain to the present day.[3]

As the longest-running Islamic dynasty, the governance of the Ottoman state was established with the concept of divine sovereignty as its ideological foundation, while also recognising that without the sovereign's administrative power(*siyāsah shar'iyyah*) Islamic law (*shari'a*) could not be adequately embodied.[4] Thus, *siyasa shar'iyya* represents the discretionary legal powers of the sultan to enforce *kanun* (imperial or sultanic law) in order to supplement Islamic law with administrative regulations. Ottoman *'ulema* (jurists) viewed *kanun* as authoritative and legitimate expressions of power, affirming that the Ottomans were morally and legally obligated to obey the sultan. However, they

1 See Paul Wittek and Colin Heywood, The Rise of the Ottoman Empire: Studies in the History of Turkey, 13th-15th centuries (Taylor & Francis Group, 2012) 45–49.

2 Gábor Ágoston, *The Last Muslim Conquest: The Ottoman Empire and Its Wars in Europe* (Princeton University Press, 2021) 9–10.

3 Baki Tezcan, 'Ethnicity, race, religion and social class: Ottoman markers of difference' in Christine Woodhead (ed.) *The Ottoman World* (Taylor & Francis Group, 2011) 159; Wittek, (n 1) 34.

4 Wael Hallaq, *Sharī'a: Theory, Practice, Transformations* (Cambridge University Press, 2009) 197–199.

 | DOI:10.1163/9789004512566_006

emphasised that the authority was not absolute; *kanun* was valid depending on whether it met the objectives of Islamic law.[5]

Following Ahmed Al-Dawoody's 'Islamic Laws of War,' this chapter argues that the Islamic rules on the use of force developed during the lifetime of the Prophet Muhammad continued to regulate and justify the means and methods of warfare by succeeding Islamic empires and states, such as the Ottoman Empire.[6] To analyse the relationship between *shari'a* and *kanun* in the context of laws of war, this chapter will examine Ottoman regulations of warfare and its adherence to the *shari'a* during the 'Golden Age' of the empire from 1452–1566 AD. Which, naturally, will centre on the reigns of *Fatih* Sultan Mehmed II, "the Conqueror", notable for establishing the distinctive character and nature of the Ottoman military; *Yavuz* Sultan Selim I, "the Grim," who raised the Ottomans to the leaders of the Muslim World; and *Kanuni* Sultan Suleyman I, "the Lawgiver,"[7] distinguished for his codification of the *shari'a* and enabling the Ottoman central administration in Istanbul to "reach its perfection."[8]

1.1 *Ottoman Political System*

Politics played a continual role in the development and application of Ottoman military power.[9] The imperial concept of 'world order' (*nizam-ı 'âlem*) was the underlying principle that guided Ottoman politics and social order.[10]

The concept of 'world order' delegated the fundamental duty of ensuring and maintaining justice and order within the empire to the sultan, a duty entrusted to the sultan by God (*cenab-ı Allahın vediası*).[11] The Circle of Justice

5 Samy A. Ayoub, Law, Empire, and the Sultan: Ottoman Imperial Authority and Late Hanafi Jurisprudence (Oxford University Press, 2019) 2–3; Halil İnalcık, "The Rise of the Ottoman Empire," in M.A. Cook, (ed.), *A History of the Ottoman Empire to 1730* (Cambridge University Press, 1976), 47– 48.

6 Ahmed Al-Dawoody, 'Islamic Laws of War' in Samuel White (ed.) *The Laws of Yesterday's Wars: Volume II* (Brill Nijhoff, 2022) 126–145.

7 Also known as "Suleyman the Magnificent" in the West. For the purposes of this chapter discussing legal matters, I will continue with the Ottoman title.

8 Gábor Ágoston and Bruce A. Masters, *Encyclopedia of the Ottoman Empire* (Facts on File, 2010) XXX, XXIX.

9 Mesut Uyar and Edward J. Erickson, *A Military History of the Ottomans: From Osman to Atatürk* (ABC-CLIO, 2009), X.

10 Gottfried Hagen, 'Legitimacy and World Order' in Hakan T. Karateke and Maurus Reinkowski (eds.), *Legitimizing the Order: The Ottoman Rhetoric of State Power* (BRILL, 2005) 55, 61.

11 Hakan T. Karateke, 'Legitimizing the Ottoman Sultanate: A Framework for Historical Analysis' in Hakan T. Karateke and Maurus Reinkowski (eds.), *Legitimizing the Order: The Ottoman Rhetoric of State Power* (BRILL, 2005) 38–39; Hakan Karateke, *Tesrifat-ı cedide: Son yüzyılında Osmanlı merasimleri* (Bamberg,1997) 15.

theory (*daire'yi adliyye*) developed by Ibn Khaldun describes Islamic political rule. Ottoman scholars in the 16th century mention this cyclical theory as the basis for ensuring justice within the imperial borders of the Empire.[12] This formulation of statecraft also implies an unending chain of causation in the functioning of the Islamic state.[13] The Circle begins with the notion that there can be no political sovereignty without the *askeri* (imperial administration consisting of the military, court officials, and clergy/*ulema*). Financial resources will be required to sustain the *askeri*. In order to receive financial resources, there must be continuous economic activity by the *reaya* (peasantry). To maintain prosperity and sustain taxable income, the sultan will need to ensure economic equilibrium and uphold justice. Justice, in turn, requires public order and social harmony. The *shari'a* is the basis in which social harmony is achieved. The *shari'a* cannot be implemented without a political authority, which cannot exist without the *askeri* or military. Thus, the Circle is joined.[14] This theory demonstrates that if justice is maintained then peace is ensured.

Ruling according to 'ancient custom' (*'adet-i qadime*) was also an important principle for the Ottoman idea of 'world order'. Despite the religious nature of the Ottoman empire, the promulgation of *kanun*, a secular legal system based on customary law (*örf*), was established by the sultan and eventually took place alongside the *shari'a*. Defined by historian, Halil Inalcık, as "the authority to legislate in the frameworks outside the *shari'a* based on the sole will of the sovereign."[15] The 'ancient custom' used by the Ottomans was a derivative of inherited structures originating from the Emirates that succeeded them, particularly the law (yassa) of Genghis Khan.[16] In fact, certain Ottoman documents used the term yassa interchangeably with *kanun* to refer to prohibitions made by the sovereign.[17]

---

12 See Cornell Fleischer, "Royal Authority, Dynastic Cyclism and 'Ibn Khaldunism' in Sixteenth-Century Ottoman Letters," in Bruce Lawrence, (ed.), *Ibn Khaldun and Islamic Ideology* (Brill, 1984).

13 John F. Guilmartin 'Ideology and Conflict: The Wars of the Ottoman Empire, 1453–1606' (1988) 18(4) *The Journal of Interdisciplinary History*, 727–728.

14 Sohail H. Hashimi, *Just Wars, Holy Wars, and Jihads: Christian, Jewish, and Muslim Encounters and Exchanges* (Oxford University Press, 2012), 200; Hallaq (n 4) 199–200.

15 Halil İnalcık, 'Le droit d'initiative du sultan et les lois de Fâtih (Mehmed II)' (2011) 39(38–39) *Cahiers balkaniques* 289–324.

16 Hagen (n 10) 69.

17 Yunus Koç, 'Early Ottoman Customary Law: The Genesis and Development of Ottoman Codification,' in *Shattering Tradition: Custom, Law and the Individual in the Muslim Mediterranean*, Walter Dostal and Wolfgang Kraus(eds.), (IB Tauris, 2005) 79; Uriel Heyd, *Studies in old Ottoman criminal law*, V.L. M.nage (ed.), (Oxford, 1973) 167.

2 Means and Methods of War

2.1 *Nature of Wars*

Ottoman "historical narratives" consisting of epic literature and hagiographies, give mention to two concepts of armed conflict: *jihad* (holy war) and *gaza* (raid).[18] The sources in which the Ottomans depicted themselves as "fighters of Islam" against non-Muslims were derived from warrior epics of medieval Anatolia as well as later texts by court historians.[19] All of which adopted a version of an early Islamic term 'ghazwa,' which refers to raiding expeditions, primarily for the sake of plunder, used by nomadic Bedouin tribes.[20] *Maghazi* (*ghazwa* plural) specifically applied to accounts of the early Muslim military expeditions which the Prophet Muhammad took part in.[21]

The Ottoman's adoption of the terms *gaza* and *gazi* demonstrates a continuity in Turco-Muslim culture and the influence of the warrior dynamics of the Arab-Byzantine frontier of South Anatolia and the Arab-Turk frontier of Transoxiana.[22] Therefore, Ottoman concepts of war were categorised into two types: war of imperial campaigns, and war of raids and counterraids.

2.1.1 Jihad

The first concept of war was formally legitimised by the Ottoman state's highest religious authority, the *Şeyhülislam*, and justified using precepts of the *shari'a*.[23] The Ottoman sultans adopted the ideology of *jihad* and assumed the role of military leaders of the holy war against infidels of Southeastern Europe – a role which legitimised their rule.[24] By the 15th century, an Islamic legal system had become well-established in the Ottoman Empire, which

18 Pinar Kayaalp, 'Frontier Warriors as Cultural Mediators: Shifting Identities of Byzantine and Turkish March Fighters as Elicited from Anatolian Epic Literature' (2012) 25 *Mediaevistik* 119.

19 Deniz Özlem Çevik, 'Gaza as "the theory of everything" of the ottoman universe: understanding contact and conflict in the Mediterranean,' MA Thesis, McGill University (2016) 8.

20 J.M.B Jones 'The Maghāzī literature' in A.F.L. Beeston et al (eds), *Arabic Literature to the End of the Umayyad Period* (Cambridge University Press, 1983) 344.

21 Ibid.

22 Eveline van der Steen, *Near Eastern Tribal Societies During the Nineteenth Century: Economy, Society and Politics Between Tent and Town* (Taylor & Francis, 2014).

23 Guilmartin (n 13), 725.

24 Viorel Panaite, *Ottoman Law of War and Peace : The Ottoman Empire and Its Tribute-Payers from the North of the Danube.* (BRILL, 2nd rev ed 2019), 54.

established the concept of holy war, *ghazw* or *jihad,* and made it compulsory upon the sultan and the state.[25]

The second concept of war was called *gaza* warfare, a perpetual war of raids along the borders of the Ottoman empire and its neighbouring Christian states.[26] Warfare in the early Ottoman period was of a continuous and religious nature between Ottomans and the Byzantines, and though both sides used their religion to justify and legitimise their aims and war, the Ottoman *gaza* was not that of a simple holy war.[27] Ottoman warriors (*gazi*) were not strictly religious fighters, but better described as raiders (*akıncı*) that held the belief of the superiority of Islam.[28]

2.1.2 Gaza

According to Ottoman historian Paul Wittek, the Ottoman state was devoted to frontier warfare, *gaza*, for the multiple purposes of plunder, territorial expansion, glory, and religion.[29] Viorel Panaite states that the *gazi* ideal, referring to it as "*jihad* with sword," was the ideology built and used by the Ottomans to justify their rule and wage war.[30] Colin Imber states:

> The most celebrated of these legitimizing ideals was the notion that the sultans and their armies were gazi's, warriors of the faith, whose war against Christians represented an Islamic holy war against infidelity. The ultimate source of this idea was the *ser'iat,* the holy law of Islam, which, to simplify greatly, makes the prosecution of holy war an obligation on the Islamic community. By invoking the *ser'iat,* Ottoman rulers were able to project their wars against Christian neighbors and their subjects' raids on Christian territories as the necessary fulfilment of a divinely imposed

25 Colin Imber, 'Frozen Legitimacy' in Karateke, Hakan T. and Maurus Reinkowski (eds.) *Legitimizing the Order: The Ottoman Rhetoric of State Power* (BRILL, 2005) 101.

26 Guilmartin (n 13), 725.

27 Uyar, (n 9), 14–15.

28 Linda T. Darling, Contested Territory: Ottoman Holy War in Comparative Texts (200) 91(1) Studia Islamica, 133–137; Cemal Kafadar, *Between Two Worlds: The Construction of the Ottoman State* (University of California Press, 1995) 79–80.

29 Wittek, (n 1); Kate Fleet, "The Rise of the Ottomans" in Maribel Fierro (ed), *The New Cambridge History of Islam*, vol 2 (Cambridge University Press 2010) 321; Bonner, Michael, *Jihad in Islamic History: Doctrines and Practice* (Princeton University Press, 2006).

30 Panaite, (n 24) 39. "jihad with sword" may be in reference to the Maliki definition of jihad to be "fighting the disbelievers with the sword".

> obligation, a claim which gave them legitimacy in the eyes both of their own subjects and of other Muslim sovereigns.[31]

The use of religion for legitimation was routinely used by Ottoman sultans throughout the 15th century, through mosque inscriptions and coins, all of which depicted the Ottomans as Muslim rulers who fought for the expansion of Islam's domains.[32] Late 14th century chronicles show that Ottoman sultans encouraged fighting by promise of both glory and booty, incentives for *jihad* and *gaza*, respectively.[33] Sultan Bayezid II (r. 1481–1512 AD) rallied his army for war by proclaiming:

> All of those wishing to enjoy the pleasure of gaza and jihad, and those who desire booty, those brave comrades who gain their bread by their sword, and those wishing to receive timar by comradeship, are requested to join me with their weapons and military equipment in this blessed gaza.[34]

It is important to note, however, that the ideology of *jihad* is interpreted as a defensive rather than offensive principle. Ahmed Al-Dawoody's chapter 'Islamic Laws of War' establishes clearly that the Islamic *jus ad bellum* is defence against aggression.[35] Though the Islamic ideology of defensive war was used by the Ottomans to repulse attacks against *dar al-Islam*, it had been offensive war that prevailed during the 15th and 16th centuries.[36] The term *gaza* implied irregular raiding activity in which the ultimate goal was the expansion of the power of Islam. Though it is uncertain when the word acquired an exclusively religious connotation, it still referred to a "predatory raid" and other offensive natures of war.[37] It is due to this difference between a defensive *jihad* and an

31 Colin Imber, 'Ideals and legitimation in early Ottoman history,' In Kunt, Metin and Christine Woodhead (eds). *Süleyman the Magnificent and His Age. The Ottoman Empire in the Early Modern World* (Routledge, 1995) 138– 139; Imber, Colin, *Ebu's-su'ud* (Edinburgh University Press, 2019) 65–73. See, Panaite, (n 24) 39.

32 Ágoston (n 2) 27.

33 Ibid 26.

34 Heath W. Lowry, *The Nature of the Early Ottoman State* (State University of New York Press, 2003) 48–49; Ibid 26.

35 Al-Dawoody, (n 6) 133.

36 Panaite, (n 24) 37–40.

37 Cemal Kafadar, *Between Two Worlds: The Construction of the Ottoman State* (University of California Press, 1995) 70.

offensive *gaza* that recent scholars oppose the religious undertone of *gaza*, asserting that *gaza* was not justified by Islamic law.

Islamic law stipulates that war is justified when there is a just cause, righteous intention, and a legitimate authority.[38] Though it has been established that the *shari'a* permits Muslims to resort to defensive *jihad* to protect themselves against aggression and religious persecution (*fitna*),[39] the permissibility of pre-emptive or offensive war initiated by Muslims in non-Muslim territories is disputed. Classical Muslim jurists agree that there are two kinds of *jihad: jihad al-daf'* (defensive war) and *jihad al-talab* (offensive war).[40] The former is a personal duty of every capable person (*fard 'ayn*) and becomes obligatory when the enemy invades Muslim territory. *Jihad al-talab,* however, is a collective duty on the Muslims (*fard kifaya*) which can be fulfilled by a number of Muslims, rather than every capable individual.[41] *Jihad al-talab* occurs when a legitimate authority has decided to initiate war outside of Muslim territory.[42] This type of offensive *jihad* cannot be waged as a means to propagate religion, given that fighting non-Muslims simply for the reason that they do not believe in Islam is a contradiction of Qur'anic injunction.[43]

Early Hanafi jurists determined that fighting to spread Islamic hegemony constitutes a just cause for recourse to war.[44] This type of offensive warfare requires that the non-Muslim enemies firstly be invited to adopt Islam. If they reject this offer, then an offer to enter into an agreement with the Islamic state will be offered, wherein they will pay *jizyah* (poll tax) in return for the protection provided. If they have refused both Islamic hegemony and to pay the *jizyah,* then this justifies war against them, and armed conflict becomes the third option.[45] Drawing from the Qur'an and the *sunnah,* hostilities by a Muslim

---

38 John Kelsay, 'Al-Shaybani and the Islamic Law of War' (2003) 2(1) *Journal of Military Ethics* 69.

39 Qur'an 2:190; 2:193; 4:75; 22:39–40.

40 Al-Dawoody, *The Islamic Law of War: Justifications and Regulations* (Palgrave Macmillan US, 2011) 76, 198–201.

41 See al-Qaraḍāwī, Fiqh al-Jihād, Vol. 1, 54, 64–114, 240, 411.

42 See al-Būṭī, *Al-Jihād fī al-Islām,* 112, 114–117; Badawi, 'Muslim/Non-Muslim Relations,' (2003).

43 Qur'an 2:256; 10:99; 16:93; 18:29.

44 Majid Khadduri, The Islamic Law of Nations: Shaybānī's Siyar (John Hopkins University Press, 1966) 95–194; Kelsay (n 38) 69–70.

45 Al-Dawoody The Islamic Law of War: Justifications and Regulations (Palgrave Macmillan, 2011) 198. See also, Abū Yūsuf Kitāb al-Kharāj tr Aharon Ben-Shemesh (Brill, 1969) 193; hadith number 4522 in Muslim Ibn al-Hajjaj, Sahîh Muslim (Darussalam, 2007) Vol. 5, 16–17.

army would only become lawful if it is preceded by an invitation.[46] Therefore, it is agreed among Hanafi jurists that along with just cause, righteous intention, and legitimate authority, an invitation to accept Islam is required.[47]

> If the army [of Islam] attacks the territory of war and it is a territory that has received an invitation to accept Islam, it is commendable if the army renews the invitation, but if it fails to do so it is not wrong. The army may launch the attack by night or by day. It is permissible to burn fortifications with fire or to inundate them with water. If the army captures any spoil of war, it should not be divided up in enemy territory until it is brought to a place of security and removed to the territory of Islam.

This is based on the reasoning that while conquests can accomplish the objective of spreading Islamic hegemony, it is not the primary or only means to an end.[48] Islamic scholar, Syed Abul A'la Maududi, writes that "Islam does not believe in war for the sake of war, rather treats it is as an instrument of diplomacy to bring about reforms and peace", therefore, "if bilateral talks have a chance of achieving the same ends, they should be given the priority."[49] The requirement for an invitation and the offering of peace is based on the Qur'anic instructions that: "If the enemy is inclined towards peace, make peace with them."[50]

Armenian historian Ignatius Mouradgea d'Ohsson defined the first invitation to enjoin and embrace Islam as a "religious summon," and the second invitation to recognise Islamic supremacy by paying the the *jizyah* as a "political summon."[51] 15th century Byzantine chronicles give mention to these "summons" and remark on the practice of sending word to surrender before

46 Qur'an 17:15–16: "We would never punish a population until We have sent a messenger to warn them. *When We decide to destroy a town, We [first] command its wealthy people [to obey God], but they disobey, so the decree of punishment is justified against them, and We destroy them utterly.*"

47 Khadduri (n 44) 95–96.

48 John Kelsay, (n 38) 69–71.

49 Syed Abul A'la Maududi, *Al Jihad Fil Islam*, transl. by Syed Rafatullah Shah (Idadarah Tarjumanil Quran 2017) 126.

50 Qur'an 8:61.

51 Ignatius d'Ohsson, Tableau général de l'Empire Othoman: Oriental antiquities, and general view of the Othoman customs, laws, and ceremonies (1788) 53, 70. See also Panaite (n 24), 82–81.

besieging cities and fortresses.[52] The Moldavian prince and scholar Demetrius Cantemir affirms the Ottomans adherence to this requirement, he states:

> The Turks are forbid by their law to wage war without acquainting the enemy of their coming. This done, (they fay), both that the Othman bravery may not be eclips'd by subduing their adversaries with fraud and stratagem, and that the enemy may be call'd to the precepts of the Koran and Mahometan faith. Upon a refusal, they think themselves not only innocent of the effusion of blood, but if they die, believe they become in God's fight, Martyrs, and if they conquer, Gazi.[53]

According to Hanafi scholars, the practice of enjoining the enemy before every attack was preferable, however, it was not an obligation that required strict adherence.[54] Cantemir mentions that the Ottomans, for the most part, complied with this type of practice prior to engaging in hostilities, but are not at fault for any failure to do so:

> However, they do not always strictly observe this custom, but often interpret the law according to urgent emergencies, nor proclaim war before they have sheath'd the sword in the bowels of the enemies [...] But it is wrong to blame the Turks for what is the common practice of all mortals.[55]

According to Hanafi jurist Al-Shaybānī, the world is divided into territory governed by Muslims, *dar al-Islam* (abode of peace), and territory governed by others.[56] Therefore, the development of the theory of a monistic caliphate as a universal policy was developed according to Muslim fighters crossing borders to 'open' *dar al-harb* (abode of war).[57] The Ottomans adopted this doctrine,

52 Chalcocondil, Expuneri, 258; Ducas, Istoria, 406; Critobul, Mehmed II, 184, 220. For example, in Ducas, Istoria, 402: Ducas mentions that the sultan's message to the envoys of Rhodos after 1453: "If you do not accept giving tribute, you will not have the sultan's friendship." (Ducas, Istoria, 402).

53 Demetrius Cantemir, T*he History of the Growth and Decay of the Othman Empire*, translation by Nicolas Tindal, (J.J. and P. Knapton, 1734) 210–211, note 94.

54 See Khadduri (n 44).

55 Demetrius Cantemir, T*he History of the Growth and Decay of the Othman Empire*, translation by Nicolas Tindal, (J.J. and P. Knapton, 1734) 210–211, note 94. See also, Viorel Panaite, *Ottoman Law of War and Peace: The Ottoman Empire and Its Tribute-Payers from the North of the Danube. Second Revised Edition* (BRILL, 2019) 81.

56 Kelsay (n 38) 66–67.

57 Panaite (n 24) 79–81.

asserting that there were no territorial limits on the sultan's sovereignty and that the ultimate objective of Islam was to subordinate the entire world to one religion and system of law, thus bringing implied order, unity, peace, and justice to territories outside of *dar al-Islam*.[58] The universalist notion of sovereignty given through divine authority was one that was also previously accepted by Genghis Khan and his descendants. Ottoman sultans upheld this Mongol-Genghisid ideal of law and sovereignty as *örf* that coincided with Islamic ideals.[59]

Sultan Mehmed II established the character and nature of the Ottoman empire based on this ideal of a universal empire and devoted thirty years of his reign to the fulfilment of this aim.[60] This primary military objective to establish a world-wide empire was demonstrated by Mehmed II's use of several legal titles to ensure his absolute authority.[61] His second title as Khan derived from a 13th century chronicle stating:

> Osman ghazi had come from the tribe of Kayi, he had been chosen sovereign by the Turkish beys of the marches. According to the tradition of the Oghuz bequeathed by Gün Khān, as long as the clan of Kayi remains in existence, none other deserves the khanate and sovereignty.

The title of Khan gave Mehmed II the legal title and ability to rebut any claims to overlordship by other Ottoman princes or by Timür and his descendants.[62] Mehmed II's third title of Caesar came after he successfully captured Constantinople in 1451:

> let no one doubt that he is by right the emperor of the Romans. For he is emperor who by right possesses the seat of the empire, but the seat of the Roman empire is Constantinople: thus he who by right possesses this city is the emperor. […] consequently, you are the legitimate emperor of the Romans.[63]

58 Ibid.

59 Guy Burak, 'The Second Formation of Islamic Law: The Post-Mongol Context of the Ottoman Adoption of a School of Law' (2013) 55(3) *Comparative Studies in Society and History* 595.

60 Halil İnalcık, "The Rise of the Ottoman Empire" in P,M, Holt, Ann KS Lambton and Bernard Lewis (eds), *The Cambridge History of Islam* (Cambridge University Press 1977) 296.

61 Ibid.

62 Ibid, 296–270.

63 Giorgios Trapezuntios' speech about Sultan Mehmed II in Franz Babinger, *Mehmed the Conqueror and His Time*, tr R. Manheim (Princeton University Press, 1978) 249.

Through all three titles of Gazi, Khan, and Caesar, Mehmed II became an embodiment of the primary goal of warfare: universal rule.

During the 16th century, Mehmed II's grandson Selim I, acquired the most important title of the Islamic world, the title of Amir al-Mu'minin "Commander of the Faithful" given to the Caliph, and *Khādim al-Ḥaramayn aš-Šarīfayn* "Protector of the two holy cities" (Mecca and Medina).[64] Religious legitimisation was used against neighbouring Muslim rulers who employed similar Islamic titles to justify their rule. Therefore, Ottoman sultans sought *fatwa* (religious rulings) to justify war against Muslim neighbours and rivals.[65] The legality of which will be discussed at a later section of this chapter.

2.1.3 Siege Warfare

For an empire to rise, another must fall. For the Ottomans, this meant the fall of Constantinople and the end of the Byzantine Empire. The fall of Constantinople is believed to have made as great an impression, both in Europe and in the East, as the fall of Rome had done almost a thousand years before.[66] By the 14th century, Constantinople, a former imperial centre, had begun its decline. Surrounded by territories under Ottoman rule and overshadowed as the principal trading centre by the Ottoman capitals of Brusa and Adrianople; Constantinople was "the dead centre of a dead empire."[67] The taking of Constantinople by the Ottomans became one of the most notable events of the 15th century, making Mehmed II's eight-week attack of the city one of the most famous sieges in history.[68] It also marked the start of a new era of warfare regarding the weapons used by the Ottomans during this siege which sparked the term "gunpowder empire."[69] Military historians suggest that the Ottoman's use of firearms during siege warfare played a crucial role in the formation and consolidation of the empire.[70] This was evident from the conquest of Constantinople, where the method of casting large siege bombards

64 Ágoston (n 8) XXXIX.

65 Ágoston, (n 2) 28.

66 Kenneth Meyer Setton, *The Papacy and the Levant, 1204–1571: The fifteenth century* (American Philosophical Study, 1976) 138.

67 Halil Inalcik, 'The Policy of Mehmed II toward the Greek Population of Istanbul and the Byzantine Buildings of the City,' (1969/1970) *Dumbarton Oaks*, 23/24, 231–232.

68 Setton, (n 66) 135–139.

69 Ágoston (n 2) 78.

70 See Ágoston 1994, 1999, 2005a, 2014; Chase 2003; Lorge 2008; Andrade 2016.

demonstrated the Ottomans superiority in siege-craft.[71] This advantageous approach meant the destruction of Byzantine fortifications and enemy property.

In line with the Islamic principle of enjoining the enemy before laying siege, Sultan Mehmed II sent out invitations to the emperor Constantine XI to surrender the city on three occasions before conquering the city by force.[72] Before the siege, the sultan commanded sixty cannons of various calibres be cast in Adrianople as a sign of the imminent attack and to give Emperor Constantine XI the time to prepare.[73] This is believed to have been done for the purpose of obeying the precepts of the *shari'a* but also because Mehmed II did not want to expose the city to pillage and cause further ruin. With victory in sight and after being thrice rejected, the sultan dismissed the emperor's belated concession to pay the annual tribute.[74] Addressing the emperor, Sultan Mehmed stated:

> If you will admit defeat and withdraw in peace, I shall give you the Peloponnese and other provinces for your brothers and we shall be friends. If you persist in denying me peaceful entry into the city, I shall force my way in and I shall slay you and all your nobles; and I shall slaughter all the survivors and allow my troops to plunder at will. This city is all I want, even if it is empty.[75]

For Mehmed II, it was incumbent upon him as a *gazi* to bring honour and pride to the house of Osman and begin his reign with a victory over the Christian infidels to fortify his political position.[76] At the time, it was speculated that Byzantium was sheltering Muslim claimants to the Ottoman throne to incite unrest, thus, Mehmed reasoned that as long as Byzantium endured, so will the possibility of a crusade.[77] In addition to his practical considerations, Mehmed II's ambition for conquest was inspired by his dream of establishing a world empire, with Constantinople at its centre; the aspiration of Islamic empires

71 Guillmartin (n 13) 734–735; Gábor Ágoston, 'Firearms and Military Adaptation: The Ottomans and the European Military Revolution, 1450–1800' (2014) 25(1) *Journal of World History* 109.

72 Inalcik, (n 67).

73 Ágoston (n 2) 75.

74 Ibid 77–78.

75 Doukas 1975, 218. See also Nicol 1994a, 65; Gábor Ágoston (n 2) 77.

76 Setton (n 66) 108.

77 Stanford J. Shaw and Ezel Kural, *History of the Ottoman Empire and Modern Turkey: Volume 1, Empire of the Gazis: The Rise and Decline of the Ottoman Empire 1280–1808* (Cambridge University Press, 1976) 55–57.

for centuries.[78] For Muslims, the conquest of Constantinople was predestined for them by God, with the Prophet Muhammad himself having ordered the first military action against the Byzantines in 629 CE.[79] Between the first military action and the final fall of the city by Mehmed II, there had been twelve expeditions against the Byzantine capital by Muslim forces.[80] The Ottomans would regularly cite *ahadith* and folk-epic material about the future Muslim conquest of the city, one of which declares: "One day Constantinople will certainly be conquered. A good *emir* ("commander") and a good army will be able to accomplish this."[81] Thus, for the Ottomans, the conquest of Constantinople was their ultimate objective as an Islamic empire, one that Mehmed II was determined to achieve: "either I take this city, or this city will take me, dead or alive."[82]

Multiple factors played a part in the Ottoman's success at breaching the walls of Constantinople, including careful planning, a larger army, abundant supplies of provisions and weapons, the absence of Byzantine reinforcements, and Mehmed II's prowess in siege warfare.[83] The siege tactics and techniques included night assaults, mining operations by the *Lağımcı Ocağı* (the hearth of miners) corps, and artillery fired in triangle formations.[84] The concept of *gaza* was central to the sultan's plan for conquest, as is demonstrated in Mehmed II's statement: "the ghaza is our basic duty, as it was in the case of our fathers. Constantinople, situated as it is in the middle of our dominions, protects the

78 Ibid 55; Setton 108; Caroline, Finkel, *Osman's Dream* (John Murray Press, 2012) 48.

79 Buhl, F, 'Mu'ta', *Encyclopaedia of Islam,* (Brill 2nd ed, 2012) VII:756a. See, halil inalcik 1–4.

80 Inalcik, Halil, 'Istanbul: An Islamic City' (Oxford University Press) (1990) 1 *Journal of Islamic Studies* 2. For further discussion on the history of Islamic-Byzantine interactions, see Hugh N Kennedy, *The Byzantine and Early Islamic Near East* (Ashgate, 2006); Ismāʿīl ibn ʿUmar Ibn Kathīr, Winning Hearts and Souls: Expeditions and Delegations in Lifetime of the Prophet, Taken from Al-Bidāya wa-l-Nihāya (Darrussalam, 2011) 21–26; Agha Ibrahim Akram, The Sword of Allah: Khalid Bin Al-Waleed, His Life and Campaigns (1970); Walter Emil Kaegi, *Byzantium and the Early Islamic Conquests* (Cambridge University Press, 1995); Peter Sarris, 'Byzantium and Islam' in *Byzantium: A Very Short Introduction* (Oxford, 2015); Angeliki E. Laiou, Roy P. Mottahedeh, *The Crusades from the Perspective of Byzantium and the Muslim World* (Dumbarton Oaks, 2001); Casim Avci, 'Military Expeditions Launched by Muslim Arabs to the Byzantine Capital of Constantinople' (2015) *Marmara Türkiyat Araştırmaları Dergisi*, 2(2), 7–24.

81 Halil Inalcik, 'Istanbul: An Islamic City' (Oxford University Press) (1990) 1 *Journal of Islamic Studies* 1.

82 Ágoston (n 2) 1–14.

83 Gábor Ágoston, 'Firearms and Military Adaptation: The Ottomans and the European Military Revolution, 1450–1800' (2014) 25(1) Journal of World History 109; Ágoston (n 2) 78.

84 Uyar (n 9) 34, 52; Ágoston (n 2) 76–77; Filiz Yildrim, 'Osmanli Devleti'nin Yeralti Savaşçilari: Lağimcilar,' (2019) *Fırat Üniversitesi Sosyal Bilimler Dergisi* 29(2), 385.

enemies of our state and incites them against us. The conquest of this city is, therefore, essential to the future and the safety of the Ottoman state". 15th century Byzantine records also report that Mehmed's speech mentioned the Islamic notion of heaven awaiting those who lost their lives in battle and the sultan's oath that Constantinople would be plundered for 3 days, permitting every soldier to keep his own spoils.[85] It is reported that the Sultan had also given a speech to the janissaries, to which he promised them rewards for their victory.[86]

As the Ottoman sultan and as a Muslim ruler, Mehmed II was obliged to act in conformity with the *shari'a,* which prohibits the unnecessary destruction of enemy property and the indiscriminate killing of non-combatants as collateral damage.[87] Under Islamic law, the targeting of enemy fortifications with weapons of mass destruction is prohibited if it is intended to kill the enemy on a large scale.[88] However, as pointed out by Al-Dawoody, damage to enemy property by an Islamic state may be carried out if it is to force the enemy to surrender or to bring an end to the fighting.[89] Classical Muslim jurists agree that it is permissible to direct weapons for catapulting large stones at the enemy, even though it may lead to casualties among non-combatants.[90] The eponymous founder of the Hanafi school, Abū Hanīfah reasons that this permissibility is based on military necessity and provided that the Muslim army intends to avoid non-combatants.[91] Additionally, based on the precedent from the Prophet Muhammad's last battle, al-Ta'if, it is permissible for the Sultan to use cannons when besieging the enemy. During the battle of al-Ta'if, mangonels were set up to be used against the besieged. Although the Muslim army did not manage to use mangonels at Thaqīf's fortress, Islamic jurists used this context of the enemy retreating or fighting from within fortifications to permit the use of such weaponry and justified the anticipated incidental harm by the

85 Pseudo-Sphrantzes, III, 269–70. See generally Halil İnalcik, 'The Rise of the Ottoman Empire' In P.M. Holt, Ann K. S. Lambton, and Bernard Lewis (eds.) The Cambridge History of Islam (Cambridge University Press, 1977) 293–323.

86 Chalcondylas, 392–393.

87 Muḥammad ibn al-Ḥassan al-Shaybāni Sharḥ Kitāb al-Siyar al-Kabīr, commentary by Muḥammad ibn Aḥmad al-Sarakhsī, ed. Muḥammad Ḥassan Muḥammad Hassan Ismā'il al-Shafi'ī, (Dār al-Kutub al-'Ilmiyyah, 1997) Vol. 1, 75–80.

88 Al-Dawoody, (n 45) 122–125.

89 Al-Dawoody (n 6) 138.

90 See, e.g., al-Shāfi'ī, Al-Umm, Vol. 4, 288.

91 See, e.g., al-Ṭabarī, Ikhtilāf al-Fuqahā', 5– 7.

military necessity.[92] Accordingly, Mehmed II's deliberate cause of destruction using cannons during the siege of Constantinople was done out of military necessity to force those inside the fortification to surrender.

Mehmed II's success at besieging Constantinople gave him 'unparalleled prestige and legitimacy.'[93] As the first Muslim ruler to accomplish the centuries-old objective of capturing the city, Mehmed was now known as Fâtih Sultan Mehmed, "Mehmed the Conqueror."[94] Constantinople, the *kızıl elma* ("red apple"), had been the symbol of universal sovereignty and therefore, the target of *gazi* warfare.[95] Therefore, for the Ottoman state, the victory brought universal recognition as an empire; for the Muslim world, the victory appointed the Ottomans as leaders of Islam; for the West, the victory forced the recognition of the *imperator turcarum* (latin: emperor of the Turks) and acceptance of another "Eastern Empire" that was established in its own right.[96]

3 Prohibitions & Restrictions

The Qur'anic directive to "*fight in the cause of God against those who fight you, but do not exceed the limits*" is considered by Muslim jurists and scholars to be the Islamic *jus in bello* permitting armed conflict against enemy combatants and prohibiting the deliberate harming of non-combatants.[97] The Qur'an also specifies that "*verily, in the Messenger of God [Prophet Muhammad] you have an excellent example*",[98] which guides Muslim armies to conduct themselves according to the sayings and practices of the Prophet during armed conflict. The obligation for Muslims to conduct warfare according to the *shari'a* is also set out the Quran'ic verse decreeing: "*O you who believe, when you meet an enemy, be firm and remember God often, so that may be successful. And Obey God and His Messenger.*"[99] Thus, the conduct of the Ottoman armies is assessed

---

92 Al-Dawoody (n 6) 142; Al-Dawoody (n 45) 117, 123–124, 164; Ali ibn Muhammad al-Mawardi, *Al-Ahkam as-Sultaniyyah: The laws of Islamic governance,* transl. Asadullah Yate (Ta-Ha Publishers, 2023) 79.

93 Gábor Ágoston, (n 2) 79.

94 Ibid. see also, Feridun M. Emecen, Osmanli Imparatorlugunun Kurulus Ve Yukselis Tarihi,1300–1600 [History of Foundation and Rise of the Ottoman Empire, 1300–1600] (Istanbul: Turkiye Is Bankasi Kultur Yayinlari,2015),141–2; Halil Inalcik, (n 67) 236–7.

95 Finkel 49; Shaw 55, Ágoston (n 2) 79.

96 See Wittek, (n 1).

97 Quran 2:190; Al-Dawoody (n 45) 58–67; Al-Dawoody (n 6) 136.

98 *Qur'an* 33:21.

99 *Qur'an* 8:45–46.

based on their adherence of the wartime prohibitions set in the *Qur'an* and by the Prophet Muhammad.

3.1 *Prohibition of Looting*

The legality of looting and plunder according to the precepts of the *shari'a* was discussed among Muslim jurists, with the Hanafi opinion being that the sultan exercises exclusive authority regarding the spoils of war.[100] Muslims have been instructed by the Prophet Muhammad that if they should conquer a city, they should not indulge in pillage or plunder: "*Do not loot, do not be treacherous and do not mutilate*".[101] The prohibition of looting (*ghulūl*) refers to a combatant from the Muslim army who takes a share from the war booty before it is divided up and distributed by the army commander.[102] Under Islamic law, the division of war booty is based on the Qur'anic verse stipulating that at the time of the Prophet, one-fifth of the spoils of war is for God and His Messenger, the near kin of the Prophet, the orphans, the poor, and the wayfarer.[103] The one-fifth share was regarded as the share of the state.[104] Some jurists held that after the death of the Prophet, the division of the *khums* (one-fifth share) should be given to the imam, the Hanafi school in particular, stating that the share should be given to Caliph.[105] Based on the Hanafi theory, *Şeyhülislam* Ebüssuûd Efendi, affirmed that the Ottoman sultan exercised exclusive authority with regard to the spoils of war and therefore plunder and enslavement without the sultan's authorisation was considered unlawful spoils of war.[106]

According to Muslim jurists, the remaining four-fifths belonged to those who participated in the war.[107] The Hanafi's held that a commander had the right to plunder enemy territory if it fit his military and political interests and enabled the defeat of enemy forces, and that after the *khums* has been

100 Colin Imber, *Ebu's-su'ud*, (Edinburgh University Press, 2019) 85.

101 Al-Muwaṭṭa, 448, see Malik Ibn Anas, Al- Muwaṭṭ a, Muḥammad Fū'ād 'Abd al-Bāqī (ed.) (Dār Iḥyā' alTurāth al-'Arabī, 1985), Vol. 2, 448. see, Al-Dawoody, 'Islamic law and international humanitarian law: An introduction to the main principles' (2017) International Review of the Red Cross 99(3) 1008.

102 Al-Dawoody, 'Islamic law and international humanitarian law: An introduction to the main principles' (2017) *International Review of the Red Cross* 99(3) 1008–9.

103 Qur'an 8:41; Khadduri (n 44) 77.

104 Majid Khadduri, *Law and Peace in the Law of Islam* (Lawbook Exchange, 2006) 122.

105 Ibid. Based on the hadith stating that "whenever God has rewarded His Apostle, the reward should go to his successors after his death." The term Imām, Caliph, and successor seem to be used interchangeably.

106 Imber (n 100) 84–85.

107 Khadduri, (n 104) 123–125.

distributed among its recipients, looting is permissible.[108] The Hanafi school also prohibits division in enemy territory, requiring that the spoils be carried to *dar al-Islam,* unless it was deemed necessary to do so by the Muslim ruler.[109] According to Islamic law, only goods obtained from a justified war and with the sultan's authorisation is considered lawful booty.[110]

It is difficult to assess the occurrence or extent of unlawful conduct in battle during the Classical Period due to the absence of historical narratives. However, unlawful looting is demonstrated in a rare account of mutiny occurring in the 1552 AD Ottoman campaign against the Safavids. An anonymous reporter described the janissaries unlawfully looting the city after a rumour spread that sultan Suleyman had died. The janissary revolt was driven primarily by the perceived opportunity to behave in a mutinous manner without incurring punishment but was aborted after the sultan made an appearance.[111] This is common of many militaries; but it can be inferred from the conducted that unordered looting and pillage by troops was prohibited. This account also suggests that the act of mutiny during military campaigns had been an uncommon incident during the early 16th century reign of Suleyman *Kanuni*, or simply was not reported on.[112]

3.2 *Prohibition of Slavery*

Ottoman military campaigns in the 15th and 16th centuries brought new territories to the empire, along with a multitude of, mostly Christian, enemy captives taken as prisoners of war. Islamic law permits the capturing of prisoners of war, however, there are strict conditions within the Qur'an regarding the end of captivity:

> When you meet the disbelievers in battle, strike their necks until you have subdued them, then bind them firmly. Afterwards either free them as a favour or by ransom until the war comes to an end.[113]

108 This is stipulated in the Qur'an 8:69: *Now enjoy what you have taken, for it is lawful and good. And be mindful of God.* See also, Abū Yūsuf, *Kitāb al-Radd 'alá Siyar al-Awzā'ī*; Khadduri (n 104) 118, 121; Panaite (n 24) 62.

109 Abū Yūsuf Ya'qūb and Abū al-Wafā' al-Afghānī, *Kitāb al-Radd 'alá Siyar al-Awzā'ī* (Lajnat Iḥyā' al-Ma'ārif al-Nu'mānīyah, 1938) 1–4; Khadurri, (n 44) 83; Khadduri, (n 104) 120.

110 Panaite (n 24) 66; Imber (n 100) 84, 89.

111 Anonymous account of the campaign against Persia, dated 1553, in Alberi, *Relazioni* vol 3, 236. See also, Palmira Brummett, 'Classifying Ottoman Mutiny: The Act and Vision of Rebellion' (1998) 22(1) *Turkish Studies Association Bulletin* 98–100.

112 Fitzgerald, Timothy J., 'Murder in aleppo: ottoman conquest and the struggle for justice in the early sixteenth century' (2016) 27(2) *Journal of Islamic Studies* 177.

113 Qur'an 47:4.

Based on this Qur'anic injunction, early Muslim jurists determined that the Muslim ruler is given the option to choose, depending on the best interest of the state, whether prisoners of war are to be released freely, held for ransom, executed, or enslaved.[114] Therefore, Muslim jurists collectively agree that Islamic law limited the many gateways to enslavement to only one: war.[115]

Had the Ottomans restricted their practice of enslavement to the lawfully captured prisoners of war, then there would be no discrepancy with Islamic law. However, the controversial practice of enslavement by the Ottomans observed in the *devşirme* system and the janissary corps were clear transgressions of the *shari'a* and exceeded the permissibility of enslavement.

The Ottoman Janissary Corps (*yeniçeri oğlanı*) were slave soldiers recruited through the *devşirme* system, or child levy system. The controversial devsirme system forcibly recruited young Christian boys to fill administrative and military ranks within the state and army and became the sultan's slave-servants.[116] This practice continued despite the fact that the *shari'a* prohibited the enslavement of *dhimmis* or "People of the Book" (*ahl al-kitab*) granted safe conduct (*aman*) by the Muslim ruler.[117]

The *devşirme* system is thought to have gradually evolved from the '*Pençik Kanunnamesi*' meaning the 'booty fifth.'[118] The *Pençik* system was based on the Qur'anic stipulation that one-fifth of war booty belongs to the state, as did one-fifth of the prisoners of war.[119] The *devşirme* system was later developed in the fifteenth century as a child levy system, where the male children of Christian families would be levied as a form of tribute instead of the poll-tax (*jizya*).[120] The levied boys were subjected to a second selection process in Istanbul, after which officers placed those they considered to be the most promising in the palace schools to be educated as administrators for various roles. These recruits were educated within the royal palace complex on Islam and the elite culture within the Ottoman state.[121] The recruits of this group are described as "the

114 Al-Dawoody, 'Al-Sarakhsī's Contribution to the Islamic Law of War' (2015) 14 UCLA Journal of Islamic and Near Eastern Law 34; Al-Dawoody (n 6) 138–9; Khadduri (104) 130–133.

115 Khaled R. Bashir, 'Islamic International Law', *Rules on the consequences of war* (Edward Elgar Publishing, 2018) 184.

116 H. Erdem Çıpa, 'Empire or Faith: Stretching the Boundaries of the Shari'a in Ottoman Institutional Practice' (2021) 8(2) *Journal of the Ottoman and Turkish Studies Association.*

117 See Khadduri, (n 104) 115, 164.

118 Hanxu Qi, 'The Devshireme System in the Ottoman Empire' (2022). 148 SHS Web of Conferences 1.

119 Ibid.

120 Gülay Yılmaz, 'The Devshirme System and the Levied Children of Bursa in 1603–4' (2015) 79(286) *belleten turk tarih kurumu* 901–930.

121 Guilmartin, (n 13) 744.

sultan's servants" and "state servitors."[122] This form of 'elite slavery' meant a privileged life amongst the higher echelon, however these privileges were only temporary as their slave status did not allow them to bequeath their wealth, status or property to their offspring, as in accordance with precepts relating to the status of a slave under Islamic law, which is accurately described by Leslie Peirce as "a paradox at the heart of the Ottoman system."[123]

Whereas the bulk of the *devşirme* recruits would be recorded as novice boys (*'acemi oglans*) and would be hired out to villagers in Anatolian towns for a period from between three to five years. The *'acemi oglans* worked predominantly as agricultural laborers and would have to learn the Turkish language and Islamic practices. After the agreed period of labour was over, they would return to Istanbul to work for three to five more years as laborers in the city before being recruited as soldiers in the janissary army.[124]

Christian subjects in the Ottoman state were officially considered *dhimmi*, which granted them protection against enslavement and the right to maintain and exercise their religion in exchange for paying the *jizya*, which was a principle that the Ottoman's used to assert sovereignty.[125] Hanafi jurist, Shaybānî, established that non-Muslims living under Muslim rule who took over their own and left Muslims unmolested could not be enslaved.[126] Therefore, the periodical levy of children from the sultan's Christian subjects and their forced conversion to Islam appear to contradict some of the essential principles of the *sharī'a*, which were conferred upon the "People of the Book" (*ahl al-kitâb*). The Qur'anic verse: "*there is no compulsion in religion*"[127] was deliberately disregarded in order for the young recruits to live within the sultan's palace.

Furthermore, the *sharī'a* expressly prohibited for Ottoman Muslims to be enslaved, however, young Muslim boys were being levied from Bosnia too, yet another contradiction caused by the *devşirme*. It is reported that following Mehmed II's conquest of Bosnia in 1463 AD, the sultan approved for the recruitment of "circumcised and uncircumcised young men," which implies

122 Leslie Peirce, *Morality Tales: Law and Gender in the Ottoman Court of Aintab* (University of California Press, 2003) 313–315.

123 Ibid 313.

124 Gülay Yılmaz, 'The Devshirme System and the Levied Children of Bursa in 1603–4' (2015) 79(286) *belleten turk tarih kurumu* 901–930.

125 Guilmartin, (n 13) 721–747.

126 Khadduri, (n 44) 219.

127 *Qur'an 2:256.*

that both Muslim and non-Muslim recruits were taken from Bosnia.[128] The 'special permission' granted by Mehmed II to allow for Muslim recruits led to the development of the *poturoğulları*, a term to refer to the Bosnian Muslim boys conscripted for the janissary army.[129]

16th century Ottoman historian, Mustafa Ali, declared the *devşirme* to be "at variance with the divine law" (*şer'e mugâyır*).[130] In his discussion on the *devşirme* system, Paul Wittek points out the incompatibility with the *shari'a*, he states:

> How is it possible, we have to ask, that such a practice could come into being, gain ground, and even become a recognized, firmly established institution in a state whose sole *raison d'etre* was, from its very beginnings, religion, whose rulers were of unquestionable piety, whose organizers and administrators, in the period when the *devshirme* must have taken root, were almost all *'ulama*? Certainly, there were very strong reasons of state which recommended the institution to the Ottomans.[131]

Members of the ottoman ruling class overlooked this contravention of the *shari'a* with the misguided belief that the system was a justifiable end to the means for the formation of an imperial "world order" (*nizam-i alem*).[132] While there is no explicit evidence that indicates how the Ottomans legitimised the practice of *devşirme*, several Ottoman chroniclers appear to have simply assumed that it was compatible with the *shari'a*, primarily because it served the needs of the state and enlarged the community of Muslims (*umma*). Ottoman historian Idris-i Bidlisi welcomed *devşirme* as a "most wise measure [which] was from the viewpoint of both law and reason a means of strengthening state and religion."[133] The Ottomans believed that the enslaved who were forcibly converted would become more efficient soldiers on account of their zealous for their new religion and hostility towards their former kin.[134] However, Ottoman sources

128 Kadrić, Sanja, 'The Islamisation of Ottoman Bosnia: Myths and Matters' in A.C.S. Peacock (ed), *Islamisation: Comparative Perspectives from History* (Edinburgh University Press, 2017) 277–295 .

129 Gülay Yılmaz, 'The Devshirme System and the Levied Children of Bursa in 1603–4' (2015) 79(286) *belleten turk tarih kurumu* 901–930.

130 Cipa, (n 116) 211.

131 Paul Wittek, 'Devshirme and Shari'a' (1955) 17(2) *Bulletin of the School of Oriental and African Studies* 291.

132 Çipa (n 116) 221.

133 Idris-i Bidlisi, as quoted in Ménage, "Sidelights on the *Devshirme* from Idrīs and Sa'duddīn," 183. See Ibid *220*.

134 Yılmaz (n 124) 901–930.

indicate that the young boys recruited for military and state service through the *devşirme* system did not forego their native language, culture, or homeland.[135] Mustafa Ali noted that the method of *devşirme* "was only adopted in the past out of need as a means to increase the number of Muslims."[136] Even though several later Ottoman scholars denounced and distanced themselves from any justifications of *devşirme*, the continued prominence of this method of compulsory recruitment suggests that Ottoman monarchs, statesmen, and bureaucrats deemed *devşirme* an indispensable institution.[137]

3.3 *Prohibition of Shedding the Blood of Another Muslim*

Islam directed the concept of war outward against the enemies of faith by prohibiting Muslim's from shedding the blood of another Muslim.[138] Islamic law justifies a state of war between *dar al-Islam* and *dar al-harb*, therefore, to wage war within *dar al-Islam* is unlawful. The Ottoman-Safavid conflict raises this issue of unlawful *gaza* as both parties followed Islam, therefore armed conflict against one another was expressly prohibited. In an authentic *hadith* of the Prophet Muhammad, narrated by Anas ibn Mālik, the Prophet said:

> I have been commanded to fight the idolators until they bear witness to *'Lā 'ilāh 'illā-llāh* (there is none worthy of worship except Allah) and that Muhammad is His slave and Messenger. If they bear witness to *'Lā 'ilāh 'illā-llāh* and that Muhammad is His slave and Messenger, and they pray as we pray and face our *Qiblah*, and eat our slaughtered animals, then their blood and wealth becomes forbidden to us except for a right that is due.[139]

This hadith establishes the prohibition of bloodshed and clarifies that fighting against unbelievers is permitted, but if they are Muslim, or if they become Muslim, then fighting them is prohibited. This prohibition is provided that they live according to Islam and bring into practice the fundamental commands. Furthermore, a hadith reported by Abdullah Ibn Mas'ud also mentions the prohibition of fighting another Muslim wherein The Prophet Muhammad said:

135 Ibid.

136 Mustafa Âli, *Nushatü's-selâtîn*, vol. 2, 30 (translation), 148 (transcription). See Çipa (n 116) 221.

137 Çipa (n 116) 220.

138 Guilmartin, (n 13) 725.

139 Hadith 3971 in *Sunan An-Nisâi'I* ed. Abu Tâhir Zubair 'Ali Za'i (Darussalam,) Vol. 5, 15.

> it is not permissible to take the life of a Muslim who bears testimony (to the fact that there is no God but Allah, and I am the Messenger of Allah), but in one of three cases: the married adulterer, a life for a life, and the deserter of his dīn (Islam), abandoning the community.[140]

The Hanafi jurist, Al-Sarakhsī argues that when balancing between a Muslim regime's aggressions against the rights of Muslims and the shedding of blood, the former should be tolerated to prevent the latter.[141] Along with other Muslim jurists, Al-Sarakhsī maintains a pragmatic reasoning that it is better to endure injustice than to resort to the use of force against a Muslim leader, which is to say that peace should be maintained and force should be used after all alternative avenues have been exhausted.[142]

4 Defences

4.1 *Defence for Looting*

The right to plunder and seize enemy territory was an essential part of Ottoman warfare during the 15th century.[143] Similar to their antecedents of the steppe, the Ottoman army functioned with the division of booty as their driving force.[144] The reward of booty was a crucial incentive for Ottoman troops, the promise of this reward was what attracted fighters to engage in armed conflict and boosted their morale.[145] Dimitrie Cantemir stated:

> It is customary with the Turkish Emperors to promise their soldiers all the goods of the enemy unless the city is taken by surrender, the walls only and the government of it reserved to themselves. It is not to be expressed what fire this gives to men naturally greedy for plunder and rapine.[146]

140 Hadith number 4375 in in Muslim Ibn al-Hajjaj, Sahîh Muslim (Darussalam, 2007) Vol. 4, 441.

141 Al-Dawoody, (n 114) 37–39.

142 Bashir, (n 115) 98.

143 Panaite (n 24) 62–63.

144 Joseph Fletcher, 'Turco-Mongolian Monarchic Tradition in the Ottoman Empire' (1979) 3/4 *Harvard Ukrainian Studies* 247.

145 Panaite (n 24) 64.

146 Cantemir, D. and N. Tindal, *The History of the Growth and Decay of the Othman Empire* (J.J. and P. Knapton, 1734), 73.

After successfully capturing Constantinople, Sultan Mehmed II granted a three-day sack to his troops.[147] As the emperor Constantine XI had not surrendered, Constantinople was considered legitimate booty according to Islamic law.[148] An Ottoman chronicle reports that the sultan regulated the looting by clarifying the terms: "the stones and the land of the city and the city's appurtenances belong to me; all other goods and property, prisoners, and foodstuffs are booty for the troops."[149] Kristobulos of Imbros also recorded that Mehmed II's first undertaking after the fall of the city, was "taking for himself the usual part of [the booty]."[150] The looting is reported to have been brought to an end by the sultan Mehmed II on the evening of the first day due to his distress caused by the destruction of property by some of his men, which supposedly led him to draw his sword on one soldier damaging the pavement of the *Ayasofya* (Hagia Sophia).[151]

Furthermore, Islamic law distinguishes between the status of combatants and non-combatants, but also between the protected status of non-believers. The *shari'a* decrees that only those from *ahl al-kittab* ("People of the Book", referring to Christian and Jewish peoples) that reject the invitation to surrender and continue to resist, those that have been subdued by force, were reduced to slavery and their goods considered to be legitimate booty.[152] The status of *dhimmi,* protected those from *ahl al-kitab* and promised not to infringe on their properties, in return for payment of the *jizya* (poll-tax).[153] Therefore, the looting of Constantinople did not include the *dhimmi* population's property or goods.[154] A *hadith* of the Prophet Muhammad states:

> If anyone wrongs a man with whom a covenant has been made [i.e. a dhimmi], or curtails any right of his, or imposes on him more than he can bear, or takes anything from him without his ready agreement, I shall plead for him on the Day of Resurrection.[155]

147 Ágoston (n 2) 78.

148 Norman Itzkowitz, *Ottoman Empire and Islamic Tradition* (The University of Chicago Press, 1972).

149 Halil Inalcik, (n 67) 232–3; tarkih-I osmani enjumeni mejmuasi, 19.

150 Critobul, Mehmed II, 158 (I, 73/1). See, Viorel, 67.

151 Duca, 298.

152 Khadduri, (n 104) 125.

153 Bashir, (n 115) 209–210.

154 Halil Inalcik, (n 64) 234, 248.

155 Hadith number in Abū Dāwūd Sulaymān ibn al-Ash'ath Sunan Abī Dāwūd (Darussalam, 2008) Vol. 3, 524–525.

Similarly, referring to the *dhimmi* population in the conquered city of Jerusalem, 'Umar ibn al-Khaṭṭāb, the second caliph, declared:

> They are granted protection for their lives, their property, their churches, and their Crosses, in whatever condition they are. All of them are granted the same protection. No one will dwell in their churches, nor will they be destroyed and nothing will be reduced of their belongings. Nothing shall be taken from their religion, nor will any one of them be troubled.[156]

Mehmed II's army adhered to this established Islamic principle that protected the inhabitants of the conquered city who had responded to the invitation to surrender.[157] After the conquest of Constantinople, the Christian population who had surrendered and agreed to pay the *jizya* obtained exactly the same rights and obligations as enjoyed by the Muslims and were protected from the looting and plundering of the city.[158]

4.2 *Defence for Campaigns against Fellow Muslims*

As previously discussed, Islamic laws prohibits the waging of war against other Muslim territories within *dar al-Islam*. However, this prohibition of internal hostility is argued not to apply to armed conflict against matters of *iman* (faith).

I will be considering the justification of the wars against the Mamluk Sultanate and the legitimacy of Selim I's conquest of the holy cities Mecca and Medina. Followed by an analysis on the prohibition of internal hostility against *ahl al-riddah* (apostates) in the context of the Ottoman-Safavid conflict and the Islamic principles justifying this resort to armed conflict.

4.2.1 Defence of Religious Orthodoxy

The overtly Sunni religious nature and institutional character of the Ottoman Empire was a factor which ensured conflict with Shi'i Islam. The friction between Shi'i and Sunni stemmed from a deep-seated religious tension within Islam, resulting in conflict over who should rule the Muslim empire.[159] The Safavid dynasty, established by Shah Ismail I (r. 1501–24) ruled over Persia from 1501 until 1736 AD. Following Shah Ismail's decision to make Shia Islam the Persian state religion, a campaign of proselytization and propaganda was carried out by

---

156 Muḥammad ibn Jarīr ibn Yazīd, Tārīkh al-Rusul wa al-Mulūk, tr Yohanan Friedman (State University of New York Press, 1987) Vol. 12, 191–192.

157 Halil Inalcik, (n 64) 234.

158 Ibid.

159 Kafadar, (n 37) 35.

the shah's agents in Anatolia.[160] Shah Ismail intended to replace all other interpretations of Islam with Shi'i Islam. He considered any Muslim who opposes his leadership, in both faith and political affairs, as guilty of disbelief (*kufr*) and thus eligible for capital punishment. His contempt for Sunni Islam led him to destroy the graves of the Abbasid caliphs and the jurist Abū Hanīfah, eponymous founder of the Hanafi school of thought which the Ottoman's predominantly followed as the legal guide. His view that Sunni Muslim's were heretics incited the attack and killing of a large number of Baghdad's Sunni population. Along with many of the city's Jewish and Christian residents (*dhimmi*) as he did not recognise a protected status for other religions.[161] Therefore, Shah Ismail's extremist Shi'ite beliefs and anti-Sunni policy constituted a threat to the Ottoman empire.[162]

Consequently, the Safavid's adoption of *Ithna-ashari* Shi'ism as the state religion of Persia was opposed by the Ottomans in accordance with the Islamic laws of apostasy.[163] In this instance, Ottoman *ulema* handled a serious internal threat to social cohesion by defining the enemies of state as enemies of religion, while also enforcing social compliance through religious orthopraxy.[164] Following the *fiqh* established by Al-Shafi'ī and Al-Ghazali, the Ottomans acted accordingly to the threat posed and rationalised that it was permissible to kill and wage war against the Safavid Muslims.

In Hungarian Scholar, Ignaz Goldziher's classic Islamic theology examination of *takfir* (accusing someone of being an apostate: *kafir*), he determines that a Muslim unbeliever is 'considered to be excommunicated' if his unbelief (*kufr*) is sufficiently proven and he has been caught. That the unbeliever should then be asked to repent and be given the opportunity to return to the community of Islam (*umma*). If he does not comply, then his punishment is death.[165] Subsequent contributions on the topic followed with an established view that the law of apostasy had its origins in the first century of Islamic history and

160 Gábor Ágoston and Bruce Masters, *Encyclopedia of the Ottoman Empire* (Facts On File, Incorporated, 2010) 280; Shaw (n 77) 78.

161 Ágoston (n 8) 71.

162 Allouche, Adel, *The Origins and Development of the Ottoman-Safavid Conflict (906–962/1500–1555)* (The University of Utah, 1980) x.

163 Shaw (n 77) 78.

164 Nabil Al- Tikriti, 'Kalam in the service of state: Apostasy and the defining of ottoman islamic identity' in Hakan T. Karateke and Maurus Reinkowski (eds.) Legitimizing the Order: The Ottoman Rhetoric of State Power (BRILL, 1st ed, 2005) vol 34, 148.

165 Ignaz Goldziher, *Vorlesungen u¨ber den Islam.* (Carl Winter's University, 1910), 182. See also, Frank Griffel, *Toleration and exclusion: al-Sha:fi"ı: and al-Ghaza:lı: on the treatment of apostates* (Yale University) 340.

that the procedure for dealing with apostates has been the same through all periods of Islamic history.[166] According to leading Muslim jurist and founder of one of the Islamic schools of thought, Al-Shafi'ī, secret apostasy, although not tolerated, is not to be treated the same as a public break from Islam. Al-Shafi'i states that:

> If one meets somebody who is still an idolater but has publicly professed Islam – whichever is the case – this does not hinder using force against him. One may oppress him, take his freedom away from him, imprison him and do similar things that do not shed his blood. His blood is granted by (the profession of) his faith. (…) we may not kill him (only) on the suspicion that he does not believe.[167]

Al-Shafi'ī establishes that someone who declares his apostasy should be harshly punished and made an enemy upon whom war must be waged as he has publicly declared his deflection from 'those whose blood is protected' and becomes from among 'those whose blood is allowed to be shed'. Al-Shafi'ī reasons that a public profession is sufficient to avoid capital punishment for secret apostasy because nobody can judge the internal disbeliefs of a fellow Muslim. He points out that *'lam yaslam illa: muta'awwadhun min al-qatli bi-l-islam'* meaning that God alone is the guardian and trustee (*wali*) and He will judge in a later trial what remains secret in this life.[168] Moreover, Al-Shafi'ī distinguished between an apostate and a Muslim unbeliever according to the *shari'a*. Unbelief (*kufr*) implies public announcement of a defection from Islam, whilst apostasy (*irtidad*) involves the outright refusal to return to Islam. Therefore, according to Al-Shafi'ī, the criteria to constitute *irtidad* is based on three necessary conditions:

1. The apostate (*murtadd*) to have had previously publicly professed Islamic faith
2. The defection from Islam involved a public declaration
3. Failure to repent when asked to do so

166 See Wael Hallaq, *A History of Islamic Legal Theories: An Introduction to Sunni usul alfiqh* (Cambridge, 1997); Syed Barakat Ahmad, 'Conversion from Islam', in The Islamic world from classical to modern times:essays in honor of Bernhard Lewis, ed. C.E. Bosworth, C. Issawi, R. Savory and A.L. Udovitch. (Darwin Press, second edition, 1991), 3–25; Rudolph Peters and Gert J.J. De Vries, 'Apostasy in Islam' (1976) *Die Welt des Islams* 17(1/4) 1–25.

167 al-Sha:fi"ı:, Kita:b al-Umm, vol. 6, 147.

168 al-Sha:fi"ı:, Kita:b al-Umm, vol. 6, 146; Frank Griffel, 'Toleration and exclusion: al-Sha:fi"ı: and al- Ghaza:lı: on the treatment of apostates' (2001) 64(3) *Bulletin of the School of Oriental and African Studies* 347.

The first two conditions are sufficient to label a Muslim as an unbeliever (*kafir*), though all three conditions are necessary to pass capital punishment for apostasy (*irtidad*).[169] The third condition, the invitation to repent (*istitaba*) is held to be the most important element in the law of apostasy.[170]

Three centuries after Al-Shafiʿī, another prominent jurist Al-Ghazali formulates a different criterion for the application of the law of apostasy. Al-Ghazali limited the obligatory application of the *istitaba*, withdrawing the right of repentance. Regarded as a representative of the fundamentalist school of thought, Al-Ghazali states:

> Apostasy seldom is a matter that only concerns one's inner self alone. If that would be the case, nobody would notice it. In most instances apostasy is a psychological pretext for rebellion against worship, traditions and laws, even against the foundations of the state itself and against its stand towards its external enemies. Therefore, apostasy is often synonymous with the crime of high treason.[171]

In doing so, Al-Ghazali shifted the weight of the public declaration of defecting from Islam to the proven existence of *taqiyya* (concealment of inner belief). Thus, Al-Ghazali held that it was permissible to kill those Muslims who spread propaganda and heterodoxy without being obligated to grant them the right to repent.[172] As Frank Griffel, a professor of Islamic studies, has pointed out, Al-Ghazali's argument laid the foundation for the broadening of apostasy rulings beyond public declarations of leaving the faith.[173] Two post-Ghazali scholars, Ibn Taymiyya and his student, Ibn Kathir argued that those who follow laws set down by humans instead of adhering to the divine law of the *shari'a* should be fought – even if they may have publicly declared their faith through *shahada* (ritual confession of faith: *'Lā 'ilāh 'illā-llāh* "There is no deity except God" and *'Muḥammadun rasūlu llāh'* "Muhammad is the Messenger of God").[174] Nabil Al-Tikriti suggests that this view, to focus purely on religious doctrine (*uṣūl al-dīn*) was established to resist the expansion of theological discourse into

169 Griffel (n 168) 346.

170 al-Mawardı, *Al ahkam al sultaniyya* (1966), 55–58.

171 Ghazali, Huquq al-Insdn bayn ta'dlim al-Isldm wa-i'ldn al-Umam al-Muttahidah. al-Qahirah: al-Maktabah al-Tidjariyyah, 1383/1 p102.

172 Griffel (n 168) 350–352; Al-Tikriti, Nabil, 'Kalam in the service of state: Apostasy and the defining of ottoman islamic identity' in Hakan T. Karateke and Maurus Reinkowski (ed), *Legitimizing the Order: The Ottoman Rhetoric of State Power* (BRILL, 1 ed, 2005) vol 34, 135.

173 Ibid.

174 Al-Tikriti, (n 164) 135.

'matters and disputes that went well beyond the "original intent" of prophetic revelation.'[175] This argument was used to justify Mamluk warfare against the Ilkhanid rulers during the early 14th century. Syed Ahmad writes that this developed law of apostasy "opened the way for religious sanction of internecine wars between Muslim rulers and repression of Muslim minority groups."[176] By the early 16th century, Al-Ghazali's understanding of apostasy was widely accepted amongst scholars as providing legitimacy for the punishment of an apostate. Hanafi scholars, Al-Shaybānī and Al-Sarakhsī also agreed with this reasoning on apostasy and justified hostility against *murtaddeen* "because his blood would be as lawful to shed as that of the inhabitants of the territory of war."[177] This argument led most Ottoman religious scholars to adopt *shari'a* justification for state-sanctioned mass violence against entire communities if *irtidad* was present among them.[178]

Şehzade (prince) Korkud, son of sultan Bāyezīd II (r.1481–1512 AD), is known for providing theological justification for an imperial policy which targeted the attack of *Kızılba*, the supporters of Shah Ismail. Korkud addressed issues of unbelief and apostasy in *'Hafiz al-insan 'an lafiz al-iman, wa Allah al-hadi ila sirat al-jinan* [*The Individual's Protector on the Basis of Articulating Faith, as God is the Guide to the Heavenly Path*],' which justified according to *usul al-din* (religious principles) and *usul al-fiqh* (Islamic jurisprudence) and the application of apostasy rulings under the prerogatives of *örf*.[179] Korkud states that absence of faith in the prophethood of Muhammad constitutes *kufr*, and that this could be displayed through wilful statements of denial, mockery, obstinacy, or exhibited through external acts.[180] External demonstrations of apostasy include scorning the *Qur'an*, wearing the *zunnār* sash (a distinctive belt required for non-Muslims to wear to show *dhimmī* status),[181] fastening *ghiyār* cloth on their

175 Al-Tikriti, 'A Contrarian Voice: Şehzāde Ḳorḳud's (d. 919/1513) Writings on Kalām and the Early Articulation of Ottoman Sunnism' in Tijana Krstić and Derin Terzioğlu (ed), *Historicizing Sunni Islam in the Ottoman Empire, c. 1450-c. 1750* (Brill, 2020) vol 177, 71.

176 Syed Barakat Ahmad, 'Conversion from Islam', in The Islamic world from classical to modern times:essays in honor of Bernhard Lewis, ed. C.E. Bosworth, C. Issawi, R. Savory and A.L. Udovitch. (Princeton: Darwin Press, second edition, 1991)13.

177 Al-Sarakhsi *masbsut* vol x, 107.

178 Al-Tikriti (n 164) 135–136; Peters, Rudolph and J.J. De Vries Gert, 'Apostasy in Islam' (1976) 17(1/4) *Die Welt des Islams* 17.

179 Al-Tikriti, Nabil, (n 164), 146.

180 Ibid 145.

181 Arthur Stanley Tritton, *The Caliphs And Their Non Muslim Subjects* (Oxford University Press, 1930) 115. According to the Pact of 'Umar, dhimmis were ordered to wear the zunnar, and were forbidden from being like the Muslims in dress.

shoulders,[182] or wearing the *qalansuwat alkuffar* (non-believers' headgear).[183] This had been a clear reference to the *Kızılba*, who were named so because of the rebel turban they adorned.[184]

Korkud's *Hafiz al-insan* was used to legitimise and justify the recourse to armed conflict, providing both *shari'a* and *kanun* justification for apostasy rulings. Justification was then issued through *fatwa* by Ottoman officials, Hamza Efendi and Kemalpaşazâde.[185] Hamza Efendi's fatwa accused the *Kızılba* of scorning the *Qur'an,* disrespecting *shari'a* texts, and attempting to subvert the Prophet Muhammad's rulings by denying the caliphate of Abu Bakr and 'Umar.[186] Kemalpaşazâde held that freely and openly wearing the red *qalansuwa* constituted sufficient evidence of one's *kufr,* which will therefore be dealt with according to *irtidad* (apostasy) ruling. It was also determined that the sultan had a religious duty to fight this group of apostates.[187]

According to Muhammad Khair Haikal, the *qital* (fighting) of the *murtaddeen* (apostates) is indeed considered to be lawful *jihad* according to its *shari'a* meaning. He states that this is because the definition of *jihad* is well-defined as "the fighting of *kuffar* to raise the word of God high" and that the apostates are *kuffar.* Therefore, fighting them is to carry out *jihad.* Even more so, Ibn *Qudāmah* states that *qital* against apostates as being of greater significance than that of disbeliever in origin: "They (the apostates) are more deserving to be fought because their leaving (of Islam) could incite others to behave similarly to them and apostasies alongside them."[188] Therefore, the Ottoman's waging of war against the Safavid and other Shi'ite Muslims was in fact, within the parameters of lawful Islamic warfare and were legitimised by the defence of religious orthodoxy.

---

182 M. Th. Houtsma, T.W. Arnold, R. Basset, R. Hartmann (eds.) 'G͟hiyār', in *Encyclopaedia of Islam, First Edition (1913–1936)*. G͟hiyār' was a distinctive mark or strip of cloth which the D̲himmīs fasten on their shoulders.

183 Al-Tikriti, (n 164) 141, 145.

184 Ibid, 136.

185 Ibid 146.

186 Ibid 146 147; Richard Repp, *The Mufti of Istanbul, :a study in the development of the Ottoman learned hierarchy* (Oxford University, 1986)218–220.

187 M.C. Sehabettin Tekinda, 'Yeni kaynak ve vesikaların ısigı altında Yavuz Sultan Selim'in Iran seferi,' (1967), *Tarih dergisi* 17(22) 54–55.

188 Almughni ibn qudaamah 10/95; Muhammad Khair haikal Doctoral Thesis on the Subject of Al-Jihaad in the Early Period of Islam, the Islamic Fiqh and the Current Era (Al-Jihaad Wal-Qitaal Fee As-Siyaasah Ash-Shar'iyah) (Amazon Digital Services, 2019) 77.

4.2.2 Internal Hostility against Dar al-Islam

In 1516 AD, Sultan Selim I, sent a letter to the Mamluk sultan Tuman Bay prior to seizing Cairo, stating: "it has been revealed to me, that I shall become the possessor of the East and the West, like Alexander the Great … You are a Mamluk, who is bought and sold, you are not fit to govern. I am a king descended through twenty generations of kings (*malik ibn malik*)."[189] Selim's justification for waging war against the Mamluks, although they were Sunni Muslims, was that they had provided aid to and allied with the heretic Safavids under Shah Ismail.[190] The *Qur'an* forbids Muslims from entering into alliances with those who fight against Muslims because of their belief and expel them from their homes:

> God forbids you from befriending those who have fought you because of your faith, driven you out of your homes. And whoever takes them as friends, then it is they who are the wrongdoers.[191]

According to this *Qur'anic* verse, the Mamluk alliance with the apostate Safavids in their war against the Ottomans, also recognised the Mamluks as enemy combatants. Thus, the sultan secured legal opinion (*fatwa*) which accused the Mamluks of oppressing Muslims, which justified armed conflict, and obligated the Ottomans to fight against them.[192] The Ottomans conquered Mamluk Egypt in 1517 AD and captured the last Abbasid caliph, after which the Levant surrendered also.[193] The transfer of title and insignia of the caliph's office was transferred to Selim, which recognised the Ottomans as the only empire worthy to assume responsibilities as commander and defender of the *ummah* (universal Muslim community), a responsibility they held for the next four centuries.[194] Thus, the Ottomans claimed the caliphate and employed the titles caliph, *Amir al-Mu'minin* (Commander of the Faithful), and the juristic

189 Karateke, Hakan T. and Maurus Reinkowski, *Legitimizing the Order: The Ottoman Rhetoric of State Power* (BRILL, 2005) 26; *An Account of the Ottoman Conquest of Egypt in the Year A.H. 922/A.D. 1516*, Translated from the *Third Volume of the Arabic Chronicle of Muhammed ibn Ahmed Ibn Iyas, an Eyewitness of the Scenes He Describes*, Translated by W.H. Salmon (London, 1981), 91.

190 Ágoston (n 8) 349.

191 Qur'an 60:9.

192 Ágoston (n 8), xxxix.

193 Mona Hassan, *Longing for the Lost Caliphate: A Transregional History* (Princeton University Press, 2017) 9.

194 Casale, Giancarlo, 'Tordesillas and the Ottoman Caliphate: Early Modern Frontiers and the Renaissance of an Ancient Islamic Institution' (2015) 19(6) *Journal of Early Modern History* 485–511.

term *imam,* along with the previously mentioned titles of *gazi,* Caesar, and Khan, all of which served to legitimise and glorify their reign and contribute to the Ottomans ideal of universal sovereignty.[195]

With his conquests, Selim I also became the custodian of Mecca and Medina, "the cradle of Islam" and given the exclusive title *Khādim al-Ḥaramayn aš-Šarīfayn* "Protector of the two holy cities."[196] 16th century Ottoman historian, Mustafa Âlî wrote about the significance of this task of protecting the annual pilgrimage to Mecca, giving the Ottomans unparalleled prestige in the Muslim world, Âlî states:

> This [Selim's] zeal was the cause of that he raised the honor of the Empire higher than under his great ancestors, and adding the noble title of "Servant of the two sacred cities" to his illustrious Friday sermin he surpassed all other sultans in rank.[197]

5 Punishments

By the 15th century, Ottoman sultans had adopted an administration of justice based on both the *shari'a* and customary law. The determination of what constituted an offence and the designation of its proper punishment rested substantially on the *shari'a.*[198] Within Islamic law, offences are divided into three categories of crime and punishment: *ḥudūd* (prescribed crimes and punishment),[199] *qiṣāṣ* (just retaliation),[200] and *ta'zīr* (crimes that require deterrent but discretionary punishments that fall outside the other two categories).[201] According to the principles of the *shari'a,* the Muslim ruler can only rule on matters for which no fixed punishment was specified and, in regulating them, he must not depart from the bounds.[202] Therefore, penalties for *ta'zir*

---

195 Hassan (n 193)

196 Ágoston (n 8), xxxix.

197 Karateke, Hakan T. and Maurus Reinkowski, *Legitimizing the Order: The Ottoman Rhetoric of State Power* (BRILL, 2005) 30; Andreas Tietze, *Mustafa 'Âlî's Counsel for Sultans of 1581,* vol. 1 (1979), 51, 142.

198 The Imperial Ottoman Penal Code tr John Strachey Bucknill and Haigh Utidjian (Oxford University Press, 1913), ix.

199 Mohammad Hashim Kamali, *Crime and Punishment in Islamic Law: A Fresh Interpretation* (Oxford University Press, 2019) 17.

200 Qur'an 2:178–179; Ibid 17.

201 Qur'an 42:16; Kamali, (n 199) 17.

202 Sarakhasi, Mabsut IX, 36.

crimes were delegated to the sultan as discretionary punishments (*siyâseten*). Regulations that were promogulated by the sultan (*kanun*) evolved into the codes of law (*kanunname*). Despite the preamble of the *kanunname* describing its sanctioning by *shari'a*, its real basis was custom (*ürf*) and continuities from pre-Islamic Turkic practices.[203] Though a general framework and basic principles of criminal law had been established, the Islamic prerogative of rulers to pass supplementary regulations gave the Ottoman sultan a greater scope to manage military and administrative affairs. This was provided that *kanun* did not transgress Islamic principles or interfere with private legal relations.[204] Celälzäde Mustafa states that the unique position of a sultan involves a heavy burden of sovereignty that only a sultan can handle (*emānet-i-hukūmet*).[205] This great responsibility is held by the Ottoman sultan as "God's shadow on earth",[206] and bestows the sultan with the power to dispense justice. As the "soul for the body of justice", the sultan is "the eternal life of the country."[207]

Ottoman historian, Ömer Lütfü Barkan's examination on the earliest surviving *kanunname* confirms the *shari'a* and sultan's decrees (*firmans*) as the sources of *kanun*.[208] Barkan ascertains the sources of *kanun* through inspecting the 1487 *kanunname* of Hüdavendigar (Bursa), which names sultanic decree as the second source of law and also explains that material extracted from Ottoman registers (*defters*) are what formed the framework of *kanun*.[209] Moreover, the

203 For example, in Barkan, Kanunlar the 1539 *kanunname* states: *"If a raiyyet lets his tenement (çiftlik) lie fallow for three years, according to kanun, his sipahi may remove his title and give it to another."* The principle that permits a sipahi to expel a tenant who fails to cultivate his land for three successive years, appears to date from late Roman times. See, Colin Imber, 'The Law of the Land', in Christine Woodhead (ed.), The Ottoman World,.

204 Baber Johansen, *Contingency in a sacred law*, 189–210.

205 Mehmet Şakir Yilmaz, 'Crime And Punishment in The Imperial Historiography Of Süleyman the Magnificent: An Evaluation of Nişanci Celālzāde's View', (2007) *Acta Orientalia Academiae Scientiarum Hungaricae*, 60(4), 430.

206 Turkish "*mueyyed min 'indi Allah*", see Celälzäde Mustafa, and Petra Kappert, *Geschichte Sultan Süleymān Kānūnīs von 1520 bis 1557, oder, Ṭabaḳāt ül-Memālik ve Derecāt ül- Mesālik* (Steiner, 1981) 143a.

207 Turkish "*Pādisāhlar 'adālet bedenlerinin rūh-i revānlari, memleket tenlerinin hayat-i cāvidānlari, canlaridir*", see Celälzäde Mustafa, (n 206) 162a.

208 Ömer Lütfü Barkan, *XV ve XVI nci asırlarda Osmanlı İmparatorluğu'nda Zirai Ekonominin Hukuki ve Mali Esasları, Birinci Cilt: Kanunlar* [*Legal and Financial Principles of the Agricultural Economy in the Ottoman Empire in the 15th and 16th Centuries, Volume 1: the laws*] (İstanbul Üniversitesi Yayını, 1943).

209 Ibid x: *"A detailed explanation of the shari'a established kanuns and the rules for the well-known customary taxes which are the foundations of the defters and the sources of firman."* See, Colin Imber, 'Law and legislation under suleyman I' in Pál Fodor (ed.), *The battle for central Europe: the siege of szigetvár and the death of suleyman the magnificent and nicholar zrínyi (1566)* (BRILL, 2019).

significance of *firmans* is found within the 1528 *kanunname* for the *sancak* (sub-province) of Aydın, which states: "whatever the sultan commands is an imperial *kanun* (*Padişahın emrettiği her şey saltanat kanunudur*)".[210]

Ottoman sultans enacted these supplementary *kanuns* in good faith and with conviction that in doing so they have not contradicted nor abrogated the *shari'a*.[211] One of the most noteworthy legal developments during Mehmed II's reign was the introduction of *kanunname* (code of law). Mehmed's *kanunname* (*Kānunnāme-i Āl-i Osman*) was established after the conquest of Constantinople regarding taxation, land tenure and criminal law.[212] In an effort to provide suitable punishment for offences, the Ottoman criminal tribunals demonstrated a tendency towards an avoidance of the rigid penalties prescribed in the *shari'a*.[213] Largely due to the desire to broaden the discretion of the criminal tribunals in the infliction of sentences.[214] Mehmed the Conqueror was, in many respects, influenced by Byzantine institutions which in turn influenced his administration system.[215] In his *kanunname,* Mehmed II presupposes that *ta'zir* punishments render *hudud* punishments obsolete. *Hudud* crimes are those that violate divinely ordained limits and have defined mandatory punishments regulated by the Qur'an and the Sunnah.[216] The state does not have the authority to pardon *hudud* crimes as they are understood as God's right to impose.[217] Thus, demonstrating an example of when *kanun* went beyond complementing the *shari'a*.[218]

Succeeding Ottoman sultans, particularly Selim I and Süleyman I, had been firmer in their adherence of Islamic law. Suleyman's influence on the evolution of Ottoman law surpassed that of Mehmed II.[219] In fact, the reign of Suleyman I saw the highest degree of compliance with the *shari'a* and efficiency possessed

210 Barkan (n 208) 14. See, Colin Imber, 'Law and legislation under suleyman I' in Pál Fodor (ed.), *The battle for central Europe: the siege of szigetvár and the death of suleyman the magnificent and nicholar zrínyi (1566)* (BRILL, 2019).

211 Joseph Schact, *an introduction to Islamic law* (Clarendon Press, 1964) 89–92.

212 Natalia Królikowska, 'The Law Factor in Ottoman-Crimean Tatar Relations in the Early Modern Period' in Jeroen Duindam, Jill Diana Harries, Caroline Humfress, and Hurvitz Nimrod (ed.) Law *and Empire: Ideas, Practices, Actors* (BRILL, 2013).

213 The Imperial Ottoman Penal Code, ix.

214 Ibid.

215 A. Heidborn, *Manuel de droit public et administratif de l'Empire ottoman* (C.W. Stern, 1908) 91.

216 Wael Hallaq, *An introduction to islamic law,* (Cambridge University Press, 2009) 155–156, 173.

217 Kamali, (n 119) 21.

218 Schact, (n 211) 91; Osmanli Devleti'nde Siyaseten Katl; Uriel Heyd, *Studies in Old Ottoman Criminal Law* (Clarendon Press, 1973) 636.

219 Ibid 91.

in a society since the Abbasid period.[220] A reputation which gave Suleyman the title *Ḳānūnī Sulṭān Süleymān* (Suleyman the Lawgiver)[221] and allowed the empire to reach the zenith of its power.[222] In his efforts to uphold the sacred law, he centred the administration of justice on the shari'a and endowed an exclusive authority and title of *seyhulislam* (Arabic: *shaykh al-Islam*) to the Grand Mufti. During his reign, Suleyman succeeded in making the *kanun* and administrative law in accordance with the *shari'a*.[223] The *Kānunnāme-i Āl-i Osman* of Suleyman demonstrated a development from that of Mehmed II, particularly in matters of penal law and law of war. Regarding penal law, Suleyman re-establishes *hadd* punishments and gives preference to imposing bodily punishments rather than fines as types of *siyâseten* (discretionary punishment).[224] According to Celälzäde, most of the *siyâseten* meted out by Sultan Süleyman represented the fulfilment of "divine justice", and as such were the direct consequence of the sins of wrongdoers. The Ottoman jurist Dede Efendi held that the Muslim ruler is given a broad discretion to deal with criminal offences for the sake of maintaining public order and ensuring the welfare of society. However, Efendi states that this is also provided that the Muslim ruler does not blatantly contradict the principles of the *shari'a*.[225] In describing the power of the Ottoman sultan, Turkish Historian, Ahmet Mumcu, states that:

> In states where sovereignty is absolutely concentrated in one hand, the last limit of the ruler's power is his ability to impose the death penalty by using his discretion. Indeed, the most severe punishment for humans is "death". Therefore, the ruler strengthens his authority to the extent that he can save the life of his subjects, and the absolute character of the state regime becomes intensified. […] especially in Islamic and Turkish-Islamic states, this institution has developed and survived by becoming an important part of Islamic public law.[226]

---

220 Ibid 89.

221 Though Sultan Suleiman I's official title is Commander of the Faithful, Shadow of God on Earth, Protector of the Holy Cities of Mecca, Medina and Jerusalem, Lorde of Lords of the World, East and West.

222 Schact, (n 211) 91.

223 Christian Lange Paradise and Hell in Islamic Traditions (Cambridge University Press, 2016) 169.

224 Schact n 211 89–92. See also, Metin M. Coşgel, et al. 'Crime and Punishment in Ottoman Times: Corruption and Fines,' (2013) 43(3) *The Journal of Interdisciplinary History*, 353–76; Özgür Yildiz, 'An Evaluation on Ottoman Prisons: the example of Karesi Prison' (2015) 9(17) Gazi Akademik Bakiş, 91.

225 Uriel Heyd, *Studies in Old Ottoman Criminal Law* (Clarendon Press, 1973) 199.

226 Ahmet Mumcu, Osmanlı Devleti'nde Siyasetten Katl, Phoenix, (2007) xix.

The principle of legality (*mabda' al-Ibahah*) in Islamic criminal law protects the interests of the individual by restricting the authority of the state.[227] This fundamental principle (*mabda al-usli*) consists of two legal principles: there is no crime without law and there is no punishment without law (*la jarima wa la 'uqubata illa bi al-nuss*).[228] Which naturally prompts the third principle of 'no retroactive application of criminal law.'[229] Therefore, prohibited conduct cannot be punishable unless there is a rule of law which has declared it to be so.[230] The Qur'an conveys that: "*We would never punish a people until We have sent forth a Messenger.*"[231] This verse is interpreted to mean that the prosecution and punishment of individuals requires that individual are informed of pre-existing law that criminalises that conduct.[232] As the Ottoman penal system is based on the principles of Islamic criminal law, it was essential that punishments for violations of laws of war are recognised in the legal system. In the case of discretionary punishments, once crimes under *ta'zir* were defined and their penalties were fixed by the sultan, the court was obliged to apply the punishment.[233]

The discretionary powers granted to the sultan and subsequently for the *qadi* (judge) to enact, are governed by the principle of judicious policy (*siyāsah shar'iyyah*) and *ta'zir*, which provides that they determine the best manner in which *shari'a* can be administered.[234] *Siyāsah shar'iyyah* is a broad doctrine of Islamic law that authorises the Muslim ruler's administration of discretionary measures in the interest of good government, provided that precepts of the *shari'a* are not violated.[235] Imposing *Ta'zir* punishments as a principle of *siyāsah shar'iyyah*, enables the sultan and *qadi* (judge) to exercise flexibility in imposing the type and severity of punishment suitable for the offence before them

227 Muhammad Munir, The Principle of Legality in Islamic Criminal Justice System (2018) *Hazara Islamicus*, 7(1); Mahmoud Cherif Bassiouni, *The shar'ia, islamic law, and post-conflict justice* (Cambridge university press, 2013).

228 Malekian, *Principles of Islamic International Criminal Law: A Comparative Search* (BRILL, 2011) 144; Ibid 108.

229 Munir, (n 227) 108–109.

230 Malekian, (n 228) 143–145.

231 Quran 17:15.

232 Abū 'Abdullāh Al-Qurṭubī, *Tafsīr al-Qurṭubī*, vol. 5, 152. See also, Matthew Lippman, 'Islamic Criminal Law and Procedure: Religious Fundamentalism v. Modern Law' (1989) *Boston college international and comparative law review*, 12(1), 47; Munir, 109.

233 Munir, 116.

234 Kamali, (n 119) 191.

235 Ibid 191, 195; Kenneth S. Gallant, *The principle of legality in international and comparative criminal law* (Cambridge University Press, 2008) 197; 51–53.

(*siyâseten*).[236] Essentially, *Ta'zir* is based on the *qadi's* ad hoc balance of the 'social, moral, and legal evaluation of a particular and unique situation.'[237] It is noted that the *qadi* does not create the offence, but may only penalise what is already an established violation under the *shari'a*.[238] The limitations of determining *ta'zir* penalties are that it cannot exceed the punishments for *hudud* penalties nor can the punishments be predetermined.[239]

'Imperial custom' (*örfi sultani*) was the term used to justify *firmans* of the late 15th and 16th centuries which related to regulations and protocol of the Ottoman ruling class.[240] The application of these juridical acts obliged subjects to live their lives and to conduct themselves according to its stipulations.[241] State officials, such as the *qādī, sancakbeg, subaşi, dizdar,* and *sipāhi* were in charge of applying the law.[242] The significance of the sultan's decrees (*firmans*) and *kanunname* depended on the strength of their application. Thus, the role of officials was to ensure that subjects submit voluntarily to the law, however, recourse to sanctions becomes necessary when subjects do not do so. The imperial 'edicts of justice' (*'adaletname*) were formulated to maintain discipline throughout the judiciary and government, ensuring that officials also abide by laws and uphold principles of justice and good governance. A special code of military conduct within the *'adaletname*, based on primarily unwritten custom (*örf*), was formulated to emphasise discipline and obedience for the military-administrative branch of government and deal with breaches of conduct.[243]

The Ottoman legal system categorised punishments into two major distinctions: punishments for 'serious crimes' and punishments for all other criminal acts.[244] This distinction is crucial as the punishment prescribed by Islamic law must correspond to the severity of the crime committed.[245] Al-Shaybānī's *siyar*

236 John L Esposito, *the oxford history of islam,* (oxford university press, 2000); Shaltūt, al-Islām, 'Aqīdah wa-Sharī'ah, 292. *Siyâseten* (*Siyâsa*) is not to be confused with *siyāsah shar'iyyah.*

237 Hallaq (n 216) 156.

238 Esposito, *the oxford history of islam,* (oxford university press, 2000); Kamali, (n 119) 191–192.

239 Hallaq 156.

240 Engin Deniz Akarlı, 'The Ruler and Law Making in the Ottoman Empire' in Jeroen Duindam, Jill Diana Harries,, Caroline Humfress, and Hurvitz Nimrod (ed.) Law and Empire: Ideas, Practices, Actors, (BRILL, 2013).

241 Koç, (n 17) 91–99.

242 Ibid 98.

243 Akarlı (n 240) 89.

244 Niki Gamm, crime and punishment: the Ottoman legal system (2014) https://www.hurriyetdailynews.com/crime-and-punishment-the-ottoman-legal-system-68371.

245 Muḥammad ibn Jarīr ibn Yazīd, Tārīkh al-Rusul wa al-Mulūk, tr Yohanan Friedman (State University of New York Press, 1987) Vol. 4, 132–133.

provides that individual punishment will be given to those who violate the rules of armed conflict, which is categorised as a 'serious crime'.[246] 'Serious crimes' consisted of apostasy, heresy, and included "offenses against public order and security, the possession of fire-arms by civilians, serious violations of market regulations, counterfeiting, acts of disobedience against the sultan and the spreading of calumnies about him, the illegal sale of grain and export of arms to foreign [Christian] countries, etc."[247] 'Serious crimes' warranted corporal punishment or banishment, while the punishment for all other crimes included fines, imprisonment or penal servitude in the galleys.[248] The *siyâseten* punishments imposed by the sultan and the *qadi* are based on the Qur'anic decree that:

> The penalty for those who wage war against God and His Messenger and strive to spread corruption in the land will be killed, or crucified, or have their hands and feet on opposite sides cut off, or exile from the land.[249]

Deterrence and incapacitation were the principal aims of *siyâset* punishment, which justified the application of these punishments as being 'an example for others.[250] A *qadi* is permitted to sentence one who has committed a *ta'zir* crime to variety of *siyâseten* punishments at his discretion, such as, a warning; summoning to the court; banishment; imprisonment; or corporal punishment.[251] The earliest record of corporal punishment in the Ottoman Empire is traced back to the reign of Mehmed II.[252] The *fatawa* of Ebüssuûd Efendi, the *Şeyḫülislām* ("chief mufti") during Sultan Suleyman's reign, indicate that corporal punishment in the form of strokes and long imprisonment were the

---

246 Muhammad ibn al-Hassan al-Shaybāni Sharḥ Kitāb al-Siyar al-Kabīr, commentary by Muḥammad ibn Aḥmad al-Sarakhsī, ed. Muḥammad Ḥassan Muḥammad Hassan Ismā'il al-Shafi'ī, (Dār al-Kutub al-'Ilmiyyah, 1997) Vol. 1, 298.

247 Heyd, (n 225).

248 Fariba Zarinebaf, *Crime and Punishment in Istanbul: 1700–1800* (University of California Press, 2011); Imperial Ottoman code, ix.

249 Qur'an 5:33.

250 Rudolph Peters, 96.

251 Recep çiğdem The Concept of Ta'zir in Theory and in Practice, (Harran Üniversitesi, 169–170).

252 Mehmet Şakir Yilmaz, 'Crime And Punishment in The Imperial Historiography Of Süleyman the Magnificent: An Evaluation of Nişanci Celālzāde's View', (2007) *Acta Orientalia Academiae Scientiarum Hungaricae*, 60(4).

two common types of *siyâseten* punishment in the Ottoman empire during the 16th century.[253]

5.1.1.1 *'Political Murder'*

In the Ottoman state, the death penalty or execution was labelled as "political murder."[254] The state imposed this penalty by *siyâseten* punishment as this was the only way to overcome the *shari'a's* standard of proof to hold a person liable.[255] Political murder was imposed for crimes against the sultan's person and the state. For the most part, the sultan would use his absolute authority to sentence rebels and state officials accused of corruption to death.[256] Ahmet Mumcu defines the measure for this crime as "doing evil to the public interest."[257] These crimes included: fleeing from war,[258] falsifying princedom, disobedience to the sultan, rebellion against the sultan, questioning the legitimacy of the sultan, attacking the sultan's throne, lying to the sultan, misleading the sultan in state affairs, or criticising and insulting the sultan.[259] The sultan could also give orders for political murder if it was for the benefit of the state. For instance, the 17th century French traveller Jean-Baptiste Tavernier writes that "if the janissaries want the head of a vizier, a *ḳāḍī'asker* (military judge), or even their own *aghas* (commander of janissary corps), the sultan must unleash the anger of those rebels. To quell them, they often strangle anyone they want and send their head to the rebels."[260] Although this punishment was scarcely enacted against members of the *ulema* (legal jurists),[261] the sultan would decree political murder for other members of the clergy, such as *qadis*. The punishment would be imposed for crimes against the state committed by *qadis*, including treason, or issuing a *fatwa* (legal opinion) against the sultan to impede his power.[262]

---

253 M. Ertuğrul Düzdağ, *Şeyhulislam Ebussuud Efendi Fetvalari Işiğinda 16. Asir Türk Hayati*, (Istanbul: Enderun Kitabevi, 1972) 47, 141; çiğdem (n 251), 171.

254 Osmanli Devleti'nde Siyaseten Katl.

255 Ebru aykut.

256 Fariba Zarinebaf (n 248).

257 Mumcu, (n 226) 45.

258 Narrated by. Abu Huraira in Sahih Bukhari volume 8 book 82 number 840.

259 Mumcu (n 226) 45–47.

260 Jean-Baptiste Tavernier, *Yüzyılda Topkapı Sarayı* (Kitap Yayınevi, 2007) 64. See, ibid.

261 This is believed to be following the practice of the Seljuks. See, Osman Turan History of Seljuks and Turkish-Islamic Civilization, (Istanbul, 1993) 136–8.

262 Feda Shamil Arik, 'Notes on the Old Turkish Criminal Law'; Osmanli Devleti'nde Siyaseten Katl; Ekrem Buğra Ekinci, 'Fratricide in Ottoman Law' (2018) *Marmara University*, 82(295), 1033.

Following Islamic procedural law, *siyâset* punishments were only imposed once there had been a proper trial, a *qadi* judgement, and the submission of direct evidence.[263] In some cases, the sultan used his absolute sovereignty to impose 'political murder', and at times the sultan would seek the legal opinion of the *şeyḫülislām* to sentence to death rebels or state officials accused of corruption.[264] It is noted that it was also acceptable for the Ottoman sultan to sentence a person to 'political murder' without an investigation or trial, on account of his absolute sovereignty and right to impose *siyâseten* as *ta'zir* punishment according to the *shari'a*.[265] To sentence a *ta'zir* crime, there will firstly be an investigation, followed by a trial whereupon a judgement will be given by the *qadi* or *şeyḫülislām*.[266] The verdict of death is given by way of *fatwa*, that would state that it is lawful to execute a person if he is a 'spreader of corruption' or a 'threat to public order' (*ehl-i fesād*).[267] If the order is to execute, then the offender would be told to perform ablution, which is the sign of a guilty verdict.[268] If the sentenced was an important statesman, then the sultan would wear a black caftan to notify the person of his execution.[269]

5.1.1.2 *Exception for Not Holding a Trial*

The Ottoman double-edged sword principle to 'rule by [martial] custom' (*örf-i idare*) was the exception to the rule that no person could be punished without a trial in a *shari'a* court, thus, it overrode the concept of public wellbeing.[270] Found in the code of conduct for the military branch, this principle authorised high-ranking military officials, primarily the grand vizier, to act on behalf of the sultan and impose *siyaset* during military campaigns or armed conflict against rebels and bandits.[271] Breach of military discipline in these situations

263 Mürteza Bedir, 'İdealizm ile Gerçekçilik Arasında Hanefî Siyaset ve Şeriat Görüşü: Hasîrî'nin Hissî ve Dinî Siyaset Anlayışı: (Siyasa ad-diniyye al-'uzma ve siyasa al-hissiyye al-'uzma) [The Hanafi View of Siyasa and Sharia between Idealism and Realism: Al-Hasiri's Conception of Temporal and Religious Politics: (Siyasa ad-diniyya al-'uzma and siyasa al-hissiyya al-'uzma)]' (2020) 10(2) İslam Tetkikleri Dergisi – Journal of Islamic Review 464.

264 Rudolph Peters, *Crime and Punishment in Islamic Law: Theory and Practice from the Sixteenth to the Twenty-First Century* (Cambridge University Press, 2005) 84–87.

265 Ibid, 101.

266 Mumcu, 96–7; İsmail Katgi, 'Osmanli Devleti'nde Siyaseten Katl' 192–193.

267 'Ibrahim Peçevi, Tarih-i Peçevi (Matbaa-ı Amire, 1281– 1284/1864–1867), 1:120 –22.

268 İsmail Katgi, 'Osmanli Devleti'nde Siyaseten Katl' 192–193.

269 Tavernier, (n 260) 107.

270 Akarlı (n 240); Engin Deniz Akarli, 'Ottoman Empire: Islamic Law in Asia Minor (Turkey) and the Ottoman Empire' in Stanley N. Katz (ed.) *The Oxford International Encyclopedia of Legal History* (Oxford University Press, 2009).

271 Akarlı (n 240).

resulted in summary trials and harsh punitive measures, including 'political murder' or the confiscation of wealth.[272]

Janissaries who violated the laws of war and were found participating in rebellions were executed, generally in the evenings and after the evening prayer, and their bodies thrown into the Bosporus.[273] A recorded instance of janissaries breaching conduct during the reign of sultan Suleyman I resulted in the execution of the highest-ranking janissary commander (*Yeniçeri ağası*), Mustafa Pasha, his senior imperial council secretary (*reîsü'l-küttab*), Haydar Çelebi, and his steward (*kethüda*), Kıran Bali, all of whom were held responsible for the breach in conduct of subordinates .[274] Janissary revolts and banditry were uncommon during the Ottoman classical period and occurred mainly throughout the 18th and 19th centuries, largely due to Ottoman military politics.[275] For this reason, the 'political murder' of janissaries for violations of warfare regulations is not found to have typically occurred within the intended timeframe of this study and is not considered in detail.

5.1.1.3 *Punishment of Protected Non-muslims*

Under Islamic law, the principle of upholding *aman* (safe conduct) granted to the *dhimmi* population is closer to divine prescription than to customary practice.[276] Although, Ottoman sources demonstrate that this principle was considered as both a custom and a stipulation of the *shari'a*.[277] The Qur'anic verses that were frequently invoked in Ottoman sources are:

> Honour God's covenant when you make a pledge, and do not break your oaths after confirming them, having made Allah your guarantor.[278]

272 Ibid.

273 Zarinebaf. (n 248)

274 Kaya Şahin, *Empire and Power in the reign of Süleyman: narrating the sixteenth-century ottoman world* (Cambridge University Press, 2013) 57–59. See, Mustafa Çelebi Celâlzade, and Petra Kappert, *Geschichte Sultan Süleymān Kānūnīs von 1520 bis 1557, oder, Ṭabaḳāt ül-Memālik ve Derecāt ül-Mesālik* (Steiner, 1981) 129a-130a.

275 For further discussion on janissary revolts and the punitive measures imposed, see for example, İsmail Hakkı Uzunçarşılı, *Osmanlı Devleti Teşkilatından Kapıkulu Ocakları: Acemi Ocağı ve Yeniçeri Ocağı* (Türk Tarih Kurumu, 1988); Patrick Balfour Baron Kinross, *The Ottoman centuries: the rise and fall of the Turkish empire* (Morrow, 1977); Y. Hankan Erdem, *Slavery in the Ottoman Empire and Its Demise* (1996) 160–73.

276 Panaite (n 24) 206.

277 Ibid, 207–208.

278 Qur'an 16:91.

> [...] Fulfill your covenants, for you will indeed be accountable for them.[279]

However, the duty to uphold this principle is not obligatory on the Muslims alone, guarantees to respect the peace were also to be observed by non-Muslims. The breach of agreement (*'ahd*) was held by Muslims to be a "legitimate cause" for terminating the *'ahd* altogether.[280] Serious penalties stipulated by the *shari'a* were imposed when non-Muslims committed violations against their *'ahd* with Muslims (*nakz-ı 'ahd*). The punishments that applied to non-Muslims that violated their *'ahd's* was distinguished by their juridical status as either: non-Muslim subjects, tributary princes, and rulers of sovereign states.[281] Firstly, warnings to honour agreements would be invoked in order to justify further sanctions to be imposed.[282] In this instance, the Qur'anic warning to *"Fulfill your covenants, for you will indeed be accountable for them"*,[283] was frequently referenced.

5.1.2 Non-muslim Tribute Payer (*Haracgüzar*)

According to Hanafi jurists, the violation of an *'ahd* by a non-muslim tributary under Muslim protection, resulted in the loss of *dhimmi* status as they became 'rebels.'[284] The violation of a covenant (*nakz-ı 'ahd*) by a population would mean that only those guilty of rebellion were punished; enslaved if they surrendered or executed if they have not.[285] Al-*Shaybānī* also gives an example of a *dhimmi* unlawfully killing an enemy combatant who was granted safe conduct (*aman*) and seizes his assets. The *dhimmi* would consequently be required to repair the damages and would also be condemned to flogging as well as imprisonment, the sentence of which would to be determined as best seen fit by the ruler.[286]

---

279 Qur'an 17:34.

280 Panaite (n 24), 205.

281 Ibid, 225–226.

282 Ibid, 226.

283 Qur'an 17:34.

284 "Rebels are those who revolts against the sovereign's authority, who rejects his orders or who attacks his properties by force." (D'Ohsson, Tableau, V, 101). See also, Panaite (n 24) 227.

285 Panaite (n 24) 228.

286 Muḥammad ibn al-Ḥassan al-Shaybāni Sharḥ Kitāb al-Siyar al-Kabīr, commentary by Muḥammad ibn Aḥmad al-Sarakhsī, ed. Muḥammad Ḥassan Muḥammad Hassan Ismā'il al-Shafi'ī, (Dār al-Kutub al-'Ilmiyyah, 1997) Vol. 1, 298; Muḥammad ibn al-Ḥassan al-Shaybāni, tr Mahmood Ahmad Ghazi, Kitāb al-Siyar al-Saghīr (Islamic Research Institute, 1987) 72–74.

5.1.3 Tributary Princes

Tributary princes suspected of *nakz-ı ʿahd* are punished with dethronement, which may be followed with execution in certain circumstances.[287] According to Al-Shaybānī, an alliance with *harbis* (enemies of war) to spy and inform them of the weak spots in the Muslim defences does not terminate the *ʻahd* between the Ottoman state and the tributary prince, but it does necessitate the imposing of punishment:

If after having entered into an agreement and having become a protected person of theirs, [the ruler] began to inform the unbelievers of the weak spots in the Muslim defenses, or provide them with guides and give refuge to their spies, would these acts constitute a violation of his pact? He replied, "No, but the Muslims should punish him for doing so and throw him into prison."[288]

5.1.4 Non-muslim Rulers

Sultan Suleyman considered non-Muslim rulers to be 'rebels' if they contested his sultanic authority. During his reign, the Wallachian, Moldavian and Transylvanian rulers became 'rebels' for this reason.[289] The punishment for rebellion during the 15th and 16th centuries was typically aimed at restoring the state of affairs through necessary military intervention. Dethronement was the punishment imposed on rebel rulers from the mid-sixteenth century.[290]

6 Conclusion

During the Golden Age, the Ottoman military forces successfully besieged fortresses and conquered enemy territories with skilfulness in siege warfare and an advanced use of weaponry, which allowed them to extend their rule across territories and expand their empire. Ottoman military dominance in the 15th and 16th centuries achieved great victories and was an effective force capable of providing and supporting the political objectives of the Ottoman state.[291] The Ottoman military was undoubtedly the linchpin of the empire.

In general, the two types of law, *shari'a* and *kanun,* seem to have coexisted reasonably harmoniously in the 15th and 16th centuries.[292] 'Reasonably

287 Panaite (n 24) 229.

288 Ibid. 227, 229, 287–289. Sarakhsi, kitab sharh al-siyar al-kabir vol IV, 86; Tabari, kitab ikhtilaf, 24–25; Majid Khadduri, 153.

289 Panaite (n 24) 227.

290 Ibid, 227–229.

291 Uyar (n 9) 66.

292 Richard Repp, 130.

harmonious', however, was not 'wholly harmonious', or even more so, it was not 'holy' harmonious, for the incompatibility of the *devşirme* system with the *shari'a* cannot be overlooked.

The forced levy and conversion of the Sultan's Christian subjects for the purposes of recruiting into his standing army was a flagrant disregard of the *shari'a*. The Ottoman's clear transgression in this instance, demonstrates their prioritisation of the state's imperial interests above all and is indicative of the forthcoming military weakness as a result of stepping away from the *shari'a* seen in later centuries, of which the loss of control and discipline of the janissary forces played a crucial part.

The Ottomans were skilled in both warfare and in finding suitable and expedient Islamic justification for their political, administrative, and military practices.[293] As an Islamic empire, the Ottomans were dutiful in continuing warfare practices of the Prophet Muhammad; aside from their *devşirme* system, all other Ottoman military institutions and operations considered in this chapter were in accordance with the governing *shari'a*. Be that as it may, the Ottoman state not only recognised the influence of the *shari'a*, but also the importance of existing customary law within the diverse communities it governed.[294] While maintaining Islamic tradition, the Ottomans also preserved political stability by upholding the practices and customs of previous existing emirates and states.[295] The Ottoman sultans, similar to the *Shahs* and Turco-Mongolian *Khans* before them, were the key authority and Lawmakers. As such, the sultans did not detach from the past, and had a tendency to preserve extisting systems into one of their own. Though this chapter did not look into the causes of longevity of the Ottoman empire, it can be asserted that a reason for its long rule is on account of building an effective bureaucracy and military, based on the principles of traditionalist Islam, pragmatism, and tolerance.[296]

293 Çipa (n 116), 223.
294 Koç, (n 17) 89.
295 Ibid.
296 Uyar, (n 9) 282.

CHAPTER 5

Ancient Malabar Laws of War

Sanoj Rajan and Sheena Sivadasan

1 Introduction

This chapter provides an overview of kalaripayattu,[1] the indigenous martial art of Kerala.[2] Kalaripayattu underpinned the norms for conflict in the Ancient Malabar region in India and then examines the practices of ankam and Mamankam on the medieval Malabar Coast from the Sangam period through the rule of the Zamorins of Calicut. Ankams were ad hoc proxy duels between professional fighters conducted to resolve inter-state disputes; Mamankam was a periodic contest designed to allow a relatively bloodless transfer of power. Both demonstrate an understanding of modern rules of proportionality, distinction and victims' protection under international war norms.

1.1 *Ancient Malabar—Social Structure and Rules*

The institution known as kalaripayattu has a very long history dating back to the Middle Ages. It is a developing institution because its shape, character, and level of popularity change in response to societal conditions. It's possible to interpret kalaripayattu in overlapping and occasionally conflicting ways. It is an 'old martial art embodying Kerala's cultural, myth-historic heritage, a traditional psycho-physiological discipline cultivating mental, physical, and spiritual benefits, practical fighting art a system of physical training beneficial to athletes, dancers, and actors.'[3]

1 Throughout history, scholars have referred to this ancient martial art as kalaripayattu, kaḷaḷrippayattu, or kalarippayatt. While all are understood to describe the same practice, for the purpose of this chapter, we will use kalaripayattu for all references except when reproducing a quote or other citation.

2 Kerala is a State in the Union of India which occupies southwestern coast of the Indian subcontinent. Until the arrival of the British, the term Malabar was used in foreign trade circles as a general name for Kerala. See, A. Sreedhara Menon, *Kerala Charithram*, 18th ed. (Kottayam: DC Books, 2019). In this chapter the names Kerala and Malabar is used interchangably to denote the same land area.

3 Ian McDonald, 'Bodily Practice, Performance Art, Competitive Sports: A Critique of Kalarippayattu, the Martial Art of Kerala,' *Contribution to Indian Sociology* 41, no. 2 (May 2007), 143–168.

 | DOI:10.1163/9789004512566_007

Kalaripayattu is a body art that can only be learned via hard practice. Kalari *gurukkanmar*, the Kalari masters, observe kalaripayattu as a divine fighting technique. Kalaripayattu is regarded as Kerala's indigenous art, the force and beauty of Kerala, and the mother of all martial arts. Kalaripayattu was largely patronised by the rulers of medieval Kerala. With the arrival of colonial powers, the practice of kalaripayattu began to dwindle. After discovering kalaripayattu's military abilities, the British began to disarm these indigenous military martial arts. Kalaripayattu was revitalized in the 1920s as part of nationalism.

C.V. Narayanan Nair, a well-known kalaripayattu practitioner, translates the term *kalaripayattu* as 'The Art of Fencing.' The phrase kalarippayattu is derived from the words *kalari* and *payattu*, according to Zaralli. 'This phrase derives from the Tamil word Kalam, which means arena, an arena for gladiatorial or gymnastic demonstrations, and assembly place of work or business in Malayalam. In Malayalam, the word Kalari refers to a unique place where martial arts are taught. Payilamil means to be trained in Tamil. Pailuka means to study or speak in Malayalam. Payattuka means to train with weapons and has the idiomatic meaning fencing exercise a trick.'[4]

In Vadakkan Pattukal, the word *kalaripayattu* was not used as a compound word. According to the Malayalam lexicon, the word kalaripayattu was first used as a compound word in Ullor Parameswaran's early-twentieth-century drama Amba.[5] Kalari and kalarividya, according to Sasidaran, are distinct: kalari, as an open place; kalarividya, a vast body of knowledge that incorporates components of fighting technique (payattu), healthcare, education, rituals, lifestyle, philosophy, meditation, the art of life, and the art of performance.[6] In modern Kerala, the term kalarividya has been supplanted by *kalarippayattu*. However, kalarippayatt refers only to fencing art and falls short of representing the wholesome activities of kalarividya as perceived in the medieval period.

Kalaripayattu is one of the world's oldest martial arts. The indigenous combat style of Ancient Malabar is often regarded as the 'mother' of martial arts.[7]

4 Zaralli, *When the Body*.

5 Zaralli, *When the Body*.

6 P.K. Sasidharan, 'Kalarippayattu: Performance Paradigm as Aesthetics and Politics of Invisibility,' published in *Performers and Their Arts: Folk, Popular and Classical Genre in a Changing India* (Simon Charley and Laxmi Narayan Kadekar eds.) (London: Routledge India, 2006), 170.

7 The historical area of Malabar, which is located on India's southwest coast, has long been noted for its commercial and cultural exchanges with other parts of the world. Malabar was used to refer to the whole state of Kerala as well as several nearby regions in Tamil Nadu and Karnataka. The history of the ancient Malabar region may be traced back to the third century BC, when the name Kerala (Keralaputra) first appeared in an inscription on

The phrase *kalaripayattu* is derived from two words: *kalari*, a 'place of exercise or gymnasium,' and *payattu*, 'to fight or exercise.' It is a personal fighting training technique that includes exercises to create acute reflexes for unarmed combat and skilful fights with sticks, daggers, knives, spears, swords and shields, *Urumi*, and so on. Kalaripayattu is known for high-flying acrobatics, beautiful motions, and mastery of lethal weaponry.

It is believed that the systems of kung fu and karate owe their origins to this martial art of Kerala. Both Indian and Chinese historical sources indicate that kalaripayattu was introduced to China in the 4th century AD by Bodhi Dharma, a Buddhist monk. Kalaripayattu was further developed in the 9th century when practised by the Nairs and Ezhavas, warrior communities entrusted with defending the state and its king. This warlike tradition held sway for centuries among the warrior chieftains of ancient and medieval Malabar, known as the Mamanka Chekavers and the Lohars, the Buddhist warriors of North Kerala. Although it dates much further back, kalaripayattu has been popular as a system of self-defence since the 12th century AD.[8]

Kalaripayattu styles can be divided into three regional subtypes distinguished by their offensive and defensive strategies.[9] *The Structure and Essence of an Indian Martial Art* by D.H. Luijendijk, which shows various kalaripayattu exercises and their applications using images, is the best resource for understanding the differences between these techniques.[10]

Parasurama is credited with creating the kalaripayattu style used in the North. Although the origin of kalaripayattu was commonly accepted to have been in the north of Malabar, this has not been verified. In the end, Chilambum, an indigenous Dravidian method, was mixed with the martial arts and ethos brought by migrants from Saurashtra and Konkan to form northern kalaripayattu. A particular subgroup of Nairs and Ezhavas, the Theyyas, was most closely associated with the right and obligation to train martial arts in the service of a monarch between the 11th and 12th centuries. To settle conflicts between rival kings, known as Vazhunnor, it is believed that at least one subcaste of Brahmins, along with certain Christians and Muslims, participated in

---

a rock by Emperor Ashoka of Magadha, and continues through the 16th and 17th centuries AD, up until the start of western colonisation.

8 See Padma Mohan Kumar, 'Kalaripayattu: The Mother of All Martial Traditions,' *Gateway for India* (2009), http://gatewayforindia.com/articles/kalari.shtml.

9 Ramon Youseph, 'Martial Art of the Month: Kalaripayattu,' *Kung-fu Kingdom* (30 May 2018), https://kungfukingdom.com/martial-art-of-the-month-kalaripayattu/.

10 D.H. Luijendijk, *Kalarippayat: The Structure and Essence of an Indian Martial Art* (Lulu.com, 2008).

a public duel called Angam. According to historian Elamkulam Kunjan Pillai, the conflict between the Cheras and the Cholas in the 11th century AD gave rise to kalaripayattu,[11] although this theory was rejected by later writers.[12]

The 13th century AD is the earliest suggested date for the existence of kalaripayattu, with the earliest reports of kalaripayattu originating from the Portuguese in the late 16th/early 17th centuries.[13] After the British outlawed it in the 18th and 19th centuries, kalaripayattu lost its lustre. However, in the past few decades, the growing interest in martial arts on a global scale has brought revitalised attention to kalaripayattu. The history of Bodhidharma, who is regarded in Shaolin mythology as the founder of the Shaolin Temples, has recently been hypothesised to link kalaripayattu with Shaolin kung fu.

This chapter explores the evolution of kalaripayattu in the Malabar Coast from the Middle Ages, deriving conclusions from a variety of historical sources, looking at the definition and evolution of kalaripayattu, explaining what kalaripayattu is and how it is used, with an emphasis on the many styles found throughout Kerala, and culminating in a comprehensive study of the regulated war tactics known as ankam and Mamankam, consistent with the concepts of 'distinction,' 'proportionality,' and other means and methods of war under modern international humanitarian law principles.

1.2 *Origin, History and Evolution*

As one of the earliest fighting styles currently practised in India and for more than 500 years, the martial art of kalaripayattu has been preserved in adherence to the *guru-sishya* tradition.[14] Kalaripayattu is a comprehensive art form that not only guides how to fight your enemy but also how to cure bodily wounds. This unique combination turns it into a thorough science and earned it the nickname 'mother of all martial arts.'[15]

The song collection Vadakkan Pattukal, (ballads) about the Chekavar of Malabar region, makes reference to kalaripayattu. The Vadakkan Pattukal

---

11 Elamkulam Kunjan Pillai, *Studies in Kerala History* (self-pub., 1970).

12 A. Sreedhara Menon, *Kerala Charithram*, 18th ed. (Kottayam: DC Books, 2019).

13 Durate Barbosa, *The Land of Malabar* (Kottayam, India: Mahatma Gandhi University, 2000).

14 The guru-sishya system is a traditional style of education in India in which a guru (teacher) transmits knowledge and wisdom to a sishya (disciple). Mutual respect, trust, commitment, and obedience underpin the guru-sishya relationship. The guru-sishya system is said to be a successful method of passing down spiritual and secular knowledge through generations.

15 Phillip B. Zarrilli, *When the Body Becomes All Eyes: Paradigms, Discourses and Practices of Power in Kalarippayattu, a South Indian Martial Art* (Oxford: Oxford University Press, 2000).

asserts that the essential principle of kalaripayattu is that one should not employ their knowledge of the art to further their own interests, but rather to support worthy causes. The martial art of kalaripayattu was developed for the battlefield and uses weapons and combat techniques that are unique to Malabar (the word 'kalari' is interchangeably used to refer both 'platform or stage where the martial art of Kalaripayattu is practised' and 'battlefield').[16] The aim of martial training, according to kalaripayattu, is to enhance a person on all levels, beginning with their physical condition and progressing to their mental and spiritual stability. In a way, it establishes a path toward living a full life guided by tradition.

1.2.1 *Kalaripayattu*: Origin

It is challenging to pinpoint the precise time when kalaripayattu developed—to sort fact from the many myths regarding kalaripayattu's beginnings and institutionalization. Two of the many genesis stories for kalaripayattu told in numerous narratives, including *Keralolpathy,* are well-known in both north and south Kerala.

The most well-known legend surrounding kalaripayattu dates to Parasurama, who was thought to have founded Kerala. In the newly reclaimed land, he brought thirty-two Brahmin families and instructed them in the skills of archery and battle. Another legend claims that Lord Siva and his *tandava* were the sources of kalaripayattu, and yet another widely held belief in south Kerala is that kalaripayattu was started by the Hindu saint Agastya. Another *Keralolpathi* source asserts that the is from where kalaripayattu originated from *Dhanurveda.*

The reality of the *Keralolpathi* and these tales, however, was disputed by historians.[17] It is believed that the authors of these Keralolpathies are Brahmins, and K.N. Ganesh, a contemporary historian, has chastised them for their strong interest in connecting all regional customs with *Brahmanism.*[18]

The first historian to attempt to determine when kalaripayattu initially appeared was Elamkulam Kunjan Pillai.[19] According to Pillai, kalaripayattu changed over during the reign of the Chola and Chera dynasties and the hundred-year war. According to Vijayakumar in *Kalaripayatt: kerelathinte*

16 A. Sreedhara Menon, *Kerala History and Its Makers* (Kottayam: DC Books, 2011), 82–83.

17 Rosmerin Mathew, *Kalaripayattum Rangavediyum* (Trivandrum: Bhasha Institute, 2009), 11–12.

18 K.N. Ganesh, *Culture and Modernity: Historical Explorations* (Trivandrum: Bhasha Institute, 2004).

19 Pillai, *Studies.*

Sakthiyum Sountharyavum, kalaripayattu evolved and developed during the Sangam period.[20] Numerous stories and narrations by travellers, including folk songs, noted the valour and skill of kalaripayattu warriors. There is a claim that early man copied kalaripayattu's techniques from animal fights.

1.3 *Legend of Agasthya and Parasurama*

The *Brahmanda Purana* claims that the sages praised Lord Vishnu to rescue them from the wicked Kshatriya monarchs on earth.[21] The sixth manifestation of Vishnu, viz., Parasurama, came to earth to exact retribution for the evil *Kashthriyas*' transgressions. Thus, Dhanurvedic guru Parasurama slaughtered the Kshatriyas and fulfilled Lord Vishnu's words.

In various puranic literature, regional mythology, and chronicles, the rise of Kerala from the oceans is narrated as a deed of Parasurama.[22] It is believed that thereafter the Dhanurveda guru Parasurama taught the martial art to the locals of this region so they could defend themselves. As a result, Parasurama is credited with developing kalaripayattu, a superior martial art style, in Kerala. A ballad in Malayalam that praises Parasurama and his deeds mentions the divine origin of the country, the founding of 108 kalaris, and how he taught twenty-one gurus the art of destroying enemies.[23]

The earliest description of warfare is found in the Dhanurveda, an upaveda to the Yajurveda.[24] A number of books on Dhanurveda have been written, including Vasishtta Dhanurveda, Visvamitra Dhanurveda, Jamadagni Dhanurveda, Vais'ampayana Dhanurveda, and Sadasiva Dhanurveda, among others. Other books on warfare and related fields include Sukraniti, nitiprakasika, Yuktikalpataru, etc. In Vasisthiya Dhanurveda Samhita, the science of warfare is taught by Vasistha to Visvamitra, where Vasistha recalls the secret teaching of Dhanurvidya as given by Sadasiva to Parasurama.[25] According to *Nitiprakasika, Brahma* composed Dhanurveda with 100,000 chapters.

Regarding the genesis of kalaripayattu, a similar mythology from southern Kerala states that Agastya, a saint and Lord Subramanian's pupil, gave kalaripayattu to humanity. Two books—*Munnool* by Agastya, followed by *Pinnool* by

---

20 K. Vijayakumar, *Kalaripayatt Keralathinte saktiyum southaryavum* (Thiruvanathapuram: Dept. of Cultural Publications, 2000), 46.

21 See Vettam Mani, *Purānic Encyclopedia* (New Delhi: Motilal Banarsidass, 1975), 568.

22 *Keralolpatti* (*The Origin of Malabar*) (Mangalore: Pfleiderer & Riehm, 1868).

23 G. Mullassery Prasannan, *Kalaripayattum Kaiyamkaliyum* (1965), 43.

24 A upaveda is a subsidiary branch of knowledge derived from one of Hinduism's four Vedas. The upavedas include Ayurveda (medicine), Dhanurveda (military science), Gandharvaveda (music and dance), and Sthapatyaveda (construction and engineering).

25 Prasannan, *Kalaripayattum*.

his student Bhogar—are regarded as the foundational works of kalaripayattu. Neither text has endured the test of time, but numerous later works cite the aforementioned sources. The primary source for the southern variant of kalaripayattu is these later writings.[26]

According to Agastya's legend, Lord Siva, who was himself a warrior, acquired kalaripayattu during his Tandava dance, and Agastya, who was Siva's pupil, got that knowledge directly from Siva. However, neither of the legends had any historical evidence to back them up, and many historians refuted them as being based on Brahmanical dogma.[27]

1.4 *Other Historical Accounts*

Kalaripayattu fighting techniques date back to the Sangam period (600 BCE—300 CE).[28] In the Sangam era, every warrior received regular military instruction in riding horses and elephants as well as shooting targets. They were experts in one or more of the key weapons of the day, such as the bow and arrow, sword, shield, and spear (*vel, Valu, vil, ambu* etc.).[29] According to other beliefs, various tribal communities in ancient Malabar are thought to have invented kalaripayattu to protect themselves from similar populations.

The native legendary ballads of Malabar, known as Vadakkan Pattugal, inspired an oral tradition narrating the adventures of warriors, highlighting the tradition of kalaripayattu.[30] These songs honour the members of two families in north Kerala called 'Puthuram Veedu' and 'Tacholi Manikkottu Veedu,' the former belonging to the Thiyya sub-caste and the latter to the Nayar caste of Hindus. These poems from Kerala, dating to the 16th century AD, depict a societal structure in which every young person must participate in martial arts training.[31]

A. Sreedharan Menon, historian, claims that kalaripayattu was one of the most significant elements of feudal Keralite culture, since it helped teach Kerala's youth military training and Spartan-like discipline, regardless of caste, community, or sex.[32] Every hamlet in mediaeval Kerala had its own kalari, which housed a presiding god known as Bhagavathy or Paradevata. After

26 Mathew, *Kalaripayattum*.

27 K.N. Ganesh, *Keralathinte Innalekal* (Trivandrum: Bhasha Institute, 2002).

28 Zarrilli, *When the Body*.

29 N. Subramanian, *Sangam Polity* (London: Asia Publishing House, 1966).

30 Kavalam Narayana Panikkar, *Folklore of Kerala* (New Delhi: National Book Trust India, 1991), 108.

31 Panikkar, *Folklore*.

32 Menon, *Kerala History*.

completing their regular academic courses in their local schools, children in Kerala would enlist in their local kalari to continue their military training.[33] This was notably prevalent among martial groups of different communities, like the Nairs and Thiyyas.[34]

In his account of Nair military instruction in kalaripayattu, 16th century Portuguese explorer Duarte Barbosa said:

> The more part of Nayars (Nairs), when they are seven years of age, are sent to schools, where they are taught many tricks of nimbleness and dexterity; there they teach them to dance and turn about and to twist on the ground, to take royal leaps and other leaps and this they learn twice a day as long as they are children and they become so loose-jointed and supple and they make them turn their bodies contrary to nature; and when they are fully accomplished in this, they teach them to play with the weapon they are most inclined, some play with bows and arrows, some with poles to become spearmen, but most with swords and are ever practising. The Nayars (Nairs) are bound, however old they may be, to always go (for training) in the winter (the rainy season or monsoon season) to take their fencing lessons until they die.[35]

Barbosa further pointed out that Malabar developed a network of martial culture during the Middle Ages, thanks to the physical training centres of the Nairs and Thiyyas.[36]

In his work *Castes and Tribes of Southern India,* Edgar Thurston said, regarding the attacking technique with a sword known as *urumi*, which is exclusive to kalaripayattu and was widely used during the mediaeval period:

> The Tiyans (*Thiyyar*) were further allowed to wear gold jewels on the neck, to don silken cloths, to fasten a sword round the waist, and to carry a shield. The sword was made of thin pliable steel and worn round the waist like a belt, the point being fastened to the hilt through a small hole near the point. A man, intending to damage another, might make an apparently friendly call on him, his body loosely covered with a cloth,

33 Jennifer G. Wollok, *Rethinking Chivalry and Courtly Love* (Santa Barbara, Ca: ABC-CLIO, 2011), 250.

34 P.K. Yasser Arafath, 'The Nadapuram Enigma: A History of Violence and Communalism in North Malabar (1957–2015),' *Economic & Political Weekly* 51, no. 15 (April 9, 2016), 47–55.

35 Menon, *Kerala History,* 82.

36 Arafath, 'The Nadapuram Enigma.'.

> and to all appearances unarmed. In less than a second, he could unfasten the sword round his waist, and cut the other down.[37]

According to Sreedhara Menon, the 'golden age' of kalaripayattu occurred throughout medieval Kerala. This period culminated with the creation of the Vadakkan Pattukkal and the emergence of folkloric figures like Aromal Chekavar, Unniyarcha, and Thacholi Othenan, who were lauded for their valour chivalry, and ideals.[38]

During this time, kalaripayattu was also widely used in the Keralite tradition of *ankam* (duel), a type of battle or combat, frequently employed in feudal mediaeval Kerala as a means of resolving conflicts that could not be resolved by local political assemblies. There was also a form of ankam known as *poithu*, which involved two people engaging in a duel. To ensure that all participants in ankam or poithu could acquire the utmost degree of competence with kalaripayattu's traditional weaponry, the participants had up to 12 years of training and preparation before the ankam was actually fought.[39] Professional mercenaries with kalaripayattu training were occasionally paid to perform ankam on behalf of others.[40]

When the use of guns and cannons became commonplace in Kerala in the 17th century, the practice and frequency of kalaripayattu started to decline. This occurred at the same time as European invasions into Kerala, which led to a decline in the use of traditional weapons like swords and spears in favour of firearms.[41]

1.5 *Bodhidharma and Kalaripayattu*

Legendary 5th or 6th century CE Buddhist monk Bodhidharma is traditionally credited with spreading Chan Buddhism in China and is considered its first patriarch. He started the physical training of the monks at Shaolin Monastery, which resulted in the development of Shaolin kungfu, according to the 17th century text *Yijin Jing*. Chinese referred to Bodhidharma as Dámó, and Japan refers to him as Daruma. Sanskrit translation of his name is 'dharma of enlightenment (bodhi).'[42] There isn't much biographical evidence about Bodhidharma

37 Edgar Thurston, *Castes and Tribes of Southern India*, Vol.7 (Madras: Government Press, 1909).

38 Menon, *Kerala History*, 82–83.

39 Menon, *Kerala History*.

40 Menon, *Kerala History*, 83.

41 Fali E. Doctor, 'Kalari Payat: Ancient Art of India,' *Black Belt* 11, no. 7 (July 1973), 23–25.

42 Ronald M. Davidson and Steven D. Goodman, ed., *Tibetan Buddhism: Reason and Revelation* (Albany: State Univ. of New York Press, 1992).

from his lifetime, and subsequent accounts became stacked with legend and questionable material.[43]

Many Chinese sources state that Bodhidharma was from the Western Regions, which are usually Central Asia but can also allude to the Indian subcontinent. He is either referred to as a 'Persian Central Asian' or a 'South Indian [...] the third son of a renowned Indian king.' Bodhidharma is portrayed as a hot-tempered, heavily bearded, non-Chinese figure in Buddhist arts. Chan's writings refer to him as 'The Blue-Eyed Barbarian.'[44]

In addition to the Chinese stories, there are several widely accepted legends about Bodhidharma's ancestry. According to an Indian myth, Bodhidharma was the third child and monarch of Kanchipuram's Tamil Pallavas.[45] Bodhidharma is constantly seen as a South Indian by the Tibetan and Southeast traditions,[46] the former in particular portraying him as a dark-skinned Dravidian.[47] On the other hand, Bodhidharma is typically regarded as Persian in Japanese culture.[48]

The narratives also dispute the date of his arrival, with one early account suggesting he landed during the Liu Song dynasty (420–479 CE) and later accounts claiming he arrived during the Liang dynasty (502–557 CE). Bodhidharma spent most of his time in the region of the Northern Wei (386–534 CE). Modern research suggests he lived in the early 5th century CE.[49]

The concept that Bodhidharma founded martial arts at the Shaolin Temple flourished in the 20th century; however, martial arts historians have established that this narrative derives from the *Yi Jin Jing*, a 17th century qigong text.[50] According its prologue, Bodhidharma left behind the *Yi Jin Jing*, from which the monks learned the martial techniques that brought them fame.[51]

---

43 John McRae, *Seeing Through Zen: Encounter, Transformation, and Genealogy in Chinese Chan Buddhism* (Berkeley: Univ. of California Press, 2003).

44 Jeffrey L. Broughton, *The Bodhidharma Anthology: The Earliest Records of Zen* (Berkeley: Univ. of California Press, 1999).

45 Kamil V. Zvelebil, "The Sound of the One Hand", *J. Am. Oriental Soc.* 107, no. 1 (Jan.-Mar. 1987), 125–126.

46 Anand Krishna, *Bodhidharma: Kata Awal adalah Kata Akhir* (Indonesian edition) (Jakarta: Gramedia Pustaka Utama, 2005).

47 Jérôme Edou, *Machig Labdrön and the Foundations of Chöd*, (Ilhaoi, NY: Snow Lion Publications, 1996).

48 Masato Tojo, *Zen Buddhism and Persian Culture* (2010), http://www.shamogoloparvaneh.com/Zen_Buddhism_and_Persian_Culture_V1.pdf.

49 *Encyclopedia of Buddhism* vol.1 (2003).

50 Meir Shahar, *The Shaolin Monastery: History, Religion, and the Chinese Martial Arts* (Honolulu: U. of Hawaii Press, 2008).

51 Boyuan Lin, *Zhōngguó wǔshù shǐ: History of Chinese Martial Arts* (1996).

Some historians, notably Tang Hao, Xu Zhen, and Matsuda Ryuchi, have questioned the validity of the *Yi Jin Jing*. 'This document is replete with errors, oddities, and unbelievable claims,' writes Lin Boyuan, 'and it cannot be accepted as a legitimate source.'[52] The earliest extant copy is from 1827,[53] while the text's composition date has been assigned to 1624.[54] Even still, the link of Bodhidharma with martial arts was only widely accepted after the serialisation of the novel *The Travels of Lao Ts'an* in *Illustrated Fiction Magazine* from 1904 to 1907.[55] According to Henning, the 'narrative is plainly a twentieth-century creation,' which 'is verified by documents dating back at least 250 years earlier, which mention both Bodhidharma and martial arts but establish no connection between two.'[56]

Meditation and the *Laṅkāvatāra Sūtra* were central to Bodhidharma's teachings and practice. According to the *Anthology of the Patriarchal Hall*, Bodhidharma is the 28th Patriarch of Buddhism in a line that stretches all the way back to the Gautama Buddha himself.[57]

1.5.1 Types of Kalaries

Kalaries were traditionally built in the proximity of aristocratic mansions. Most aristocratic families owned their kalaries, constructed using Tachu Sastra, the local science of architecture. The *cerukalari* and *kuzhikalari* (or *pitkalari*) are two types of kalaries designed for physical and weapon training. Kuzhikalaries are still in use today. A kalari is located in the plot's southwest corner, with its face oriented eastward as per the Vastushastra.[58]

> Earth is dug up to a depth of around three feet from a rectangular plot of ground about forty-two feet in length in an east westerly direction and twenty-one feet in breadth. The excavated soil is stacked around the pit

52 Lin, *Zhōngguó wǔshù shǐ.*

53 Matsuda Ryuchi, *Zhōngguó wǔshù shǐlüè A Brief History of Chinese Martial Arts* (Chinese edition) (1986).

54 Ryuchi, *Zhōngguó wǔshù shǐlüè*, 48.

55 Stanley Henning, 'Ignorance, Legend and Taijiquan,' *Journal of the Chen Style Taijiquan Research Association of Hawaii* 2, no. 3 (Autumn/Winter 1994), 1–7.

56 Stan Henning and Tom Green, 'Folklore in the Martial Arts,' Thomas A. Green, *Martial Arts of the World: An Encyclopedia* (Santa Barbara, Calif: ABC-CLIO, 2001).

57 Philippe Cornu, *Dictionnaire Encyclopédique du Bouddhisme* (Paris: Seuil, 2006).

58 Vastushastra is a traditional Indian system of architecture that is based on ancient texts. It describes the principles of design, layout, measurements, ground preparation, space arrangement and spatial geometry for various types of buildings. It aims to integrate architecture with nature and create harmony and balance in the environment. Vastushastra is also known as the science of dwelling.

> and pushed into solid ridges. The floor has been levelled and pushed as well. The space is thatched roofed with the support of two main pillars one in the east and the other in the west.

Anka kalari is the location where fighting used to take place. These types of kalaries help practitioners regulate their body temperature; also, the mud in these types of kalaries is considered healthy as it does not induce skin disease in practitioners.[59]

Kalaripayattu techniques and training vary from region to region. Three basic types of traditional kalaripayattu are generally recognised and are based on the regions in which they are practised. They are:

- the Northern style, also known as Vadakkan Kalari;
- the Central style, Madhya Kalari, and
- the Southern style, also known as Thekkan Kalari.[60]

The Northern kalari itself was divided into three types concentrated on the hero battle with Arappukkai, Pillathangi, and Vattenthiruppus[61] Weapon training was the major technique used in those areas.[62] The Central style of kalaripayattu is based on the square pattern of footwork and is linked to the Chaver and Mamangam.[63] Northern and Central kalaripayattu mythology is linked to Parasurama, whilst the southern tradition is linked to the Agastya saint. The Southern style encourages spontaneous combat, also known as Dranam Palli Sampradaya, with little emphasis on weapons.[64]

Diverse parts of Kerala had different kalaripayattu training customs and practices taught in a kalari, or specialised training facility. Each kalari's location and construction are in accordance with numerous Kerala-based religious practises and architectural treatises like the Vastu Shastras (Hindu architectural treatises).[65] There are requirements for the kalari's physical dimensions, the depth of the ground therein, and the type of material that must make up

59 Chirakal T. Sreedharan Nair, *Kalarippayatt: The Complete Guide to Kerala's Ancient Martial Art* (New Delhi: Westland, 2007), 3.

60 A. Vinodan and S. Meera, 'Exploring the Relevance of Cultural Resource Management: A Case Study of Kalaripayattu,' *Journal of Heritage Management* 3, no. 1, (2018) 71–86.

61 George Pati, 'Kalari and Kalarippayattu of Kerala, South India: Nexus of the Celestial, the Corporeal, and the Terrestrial', *Contemporary South Asia* 18, no. 2 (2010), 182.

62 Vijayakumar, *Kalarippayatt*.

63 Pi Balakrishnan, *Kalarippayattu: The Ancient Martial Art of Kerala* (C.V. Govindankutty Nair Gurukka, 1995), 13.

64 Zarrilli, *When the Body*.

65 Shaji K. John, *Kalaripayattu: The Martial and Healing Arts of Kerala* (self-pub., 2011), 21.

the floor: red sand blended with particular herbs to help repair minor injuries sustained while training. The site of ritualistic structures, such as the Poothara, Ganapatithara, and Guruthara, are to face the west, and the entrance of the kalari must face east.[66] Salutations are offered to the presiding gods before each kalari training session, and the kalari temple is honoured by paying respect. Students use soil from the kalari site to apply tilak or tikka to their foreheads and the forehead of the idol of the presiding god.[67] The traditional training clothing is a red and white or red and black loincloth. During training, oral orders, or vaithari, are provided by the guru in Sanskrit or Malayalam.[68]

In the past, kalaripayattu instruction was required for all Keralites belonging to the Hindu community, men and women, starting from age 7 or 9 and continuing until they completed their education. Members of other communities started using the art by the 11th century AD.[69] According to noted historian Professor A. Sreedharan Menon, 'each *desam* or locality had a Kalari with a guru at its head and both boys and girls received physical training in it.'[70] Warriors, soldiers, and anybody else interested in a career in martial arts would continue their training throughout their entire lives. The Northern style and the Southern style of kalaripayattu are typically recognised among kalari practitioners. These two systems share striking similarities in their *vazhi* (Malayalam for 'way' or 'method'), which include, among others, the styles of Hanuman, Bhim, and Bali. In kalaripayattu, each vazhi has a distinct function. Hanuman Vazhi, or 'The Way of Hanuman' in Malayalam, is one style that emphasises technical application, speed, and a variety of tricks and outsmarting tactics. The main goal of Bali Vazhi ('The Way of Bali' in Malayalam), is to use the opponent's technological applications against them in a way that puts them in danger. The use of physical power is prevalent in Bhiman Vazhi ('The Way of Bhiman' in Malayalam).[71] Various masters have adjusted and adapted the styles in accordance with their understanding of the art. The tradition of continuously learning, modifying, and perfecting the techniques by looking at what is workable and efficient is where kalaripayattu practitioners develop and achieve mastery. While adhering to tradition is important, gurukuls of

66 Sebastian, Shevlin, 'Warrior on The Stage,' *The New Indian Express*, (9 March 2014).

67 Gagan Khullar, 'The Ancient Martial Art of Kalaripayattu in Delhi,' *The Hindu* (25 June 2019).

68 E.M. Manoj, 'When Kalaripayattu Dons New Attire,' *The Hindu* (3 October 2015).

69 M. Sujatha and K.G. Jose, 'Health Tourism With Reference to Kalari' (Kottayam: Mahatma Gandhi Univ., 2015), 19.

70 Supriya Unni Nair, 'Defying Age with a Sword: Meenakshi Gurrukkal, Kerala's Grand Old Kalaripayattu Dame,' *The News Minute* (6 February 2016).

71 John, *Kalaripayattu*.

kalaripayattu have used their knowledge and logic to help evolve the artform[72] An adversary combatant's surprise technique might teach a kalari practitioner new fighting moves. The kalari practitioner would need to develop the ability to recognise, accommodate, and counteract these novel approaches. This is particularly evident in the Southern style of kalaripayattu, which is thought to have undergone adaptations and modifications during battles with Tamil kingdoms to combat fighting styles like Silambam, one of the main fighting styles used by Tamil warriors at the period.

However, compared to its northern and southern counterparts, the third form—the Central style, or Madhya Kalari—is less frequently practised. Although it is primarily limited to the Tulu Nadu region in northern Kerala and southern Karnataka, a smaller, localised variation of kalaripayattu known as Tulunadan Kalari is mentioned in literature like the Vadakkan Pattukal. In remote areas of Kerala, there are allegedly still some smaller, regional types that can be seen, but they are becoming harder to locate. Dronamballi, Odimurassery, Tulu Nadan, Shaiva Mura, and Kayyangali are a few examples.

2 Means and Methods of Warfare

In ancient India, the major religions served as the states' guides in implementing the laws of international behaviour.[73] Buddhism and Hinduism both promoted a number of humanitarian ideals that were fundamental to this region's way of life, comparable to contemporary notions of human rights and humanitarianism.[74] Classic instances of this include the Buddhist teachings on 'wars of self-defence and the peaceful resolution of disputes' and the concept of 'Desha Dharma' held by Hindus in ancient India and practised throughout the nation.[75] Beyond this, the rules established in Chainarole by the warriors of ancient Manipur and those of the Chekavars, the kalaripayattu-practising warriors of medieval Malabar, contain behaviours that are obviously in accordance with contemporary laws of war.

Ankam and *Mamankam* were types of controlled combat that were the traditional means to resolve claims and disagreements amongst the local rulers

72 John, *Kalaripayattu*.

73 James Bryce, *The Holy Roman Empire* (1871).

74 C.J. Chacko, 'International Law in India,' *Indian Journal of International Law* 1. (1960), 184, 199.

75 C.G. Weeramantry, 'Buddhism and International Humanitarian Law,' in V.S. Mani (ed.), *Oxford Handbook of International Humanitarian Law* (Oxford: Oxford Univ. Press, 2007), 5.

on the mediaeval Malabar Coast, preventing full-fledged war. Such battles were fought for their masters by highly skilled kalaripayattu warriors who were paid by local rulers for their services. Sword and hand-to-hand combat took place in front of large crowds with important people invited. Similar to the tenets of contemporary international laws of war, violation of rules of combat was forbidden and participants in the conflict were expected to uphold the highest ethical standards.

2.1 *Historical Origin of Ankams and Mamankams*

'War was in fact the natural state of Malabar prior to the emergence of the Ankams and Mamamkams,' and wars were long-lasting.[76] Malabar kingdoms, like other kingdoms of the period, practised pillage, destruction, death of civilians, and targeted sexual violence. During conflicts, it was common practise to destroy captured areas by burning and plundering everything found there. To protect themselves, civilians were forced to either take up weapons and fight the invading forces or forsake their lands and professions and flee. This shattered the region's thriving economy, which was dependent on trade and commerce of spices, crafts, gold, and diamonds with Europeans, Chinese, and Arabs.[77]

To this end, two forms of conflict resolution emerged to mitigate, shape and control armed conflict. They were concurrently a form of warfare, as well as laws of war. The ankam and Mamankam conflict resolution system is reported to have flourished during the Chera rule.[78] It began to evolve in the 12th century BC when the Chera dynasty was defeated by the Chola dynasty.[79] This resulted in the development of tiny kingdoms within the Chera Empire, some of which were subject to the system of ankam and Mamankam conflict resolution. The new system evolved as a means of distinguishing combatants and non-combatants, which in turn protected the civilian population, who were primarily farmers, artisans, goldsmiths, and traders, from the effects of armed

---

76 A. Galleti, *The Dutch in Malabar* (Madras: Supr. Govt. Press,1911), 19.

77 Evidence shows that the Malabar Coast had a flourishing trade with Greeks, Romans, Chinese and Arabs from as early as 3000 BC. See Srikumar Chattopadhyay and Richard W. Franke, *Striving for Sustainability: Environmental Stress and Democratic Initiatives in Kerala* (New Delhi: Concept Publishing, 2006), 79. Also see K.M. Panikkar, *India and the Indian Ocean: An Essay on the Influence of Sea Power on Indian History* (New York: Macmillan, 1945).

78 Reigned between 3rd century BC and 12th century AD, ruling over an area corresponding to modern-day western Tamil Nadu and central Kerala.

79 K.K. Nair, *By Sweat and Sword: Trade, Diplomacy and War in Kerala Through the Ages* (New Delhi: Manohar Publishers, 2012).

conflicts, thereby protecting the kingdoms' and the region's economic interests. This is supported by the records of foreign visitors such as Benjamin of Tudela (AD 1170), Chau Ju-Kua (AD 1225), Abul Feda (AD 1273–1331), Marco Polo (AD 1293), Ibn Battuta (AD 1333–45), and Friar Jordanus (AD 1323–30), who visited the region between the 12th and 16th centuries AD. Their texts emphasise the absence of serious turmoil between local rulers resulting in violent conflicts throughout this period, which aided the growing overseas trade and commerce.[80]

Throughout the new system's evolution, the people were gradually separated into two categories: Chaver Padas (death squads ready to die in war) and civilians. The Chaver Padas, which eventually evolved into a group that ceremoniously participated in Mamankams, were originally part of an effort to distinguish between combatants and non-combatants. A subset of the Malabar people, particularly from specific castes such as Nairs and Ezhavas, were enlisted in the Chaver Padas, and their sole *avakasham* (right and responsibility) was to participate in internal and external battles and safeguard the kingdom. Later records show that persons of various religions, such as Mopila Muslims and Portuguese Christians, enlisted in the Chaver Pada of Zamorin.[81] Since it was unlikely that Chaver Padas members would survive the war, they were not expected to establish committed marriage relationships or take care of their homes.[82] As a result, there was a distinct social, cultural, and political division between combatants and non-combatants. In addition, there was an unwritten but strictly followed code of chivalry among the warring parties, according to which only the actual combatants were allowed to engage in battle and suffer its consequences. Women and children, in particular, were to be protected and not targeted as non-combatants.[83]

2.2 *Ankam*

Ankams were a type of duel fought on an Ankathattu, a four to six-foot-high temporary platform created expressly for the purpose. Duels for settling personal feuds were not uncommon in different civilizations around the world during the same period, but what distinguishes ankams from other duels of the time is that they were usually performed to settle disputes between local

80 Nair, *By Sweat*, 75–76. Also see K.A. Nilakanta Sastri, *Foreign Notices of South India: From Megasthenes to Ma Huan* (Madras: Univ. of Madras, 1972).

81 Francis Werdr, 1 *Transactions of the Literary Society of Bombay* 4–5. (London: Longman, Hurst, et al, 1819).

82 Nair, *By Sweat*, 65.

83 Nair, *By Sweat*, 67.

rulers as an alternative to full-fledged war, thereby avoiding civilian casualties and unnecessary cost.[84] The ruler represented by the surviving fighter was considered the winner.

The Maha-Magha-Ankam, also known as Mamankam, was a far more extensive exercise held once every twelve years, during which the king's throne was available to challenge by aspiring local kings and chieftains. Mamankams, like ankams, were held in a specially designated location and under stringent control, so that casualties were confined to the prospective soldiers who chose to accept the challenge. If an aspiring local ruler's combatant was successful in winning the Mamankam and killing the monarch, that local ruler would be appointed as the next king. There was a clear divide between combatants and non-combatants in both Ankams and Mamankams, and civilian protection was prioritised.

The word '*ankam*' is loosely translated to mean 'duel' and originated as a battle between two parties to settle a score in feudal Malabar society. The participants in ankams, known as Chekavar, belonged to the warrior branch of some Hindu castes in Kerala, such as the Nairs, Ezhavas, and Thiyyas. These fighters were masters of kalaripayattu and were contracted to fight to the death in an ankam to settle conflicts between regional rulers. The Chekavars were reputed to be the guards of the kingdom and were known to be lethal killers. Before taking part in his first ankam, a man prepared and practised for at least twelve years. 'One became a Chekavar only after fighting an ankam,' the legend goes, and 'a Chekavar's food was on the point of the sword.'[85] Because the ankam ends with the death of one of the warriors, participants frequently charged exorbitant fees for their fights. The payment per combatant was approximately 1,000 fanams, a substantial sum in those days.[86] A portion of this money was given to the local monarch, known as *Naduvazhi*, who had the authority to oversee and perform the ankam. Furthermore, it was traditional to compensate the family of a Chekavar who died in combat.

When a Chekavar was killed in an ankam, his kith and kin were obligated to seek revenge on the slayer or a member of the killer's family, a responsibility carried down from generation to generation. This is referred to as *Kudipaka*.[87]

84 Malabar in those days also had individual duels, known as *poithu*, which were the same as classic duels between two individuals in other parts of the world.

85 Nair, *By Sweat 67*.

86 A gold coin in circulation during the period.

87 Balakrishnan Nayar, 'The Sterner Aspects of Nayar Life', *Calcutta Rev.* CIV, no. 208 (April 1897) and Balakrishnan Nayar, 'The Origin of the Malabar Nayars,' *Calcutta Rev.* CVII, no. 72 (1898).

According to Sangam literature and hero stones discovered in Tamil Nadu, Chekavars were frequently engaged in war on behalf of a local king, and the Chekavars in these generally depict an image of an armed man alongside a *Shiva Linga*.[88] It was customary to erect a hero stone for each man who died in combat on behalf of the local king. The ruler represented by the winning duellist was declared victorious. Almost all disputes were resolved satisfactorily with an ankam, which spectators appreciated, rather than a full-fledged war with the chance of violations. The date and location of ankams were advertised in advance and served as festivals to which thousands of observers gathered. In some circumstances, ankams included Chekavar betting, in which civilians deposited wager money with the Naduvazhi on their favourite Chekavar, not unlike the gladiators of ancient Rome.

Ankams were also used to settle disputes involving foreigners; in one reported case, a specific protocol was devised for foreigners. A dispute with the Portuguese became so serious that it was decided to settle it with a duel, with the victor's side winning the argument.[89] The local monarch chose his most capable Chekavar, a skilled fighter with a sword and shield. The Portuguese chose their bravest member to be their champion, clothing him modestly to minimise the impact if he lost. In the end, he triumphed over his opponent, and the local king was astounded by the talent of a man he assumed to be a simple sailor. Following the defeat of his Chekavar, the king granted the contested right of way to the Portuguese.[90]

Another incident occurred in 1661 when the influence of ankam had rubbed off on the European troops stationed in Malabar when the besieged commander of the Portuguese garrison at Cochin challenged his Dutch opponent to a fight between a single Portuguese champion and five Dutchmen.[91]

The concept of ankam spread to nearby larger kingdoms with huge standing armies in various forms. Even when both sides had enormous armies queued up for combat, they practised a modified version of ankam. In one documented example in Calicut, both armies agreed to fight a hundred warriors from each side, and after roughly five or six warriors from each side were slain, to cease the fight and determine who had won or to arrange a peace. For such

88 A symbol of Lord Shiva, a Hindu god.

89 Jean de Thévenot and Archibald Lovell, *The Travels of Monsieur de Thevenot into the Levant in Three Parts: The East-Indies*, vol. 3 (2013).

90 Jacob C. Visscher and Heber Drury, *Letters from Malabar* (Madras, 1862), 26.

91 S. Parameswaran Aiyar, *Pattapattu: The War Ballads of Kerala*, 49.

agreements, special mediators from the Brahmin caste were hired. This helped to avoid a total onslaught by all armies and any potential violations.[92]

2.3 *Mamankam*

Mamankam is a vestigial version of the word Maha-Magha-Ankam, which refers to the great ankam in the month of Magha.[93] This was done in the form of a celebration, and its origins may be traced back to the 12th century BC when the second Chera Empire began to fall apart. According to history, Malabar's rulers, known as Perumals, were only supposed to govern for a cycle of twelve years, after which they were expected to stand down for a newly elected monarch. This event was celebrated for 28 days, and on the 28th day, the monarch put down the state sword, and the assembly declared the throne vacant and chose a new king.[94]

However, as time passed, the Perumals' authority grew, and they became hesitant to step aside for the next monarch after the traditional tenure of twelve years. However, the custom of celebrating the completion of twelve years persisted, and instead of abandoning the throne, the monarch would accept the challenge of aspiring candidates to defeat him and take the throne. The contestants had to make their way through the monarch's guards and assassinate the king, which was no easy feat. Thus, what began as a peaceful transition of power became a deadly fight in which aspiring candidates challenged the king. In one such successful attempt during a Mamankam, the Zamorin of Calicut challenged the then-Perumal, the Walluvanadu Raja, and achieved dominance over all Malabar kings. Nobody could challenge his authority after that, and the Zamorin presided over the Mamankam until the final one was held in the 18th century.[95]

The 28-day Mamankam celebrations included religious events, military games, festivals, and other activities. The entire riverside where the event took place was lavishly decked with silk, gold, and other ornaments, and cannon were fired at all hours of the day and night. On these days, the Zamorin would stand in the midst of the festivities, carrying the emperor's sword on a raised platform known as a *Manithara*, approximately 40 feet above the

92 Lodovico de Varthema, *The Travels of Ludovico Di Varthema* trans. John W. Jones (London: The Hakluyt Society, 1863), 150.

93 A month in the Hindu calendar corresponding to January-February in the Georgian calendar.

94 Jonathan Duncan, *Transactions of the Literary Society of Bombay* (London: Longman, Hurst et al, 1819), 4–5.

95 A. Sreedhara Menon, *A Survey of Kerala History* (Kottayam: DC Books, 2022), 151–152.

ground, flanked by his bodyguards, and accepting challenges to his title. At this time, anyone may penetrate the Zamorin's bodyguards, kill him, and take his crown.[96] According to records, as many as 55 Chaver Pada members died in vain attempts in a single day, and this continued until the final day of the Mamankam. In one such case, a Chaver warrior nearly killed the Zamorin, who was only saved at the last moment by his Muslim bodyguard.[97]

The Mamankam, despite being a horrific celebration of death and violence, had a significant humanitarian meaning. It reduced civilian casualties by conducting the military conflict in a planned location under strict control. Countries around the world have routinely vied for their neighbouring thrones, and in Malabar, this reality was codified, with the throne open for the challenge every 12 years. This avoided unforeseen attacks and confrontations, which may have resulted in innocent casualties and avoidable suffering.

2.4 *Decline of Ankam and Mamankam*

The arrival of European colonists, particularly the British in the 16th century, signalled the beginning of the downfall of kalaripayattu, the martial arts theory underpinning both ankam and Mamankam. The physical strength and training provided at the kalaris were ineffective against the Portuguese's greater weaponry. The Europeans' sophisticated armaments completely overwhelmed kalaripayattu warriors. Furthermore, many of the invaders were not interested in a less-bloody conflict resolution, which was the main principle underlying ankam and Mamankam. Invasion by Muslim rulers from Mysore in the second half of the 18th century also harmed the supremacy of the native kings. The power and prestige of the kalaripayattu and Chekavars diminished, and the kalaripayattu institution suffered a blow under the authority of the Mysore rulers. Toward the end of the 18th century, the rulers of Kerala's many regions handed the responsibility of safeguarding the region to a standing army, further undermining this system of conflict settlement.

But it was British political dominance that killed the kalaripayattu and Chekavar traditions. The British consolidated their rule over Malabar in northern Kerala in 1792. After putting down a local revolt, the new rulers outlawed

96 Vivid explanations of the *Mamamkam* festivals of 1683 and 1695 were made in their respective books by William Logan, the then British Collector of Malabar, and Alexander Hamilton, a Scottish naval captain. See Logan, vol. 1, 306–308 (1727).

97 J. Duncan and M. Derrett, 'Maintenance of Peace in the Hindu World: Practice and Theory,' in *Indian Y. B. International Law* (1958), 361. Also see A.L. Basham, *The Wonder That Was India: A Survey of the history and Culture of the Indian Sub-Continent before the coming of the Muslims* (London: Ingram, 1981), 8–9.

kalaripayattu in 1793. In 1804, the British government issued an order declaring that anyone who concealed weapons or violated the ban on carrying arms would be deported for life. Similar techniques were used to quell a rebellion in Travancore, Kerala's southernmost region. The British were successful in ending this ancient military structure by outlawing it entirely. However, a group of devoted followers covertly trained and taught this martial technique to ensure its future. At the beginning of the 19th century, practioners and scholars codified the traditional knowledge of kalaripayattu. As a result, this art was preserved for the benefit of future generations.[98]

3 Conclusion

Kalaripayattu is a martial art designed on the ancient battlefield, with weapons and fighting tactics that are unique to Kerala. Unlike in other martial arts, combatants in kalaripayattu came from all castes (especially Nairs and Tiyyas) and religions, as well as women. Because of the prevalent social, cultural, and economic conditions in Malabar at the time, *ankam and Mamankam* emerged as conflict resolution methods. They have significant humanitarian values and can be compared to the modern laws of war:

- Because full-fledged conflict is reduced to combat between two skilled martial arts practitioners in an ankam, casualties are kept to a minimum. Casualties are also decreased in the case of Mamankam because the number of warriors is limited and the battle is performed in a regulated manner.
- Fighters and non-combatants are kept separate. Non-combatants cannot be wounded in an ankam since it is a duel. Citizens are permitted to view ankams, but the separation is clear, and numerous scholars have noted that even the highly-guarded mansions of the warfare elite, known as the taravattus, were kept well apart from civilian populations.[99] Unlike then-contemporary forts, which housed entire civilian populations, the taravattu system ensured that in the event of an attack, only the combatant class was impacted. Although fighting occured during festivals in the sight of civilian viewers in Mamankam,

98 Padma Mohan Kumar, *supra* n. 67.

99 Logan, *supra* n. 50, at 82–83. Also see Francis Day, 'Land of the Perumals or Cochin: Its Past and Its Present' (Madras, 1863), 319 and James S. Buckingham (ed.), XXII The Oriental Herald and Journal of General Literature (1829).

a clear demarcation between fighters and non-combatants is firmly enforced.

- Both ankams and Mamankams adhere to strict restrictions regarding weapon balance and use. Both situations involve low-intensity conflict in a controlled area; therefore, there are no environmental consequences.
- The victims, who are mainly Chekavar's relatives, are amply rewarded and cared for by the local ruler. The family of a contender who confronts the king is never injured in the Mamankam; they are saved so that a family member may battle the king in the future if he so wishes.

Though reinstituting Mamankam in today's war scenario would be nearly impossible, ankam does contain ideals that may be aligned with present day internationally accepted war practices. Since the medieval period, duels have been fought in various civilizations to settle personal vendettas. Ankam was distinct from its counterparts in that it was waged in place of actual wars to resolve disputes between nations. Ankam was improved throughout the years by the creation of rules making it a fair competition under the norms of kalaripayattu. These guidelines were consistent with modern-day laws of war concepts like proportionality, distinction, and victim protection. Though it may appear impossible to create a perfect war that virtually eliminates the impacts of war, ankam demonstrated that it is feasible to limit deaths and crimes.

CHAPTER 6

Iban Laws of War

Angeline Lewis

> Agi idup, Agi ngelaban (Still alive, still fighting).
>
> RENTAP TANAH RUNTUH MENUA[1]

The customs of war in western Borneo during the nineteenth century, particularly among the Iban people in their famed engagements with James Brooke and the Royal Navy, are in many ways a product of place. Unlike many studies in these volumes, where customs regulating war emerged strongly from conflict on land, Borneo was part of an essentially maritime zone, defined by its own difficult geography and climate, located at the confluence of regional maritime trading, raiding and slaving routes, and subject to shifting settlement and rule throughout its coastal and riverine areas.

The maritime character of the Bornean zone is the first defining aspect of Iban warfare. It emerged not because all the peoples of the island were dependent on the water, but because most of their primary interactions were. The Iban emerged among them as an essentially maritime/riverine power, whose shallow-draughted *bangkong* boats were particularly suited to coastal raiding, during a key phase of their history during the nineteenth century. Theirs were forms of power, influence and war that were not recognised as legitimate by Britain, who characterised them instead as unlawful piracy. Describing the region as a maritime 'zone' provides the opportunity, as Warren has put it, of presenting this 'ethnohistory' on 'its own terms, rather than merely as a corollary of the history of Western imperial expansion in East Asia.'[2] In doing so,

1 War cry of Libau anak Ningkan, a warleader of the Skrang Iban renowned for fighting against Brooke rule in Borneo during the period of the 1840s-60s. His praise name, Rentap Tanah Runtuh Menua, means 'Earth-tremor, World-shaker,' and his battlecry is now the motto of Malaysia's Royal Rangers Regiment.

2 James Francis Warren, *The Sulu Zone 1768–1898: The Dynamics of External Trade, Slavery, and Ethnicity in the Transformation of a Southeast Asian Maritime State,* 2nd edn (Singapore: National University of Singapore Press, 2007), pp XXVII–XXIX.

 | DOI:10.1163/9789004512566_008

Warren interprets a dynamic and unstable 'spatial system' specific to its own time and ethnic context,[3] in which any study of Iban *adat* on war and raiding must be contextualised.

The second key characteristic of Iban warfare, headhunting, poses a starker challenge to the central premise of this volume because, while it was 'regulated' in Iban practice, the act of taking human trophies must also be recognised as one fundamentally at odds with both the rules and the principles of the modern laws of war. Third, the Iban concept of *adat,* regulating both the resort to and practice of raiding and headhunting (what might be loosely framed as *ius ad bellum* and *ius in bello*), is considerably broader and spiritually deeper than its traditional translation as customary law.

An Iban case study during the nineteenth century therefore challenges the reader to consider how a system of life, which was reliant on rules and customs to maintain the cosmic balance, regulated practices rejected as illegitimate both by contemporary British law (albeit subject to Parliamentary scrutiny for its propriety in Borneo), and by modern laws of war. Direct analogies between today's legal principles and structure on the one hand, and Iban *adat* and warfare on the other, must therefore be treated with caution, but still warrant exploration to understand how different peoples have chosen to regulate conflict over time.

1 Western Borneo and Its Peoples in the Nineteenth Century

The geographic and climatic features of Borneo which lent themselves most readily to maritime power are shared with much of the archipelago: rough seas from October to March as a result of the north-east monsoon; a multitude of islands, many of them sparsely inhabited; gulfs and deep estuaries. In Borneo itself, a complex river system is protected by broad sand bars along the western coasts, limiting access to ships with deep draughts and causing unpredictable currents. This area, where Iban raiding was focussed, stretched from Tanjung Datu at the mouth of the Sarawak river, north to the seat of the Sultan of Brunei and then to Marudu Bay, where a strait separates Borneo from the islands of the Sulu archipelago, another regional maritime power (see Map 1, FO 925–2657).

Ashore in the Sarawak area, the land proved difficult both to navigate and develop. It is dominated by a swampy coastal plain, rising into steep hills and

3 Warren, ibid, p XXVIII.

MAP 6.1

thick jungle, where movement of people, goods and information was historically limited to the many navigable river systems.[4] For example, the Rejang river is over 300 miles long, and navigable, for shallow-draughted vessels at least, as far as 160 miles from the coast. The Saribas river system, home for a key Iban group, is 52 miles long, and the Batang Lupar system, of which the Skrang (where another powerful Iban group lived) is part, is over 70 miles (see Map 2, FO 925–2736).[5] Even in these navigable rivers, tides change swiftly and only the flood tide traditionally allowed upriver access.[6] This geography fostered an economy founded on subsistence fishing and wet-*padi* agriculture largely

4 Ulla Wagner, *Colonialism and Iban Warfare* (Stockholm: O.B.E.-Tryck, 1972), p 13; Colin N. Crisswell, *Rajah Charles Brooke: Monarch of All He Surveyed* (Kuala Lumpur: Oxford University Press, 1978), p 6.

5 Ho Ah Chon reported navigable distances in miles in: *Kuching in Pictures 1841–1946* (Kuching: See Hua Daily News, 2000), p 1. The Lembaga Sungai-Sungai Sarawak (Sarawak Rivers Board) has gazetted major rivers and their measured length: see Sungai Diwartakan (Rivers Gazetted under the Sarawak Rivers Ordinance 1993 and Major Tributaries),' https://srb.sarawak.gov.my/page-0-159-50-Gazetted-Rivers.htm, accessed 4 October 2022.

6 See Edwin H. Gomes, *Seventeen Years Among the Sea Dayaks of Borneo: A Record of Intimate Association with the Natives of the Bornean Jungles* (London: Seeley and Co, 1911; republished Kota Kinabalu: Natural History Publications, 2004), p 145.

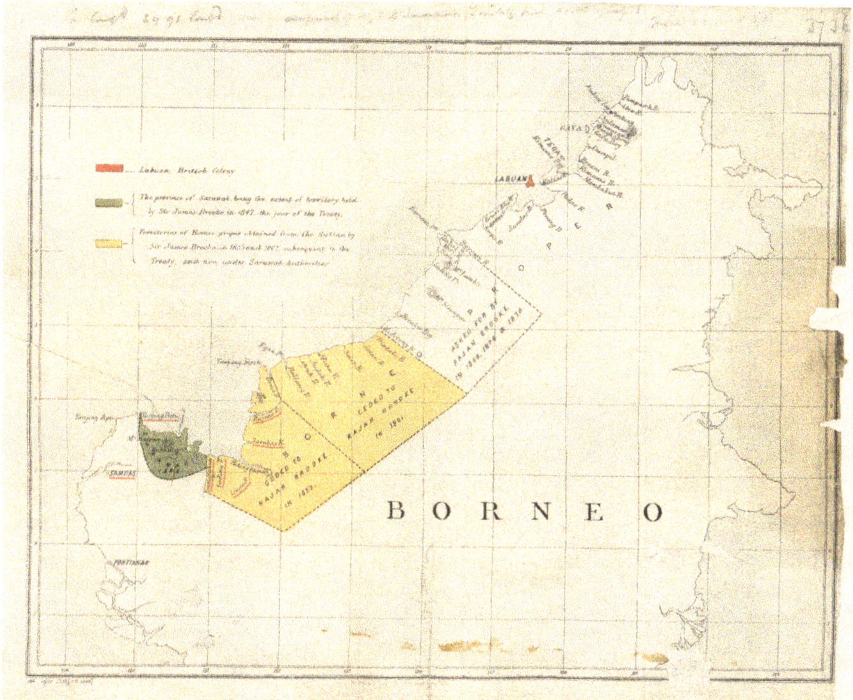

MAP 6.2

by regional peoples, plus a waterborne trade mainly in jungle products, which was controlled by Malays in coastal settlements.[7]

The Iban came to this difficult and distinctive environment as migrants from the Kapuas river, south of the Sarawak basin. Their primary movement north began around the seventeenth century,[8] in search of new *padi* (rice) fields to clear for their swidden agricultural practices.[9] This particular migration ended

7 Wagner, above n 4, p 18.

8 Wagner, ibid, p 14. Sandin noted that the Kapuas migration was the 'most important' Iban movement into western Borneo, but that there were also two previous migrations mentioned in oral tradition: one from Java landing on the coast near Brunei, and the other landing at Tanjung Datu in the Sarawak region, from whom descended Ibans, Melanaus and others. He also described Iban oral traditions of an ancient origin for their people in the Middle East area, migration to Sumatra and from there to the Kapuas: Benedict Sandin, *The Sea Dayaks of Borneo Before White Rajah Rule* (Melbourne: McMillan, 1967), pp 2–4, 26.

9 Charles Brooke, writing of Iban in the Kanowit river region: *Ten Years in Sarawak* (London: Tinsley Brothers, 1866), vol 1, p 327. For a review of Iban agriculture generally, see Wagner, above n 4, p 15.

around the beginning of the eighteenth century with new Iban settlements established in the Batang Lupar/Skrang and Saribas river systems.[10] There, the Iban migrants displaced Seru and Bukitan people, of whom the latter migrated north, where the Iban would later follow.[11] The continued Iban migration pattern was a key element of their culture and agricultural practice, as well as a response to pressure from conflict following the arrival of adventurer James Brooke in the Sarawak region in 1839.[12] Then, the Iban numbered around 50 000 in their 'heartland' in the Skrang, Saribas and Rejang rivers, with perhaps as many as 30 000 more further north towards Brunei.[13] However, in terms of group identity, Pringle argues that at that time the Iban 'had no word which expressed their relative cultural unity' across their settlements. Instead, they 'identified themselves by river: "We of Skrang" (*kami Skrang*) or "We of Undup" (*kami Undup*), or sometimes merely as "we of this area" (*kami menoa*).'[14] Sandin considered that the name Iban was conferred by the Bukitans, another Bornean people, after the settlement of a battle between them by marriage, 'due to the fact that [the Iban] were pushing other races out, and taking all into their possession.'[15]

The Iban were not alone in their newly settled river systems. In fact, a 1940 census in Sarawak 'classified a population of three-quarters of a million into fifty-one "races," three of which were subdivided into eighty-one "tribes".'[16] Other tribal groups included the sago-farming Melanaus, who had once practised headhunting but had given it up by the time of Brooke's arrival in 1839,[17] and the Bidayuh, although the latter did not become 'fully established' in the Sarawak area until around 1840.[18] British sources from the colonial area created confusion by calling both Iban and Bidayuh people 'Dayaks,' sometimes

10 Sandin, above n 8, p 20. Sutlive described Iban movement into the Katibas river system in the 'first decades of the nineteenth century:' Vinson H. Sutlive, *Tun Jugah of Sarawak: Colonialism and Iban Response* (Kuala Lumpur: Penerbit Fajar Bakti, 1992), p 13.

11 Sandin, ibid, pp 33, 35–9.

12 Sutlive, above n 10, p 12.

13 Ooi Keat Gin, 'Brooke Rebels or Iban Nationalists? Revisiting Anti-Brooke Struggles 1841–1941,' *Sarawak Museum Journal* 61, no. 82 (December 2005): 187–205, p 190.

14 Robert Pringle, *Rajahs and Rebels: The Ibans of Sarawak under Brooke Rule, 1841–1941* (New York: Cornell University Press, 1970; republished Kuala Lumpur: S.A. Majeed and Co, 2007), p 25.

15 Sandin, above n 8, p 19. See also Erik Jensen, *The Iban and their Religion* (Oxford: Clarendon Press: 1974), p 17.

16 Jensen, ibid, p 3, citing E.R. Leach, *Social Science Research in Sarawak* (London, 1950), p 15.

17 Wagner, above n 4, p 21.

18 Tom Harrisson, *The Malays of South-West Sarawak Before Malaysia: A Socio-Ecological Survey*, (London: MacMillan, 1970), p 147.

divided into Sea Dayaks and Land Dayaks respectively. Punans, another group who relied on swidden cultivation and jungle resources, lived in the northern rivers, including the Rejang. The Rejang also received migrations from Kayans during the early nineteenth century, who came from eastern Borneo via the Baram river and, like the Iban, were reputed as riverine raiders.[19] British observers in the Brooke period considered that all these peoples were victims of raiding by the Skrang and Saribas Iban; even their larger communities were targeted if 'small parties were discovered at a distance from their villages, or living at their farmhouses.'[20] They too were therefore part of the maritime dynamic of the north-west coast of Borneo during the period, although for many groups, a lack of maritime prowess contributed to their lack of political power in terms of the primary interaction between Iban groups, Malay chiefs and the ruling court in Brunei.

The coastal settlements were dominated by Malays, led by such chiefs. Unlike the Iban, the Malay group does not appear to have migrated to Sarawak at any particular time.[21] Rather their group identity as Sarawak Malays came from their shared adherence to Islam.[22] While the Malays tended to control the coastal area, their control came as much from their role as tax collectors for the Sultan of Brunei as from their maritime power – jointly with the Iban, as will be seen. The Sultan claimed suzerainty over the coast, including the Sarawak area, where he founded the town of Kuching as a provincial capital in the 1820s, after the discovery of antimony there.[23] After Kuching was founded, taxes began to be collected in rice and goods from all, including Malays and Iban, by Malays appointed by the Sultan.[24] The process was often administered using false rice measures, although the Iban cut the false baskets with their knives and, in response to the corruption, 'felt justified in plundering many

19 Wagner, above n 4, p 21; for Kayan raiding, see Spenser St John, *Life in the Forests of the Far East; or Travels in Northern Borneo*, 2nd edn (London: Smith, Elder and Company, 1863), vol 1, p 38.

20 Hugh Low, *Sarawak: Its Inhabitants and Productions being Notes During a Residence in That Country with H. H. the Rajah Brooke* (London: Bentley, 1848), p 278.

21 Craig A. Lockard, *Chinese Immigration and Society in Sarawak, 1868–1917* (Sibu: Sarawak Chinese Cultural Association, 2003), p 16.

22 Lee Yong Leng, *Population and Settlement in Sarawak* (Singapore: Asia Pacific Press, 1970), p 55.

23 John Crawfurd, *A Descriptive Dictionary of the Indian Islands and Adjacent Countries* (London: Bradbury and Evans, 1856), p 377; see also George Windsor Earl, *The Eastern Seas; or Voyages and Adventures in the Indian Archipelago, in 1832-33-34* (London: William H. Allen, 1837), pp 310–11.

24 Sandin, above n 8, p 61. The taxation system is described in detail in Nicholas Tarling, *Britain, The Brookes and Brunei* (Kuala Lumpur: Oxford University Press), p 5.

Malay settlements at various places along the coast.'[25] Moreover, the dynamic of Malay control varied between areas. In some, there is evidence of unfavourable terms – 'forced trade' – being enforced by Malays on others, including Iban.[26]

By the nineteenth century, notwithstanding the founding of Kuching, the sultanate of Brunei is widely considered to have been in decline. The Sultan's increasingly weak rule led to competition for control among Malay chiefs in Brunei's regions of interest, each seeking to 'attract both Illanun pirates and Iban marauders to their cause.'[27] Around this time, a pattern of joint Iban-Malay maritime raiding became established, approximately two to four generations before Brooke's arrival, which appears to have been connected to Brunei's political weakness. Iban in rivers north of Sarawak, especially the Saribas and Skrang, were amenable to joint raiding with local Malay leaders, although they deliberately limited the support they gave to any one of them so as to limit Malay political and trade control.[28]

Early observers thought coastal Malay influence developed into a deliberate recruiting of Iban to train them to piracy, first as rowers then as experts to design and operate *bangkongs*, which became synonymous with the Malay term *prahu*.[29] The closeness of this interaction is evident in the adoption and use of Malay titles such as 'Temenggong' and 'Orang Kaya' by Iban war leaders.[30] Around this period of time, there is also a development in Iban oral tradition from a focus on heroic figures engaged in pioneering migration and clearance of new *padi*, to a new 'pattern of raiding and retaliatory intra-Iban warfare carried on along the coastlines' around Sarawak and Brunei.[31]

25 See further, Tarling, ibid.

26 Tarling, ibid.

27 Sophia Raffles, *Memoir of the Life and Public Services of Sir Thomas Stamford Raffles Particularly in the Government of Java, 1811–1816, and of Bencoolen and its Dependencies, 1817–1824* (London: James Duncan, 1835), p 78. More recent concurrence is found in, for example, Andrew P. Vayda, 'Headhunting Near and Far: Antecedents and Effects of Coastal Raiding by Iban in the Nineteenth Century,' *Sarawak Museum Journal* 2, no. 44 (July-December 1975): 111–138, p 121; Pringle, above n 14, pp 58–9.

28 Vayda, ibid, p 124; see also Pringle, ibid, pp 67–9.

29 Eg, Henry Ling Roth, *The Natives of Sarawak and British North Borneo*, vol 2 (London: Truslove and Hanson, 1896), Appendices, 'Sea Dyak, Malay by H. Brooke Low,' p iv, and 'Sea Dyak (and Bugau), Malau by Mr. Brereton,' p cxviii. A prahu is a sailing vessel characterised by a large triangular rig and outrigger, typical of the Bornean and Indonesian region. It is sometimes also spelled *prau*.

30 Sandin, above n 8, p 60.

31 Ibid, p 68.

A further contributor to instability was the establishment of satellite outposts on the north-west coast of Borneo by Sulu and Iranun raiders.[32] The latter 'burst quite suddenly' into Borneo seas from their home in Mindanao in the late eighteenth century and built a 'clientage' relationship with Sulu.[33] The Iranun incursion into Borneo meant initially they clashed directly with Iban raiders seeking to raid in the same waters.[34] However, as time went on, Iban warriors were reported sailing in Iranun warboats in the Gulf of Thailand and off modern Vietnam, leading Vayda to suggest that by the 1820s, they had actually adopted 'some of the ways' of the Iranun as their own.[35]

In addition to regional maritime powers, the Sarawak region in Borneo also reflected a long history of Chinese trade influence, beginning in the prehistorical period and continuing to the Ming dynasty, before disruption and re-emergence in the nineteenth century.[36] By 1839, the British thought there to be thousands of Chinese settlers in Sarawak, engaged in gold mining, trade and agriculture.[37] Notwithstanding, direct Chinese contact with the Iban was limited, including because of the risks of Iban raiding and headhunting.[38]

The arrival of European powers reconfigured the balance of maritime power between Chinese trade, regional sea powers, Brunei and the other peoples of western Borneo. European interest was focussed on maritime trade, and at times it extended to colonial acquisition. In Borneo, nineteenth century Dutch interests were focussed south of Sarawak, in Sambas. British colonialism had extended as far as Raffles' Singapore, but two failed efforts to settle the offshore island of Balambangan had exhausted any territorial interest in Borneo.[39] Indeed, an 1824 treaty with the Dutch delimited spheres of maritime

---

32 Warren, above n 1, pp 77–8; Tarling, above n 24, p 8.

33 James Francis Warren, *Iranun and Balangingi: Globalisation, Maritime Raiding and the Birth of Ethnicity* (Singapore: Singapore University Press, 2002), especially p 130; Warren, *Sulu Zone,* above n 1, p 151. Iranun is often rendered 'Illanun' in nineteenth century British reports.

34 Sandin, above n 8, p 63.

35 Vayda, above n 27, p 117; Pringle, above n 14, p 68; cf Parliamentary Papers (UK), House of Commons, Command Papers, 1854–5 XXIX.1 [1976], *Reports of Comms to inquire into Position of Sir J. Brooke* ('Parl Papers, *Reports of Commrs*'), Testimony of Orang Kaya Dana Makota, 12 October 1854, p 183.

36 Harrisson, above n 18, pp 118–9, 132.

37 John Crawfurd, *History of the Indian Archipelago: Containing an Account of the Manners, Arts, Languages, Religions, Institutions and Commerce of its Inhabitants* (Edinburgh: Constable, 1820), p 473; Earl, above n 23, p 250.

38 Sutlive, above n 10, p 17; Lockard, above n21, p 8.

39 Alexander Dalrymple, an hydrographer with the British East India Company, secured the Sultan of Brunei's cession to establish a Company factory at Balambangan in 1762, but it

and colonial interest in what the British called 'the Eastern Archipelago', while also mandating cooperation to suppress piracy. In part, the Anglo-Dutch treaty attempted to resolve competing legal views, and resulting diplomatic pressures, regarding the exclusivity of trade in the nations' respective areas, as well as British concern about access to China trade routes.[40] In general, though, the arriving Europeans 'did not at first wish to control the land, only the sea. ... What they mainly wished to do was ensure that no one else should go freely and independently to or fro across it.'[41]

The means by which this form of dominion was justified was through the delegitimisation of non-European access to the sea, which turned on a narrative of regional piracy. A theme in later British colonial history is that the Iban 'owed allegiance to no authority but themselves,'[42] and thus turned to piracy outside the bounds of legitimate maritime power, but the reality of power relationships involving Iban, coastal Malays and Brunei in Borneo is considerably more complex. The Iban constituted a riverine-focussed group capable of exercising maritime power, under the nominal suzerainty of a decaying but similarly maritime-based power in Brunei. While Brunei ruled the coast through local Malay elites, those chiefs were involved in both Iban repression through tax collection and forced trade, and the encouragement of Iban coastal raiding, which in turn contributed to Brunei's continuing decline.

By the mid-1830s open revolt against the Sultan's rule in the Sarawak area had broken out. It was particularly focussed on Pangeran (Prince) Mahkota, representative of the Sultan, who was reputed to be corruptly involved in the antimony trade as well as forced trade generally.[43] In 1837, things had deteriorated so much that the Sultan sent his heir apparent and uncle, the Rajah Muda Hassim, to Kuching to quell the revolt. This environment was the scene setter for the arrival of James Brooke in his yacht *Royalist* in 1839, his direct confrontation with the Saribas and Skrang Iban 'pirates' and his enlistment of the Royal Navy to help suppress them.

---

was sacked by Sulu raiders in 1775. Re-established in 1803, the British settlement proved not to be viable and was abandoned in 1805.

40 Ronald Hyam, *Britain's Imperial Century 1815–1914; A Study of Empire and Expansion* (London: B.T. Batsford, 1976), p 343.

41 Harrisson, above n 18, pp 135–6.

42 See Pringle, above n 14, pp 38–65.

43 Ooi Keat Gin, *Of Free Trade and Native Interests: The Brookes and the Economic Development of Sarawak, 1841–1941* (Oxford: Oxford University Press, 1997), p 14.

2 How Did Iban Society 'Regulate' Itself?

Before turning to Iban warfare in the Brooke period, the Iban approach to self-regulation should be set out, first generally, and then with respect to warfare – although putting the question in these terms frames the Iban *adat* out of its own context, and within a modern, Western-influenced concept of regulation as law or rules. However, while often translated as 'customary law,' *adat* represented much more than a code of law. As Jensen writes, Iban *adat*

> involved the basic values of life, their system of agriculture, as well as the code according to which their society is ordered. It also [concerned] the "correct" manner of behaviour. *Adat* is applied not only to men but also to animals and to natural phenomena.[44]

Thus, an Iban might speak of a person as having

> either good or bad adat. To have good adat [implied] not only that a person's behaviour [was] in accordance with the specific rules of adat accepted in his community, but also that it [exemplified] more abstract ideals, such, for example, as generosity or personal courage.[45]

Rules of behaviour were essential among people, such as the Iban, who lived in remote, multi-family longhouses. However, *adat* sought not only to 'assure harmonious relations' within the longhouse community, but also to

> maintain a community in a state of ritual well-being with respect to the gods and spirits. Any serious breach of *adat* [threatened] this relationship and [was] dealt with accordingly, not only by secular means, but ... often by super natural sanctions or forms of ritual propitiation as well. Thus the correctness of *adat*, when properly adhered to, [was] demonstrated by a continuing state of spiritual well-being expressed outwardly in terms of health and material prosperity.[46]

---

44 Jensen, above n 15, p 5. As this is an historical study, references to *adat* are in the past tense, but the author acknowledges the continuing practice of *adat* as an evolving belief system to this day.

45 Professor Clifford Sather, 'Introduction,' in Benedict Sandin, *Iban Adat and Augury* (Penang: Penerbit Universiti Sains Malaysi, 1980), pp xii-xiii.

46 Sather, ibid, pp xi-xii.

A breach of *adat* could be detected through the disruption of this balance, for example through the experience of illness or calamity.[47]

Adat was, in the nineteenth century, an 'unwritten, but highly codified' system recorded in oral traditions,[48] 'remarkably uniform' among different Iban groups – although there are some differences in religious practice, particularly in the Saribas region, attributed to intermarriage with other peoples.[49] It was this shared system of belief that allowed the wider collective of Iban longhouses, each of which was independent, to cooperate for survival in the absence of any centralised Iban political authority.[50] In so doing, *adat* reflected the importance of the kinship ties in longhouses, in each of which leadership was given to 'senior warriors and warleaders, the *raja berani, tau kayau* or *tau serang*.' Each was chosen for his personal qualities. For *adat, tau serang* in particular was a leader who was 'able to attack,' the meaning of the phrase, but it also imported a religious meaning of one who had 'dreamed the necessary dreams' – not all great war leaders needed the religious quality, but all required personal qualities of leadership.[51]

Adat, as Sather and Sandin emphasise, was complemented in Iban tradition by the practice of augury, focussed on 'interpretation of divine revelation in the behaviour of birds, reptiles, and animals.'[52] That is, while *adat* regulated matters capable of human control and certainty, within that framework 'choices' had 'to be constantly made in which success or failure' were unpredictable. Augury provided guidance against such uncertainty, making reading omens from birds an essential part of being 'on the warpath' in the Iban way of life.[53] For example, the story of Siu and Sera Gunting's visits to the longhouse of Sengalong Burong (the king of the gods) is an important Iban oral tradition. On his arrival, Siu encountered Sengalong Burong's daughter alone 'because the men had all gone off to obtain the head which was necessary to conclude the mourning period for many of their relatives who had recently been killed.'[54]

47 Jensen, above n 15, p 114.

48 Sather, above n 45, p xv. For a description of the different forms of Iban oral tradition, including poetry and prose forms, see Jensen, ibid, p 64 et seq.

49 Jensen, ibid, pp 56–8. Jensen identifies the key differences in the *gawai antu* (feast of the dead): p 58. See also Freeman: Derek Freeman, *Some Reflections on the Nature of Iban Society*, Occasional Paper, Research School of Pacific Studies (Canberra: Australian National University, 1981), pp 6–7.

50 Sather, above n 45, p xiv. *Raja berani* was the name given to a wealthy and brave man, or alternately war leader, *tau kayau* was a raid leader, and *tau serang*, a war leader or general.

51 Pringle, above n 14, p 44.

52 Sather, above n 45, pp xi-xii.

53 Sather, ibid.

54 As retold in Jensen, above n 15, p 86.

They were married, and had a son, Sera Gunting, who later travelled back to his grandfather's longhouse. Sengalong Burong explained to Sera Gunting that omens had to be taken (the practice of *beburong*) in all things except fetching water and defecating, and explained that good omens came only from his seven sons-in-law, all represented by birds. A few days afterward, one of the sons in law, Ketupong, 'led a head-hunting expedition' and Sera Gunting was 'invited to learn the significance of bird omens on the warpath. Upon the expedition's successful return, Sengalong Burong taught his grandson the correct procedure for the major festivals (*gawai*) and some key verses of the *pengap* incantations.'[55]

Sandin's descriptions of *adat* and augury match the breadth of the guidance given by Sengalong Burong in this tradition. His collection of practices included building a longhouse, agriculture, hunting, fishing, fruit and honey collection, incest and adultery, death and mourning, childbirth, lullaby singing, religious festivals (*gawai*), bachelor and maidenhood, courtship, weaving, marriage, adoption, manumission of slaves, general etiquette, war leaders, trading ventures and sailing overseas.[56] Both *adat* and augury were also specifically connected to Iban warfare practices of raiding and headhunting.

3 Iban Warfare: Maritime Raiding and Headhunting

Iban means and methods of warfare centred on maritime raiding and the practice of headhunting – the latter both as a reason to raid, and the result of raiding. It became established as a defining Iban practice once the main migration into the north-western rivers of Borneo was completed, as their control of the new river systems was established. In an oral tradition recorded by Sandin, for example, Unggang built a large war boat to guard the mouth of the Saribas river, guided by a dream. His purpose was to prevent the Iranun 'and other pirates from entering and to attack other strangers who came to sail in that part of the South China sea.' He 'did not like to be accompanied by other Iban boats, as his own could easily carry over 100 warriors. At this time no one dared to attack any boat commanded by Unggang.'[57] Unggang's maritime success encouraged him 'to attack trading ships and other vessels in the South China

55 Ibid, p 89.
56 See further Sandin, *Adat and Augury*, above n 45, table of contents.
57 Sandin, *Adat and Augury*, ibid, p 64.

Sea and to take the heads of their crew members.'[58] Sandin dated the first great Iban coastal raids to the period of this oral tradition.[59]

Iban raiding included intertribal conflict, but also extended 'indiscriminately' throughout their rivers and further along the coast, targeting non-Iban villages and boats.[60] Unggang, the same chief as above, reached agreement with Chinese traders in the Sarawak river around the start of the nineteenth century, for example: the Chinese could trade pots, shells and beads for *padi*, provided they flew a white flag from their vessels at all times. However, anyone who ventured into the river without such a flag, and who was not a Saribas Malay, would be killed and their head taken.[61]

The warlike tendency of the Iban was reflected in the development of vessels suited to the geography of the Bornean coast. Their *bangkongs* had a shallow draught and were readily manoeuvrable by oar. Once the target area was reached, the boats could be beached for the attack on local settlements, although this did tend to leave war parties open to ambush if the lead vessel proceeded too far ahead.[62] The boats were lashed with rattan, and could be readily disassembled and stored in longhouses between raids.[63] The oarsmen and fighters primarily carried spears, swords and shields but were also armed with the *sumpitan* (blowpipe) and occasionally *leelas* (brass guns).[64]

Evidence of resistance to Iban raiding – including by other Iban groups – is uncommon but, where it exists, it was creative. Measures included a system of alarms, deployment of an armed patrol vessel by Mukah river settlements, consolidating trading vessels into convoys, and arming trading vessels with *leelas*.[65] A joint expedition of coastal Malays and Bidayuh attempted to block the mouth of the Saribas and prevent the egress of Iban warboats,[66] while the Sebuyau Iban floated a boom across the Lundu river and erected 'stockades' around their settlement.[67] As a result of continued raiding, some Iban groups

58 Vayda, above n 27, p 117.

59 Sandin, *Sea Dayaks*, above n 8, pp 44, 60.

60 Pringle, above n 14, p 62–3.

61 Sandin, *Sea Dayaks*, above n 8, pp 64–5.

62 Gomes, above n 6, pp 81–2.

63 Ibid, p 80.

64 Harry Miller, *Pirates of the Far East* (London: Robert Hale and Company, 1970), p 20.

65 Parl Papers, *Reports of Commrs*, above n 35, Testimony of Abdullrahim, 14 October 1854, p 197; and Testimony of Nakodah Moora, 25 October 1854, pp 216–217.

66 Ibid, Testimony of Datu Patinggi Gapoor of Sarawak, 28 September 1854, p 132; Testimony of Moosah, 11 October 1854, p 178.

67 Spenser St John, *The Life of Sir James Brooke: Rajah of Sarawak* (London: William Blackwood and Sons, 1879; republished Oxford: Oxford University Press, 1994), p 17.

later joined with James Brooke in his efforts to suppress the Saribas and Skrang Iban, who comprised the main raiding groups, claiming them to be pirates.[68]

Iban maritime raiding was tied to a second practice: headhunting. It was carried out ashore as well as during raids at sea, by attacking individuals at work in the fields or residents of remote villages reached by river.[69] Headhunting has been described as originally a 'localised' phenomenon in the upper reaches of Sarawak river systems, moving slowly with Iban migrations towards the coast in the mid or later eighteenth century.[70] However, anthropologist Sutlive identifies it as a deeper social cause of Iban migration itself: there 'was an intangible cultural force which produced very tangible consequences,' he wrote, and this was the social desire to engage in warfare, and particularly headhunting.[71] Vayda and Wagner similarly suggest that headhunting might also have 'worked as part of a process regulating land use and the territorial expansion and dispersion of populations,'[72] and as a means to boost individual prestige, encouraged by women in the longhouse.[73]

Headtaking was both a foundation for warfare and part of it. For example, taking a new head was required to end the mourning period for a deceased person, as instructed by the 'spirit-hero *Puntang Raga*.'[74] It also played a role in key parts of the agricultural cycle,[75] and was essential for the status of *raja berani* (wealthy and brave)[76] – the latter an important step in securing a high value bride. The return from a raid with a head was the start of an important ritual process. The returning warriors, if successful, were met with the 'traditional festival of Enchaboh Arong to celebrate the enemies they killed and the loot they had brought home.' Enchaboh Arong was the first stage of the *Gawai burong*, the bird festival and 'greatest of all Iban ceremonies' – there were a further eight stages.[77] The heads (*antu pala*) 'were formally received with the best blankets (*pua kumbu*) by the mothers, sisters or sweethearts of the warriors at

68 Sandin, *Sea Dayaks*, above n 8, p 65. The Sebuyau were well-settled in the vicinity of Kuching and although they described themselves as 'quite unlike' other Iban, Sandin considers this untrue: ibid, p 9.

69 Parl Papers, *Reports of Commrs,* above n 35, Testimony of C.F. Bondriot of Java, p 110.

70 Sandin, *Sea Dayaks*, above n 8, p 59; Vayda, above n 27, pp 114–6.

71 Sutlive, above n 10, p 15. J.H. Walker, *Power and Prowess: The Origins of Brooke Kingship in Sarawak,* (Sydney: Allen and Unwin, 2002), pp 12, 20; Vayda, ibid, p 113.

72 Vayda, ibid, p 112; Wagner, above n 4, pp 142–3.

73 Wagner, ibid, pp 107, 121.

74 'Headhunting,' Vinson and Joanne Sutlive (eds), *Encyclopaedia of Iban Studies,* Vol 2 (Kuching: Tun Jugah Foundation, 2001), p 679.

75 Ibid.

76 Freeman, above n49, pp 38–41.

77 See Sandin, *Adat and Augury,* above n 45, pp 41–2.

the landing place of the longhouse',[78] and then kept in hanging baskets in the longhouse. Raiding facilitated headtaking to these proper ends. However, *adat* also regulated the conduct of raiding, identifying proper conduct and imposing penalties for wrongful actions.

4 What Conduct Did Adat Prohibit?

Iban oral traditions relating to the conduct of war identified key principles for both the proper resort to force, and the manner in which it was to be conducted, including the proper disposition of heads taken. For example, a tradition recorded that:

> after the submission of the Kantu tribe, Rukok instructed Sampar in the following war regulations:
> - If a warleader leads a party on an expedition, he must not allow his warriors to fight a guiltless tribe that has no quarrel with them.
> - If the enemy surrenders, he may not take their lives, lest his army be unsuccessful in future warfare and risk fighting empty-handed war raids (*balang kayau*).
> - The first time that a warrior takes a head or captures a prisoner, he must present the head or captive to the warleader in acknowledgement of the latter's leadership.
> - If a warrior takes two heads or captives, or more, one of each must be given to the warleader; the remainder belongs to the killer or captor.
> - The warleader must be honest with his followers in order that in future wars he may not be defeated (*alah bunoh*).[79]

This tradition is indicative of a system less about prohibited conduct in war, than the following of the *right* means and methods, right intent, and right omens. An interesting aspect of this is the social requirement that fighting, while expected, was nonetheless voluntary: 'when an Iban became a member of a fighting group it was *by his own choice*, and that in joining an attack (always in hope of taking a head) he was doing what he most wanted to do.' Further, 'Any mature man who had occasion to mount an attack … could become a

78 Ibid, p 40.

79 Gregory Nyanggau Mawar, 'Origin of Adat Iban: Part 4, Adat Creation – The Rules of Engagement, Code of Conduct and Omen Birds,' https://gnmawar.wordpress.com/adat-iban/origin-of-adat-iban-part-4/, 26 February 2023.

pun ngayau (lit. originator of war),' whom others could choose to join if they wished.[80]

Similarly, while captives could be taken during war, Iban treatment of them reflected the egalitarian nature of longhouse society, and the lack of a formal political structure or hierarchy beyond each longhouse. A series of customs addressed "ritually enfranchising and adopting captives in war;'[81] similarly to customs dealing with the keeping of slaves who, whose 'status was theoretically heritable,' but in fact they 'usually enjoyed eventual emancipation, so that the Iban 'never developed a significant slave class.'[82]

5 What Were the Consequences for Breaching Adat Related to Warfare?

In addition to rules of conduct and behaviour, *adat* also defined the punishment and propitiation required to make good wrongful conduct (*penyalah*).[83] For many transgressions punishment took the form of fines, or 'reparations of value.'[84] Ceramic jars, examples of which in Borneo have been traced to Chinese, Vietnamese, Thai and Khmer producers, and are up to a thousand years old,[85] entered into Iban use as currency, including for payment of *adat*.[86] For example, if 'a warrior killed his fighting mate by mistake while on the warpath, the killer must also pay a *pati nyawa* compensation of two valuable jars to the deceased's family. Failing to pay this, he must surrender himself to become their slave together with his descendants.'[87]

When the perpetrator was unknown or could not pay the fine, the *tuai rumah* (headman) of the longhouse might '"fine" himself and restore order in the universe of man-spirit relations.'[88] If a known person refused to pay the

80 Freeman, above n 49, p 36.

81 Ibid, p 47.

82 Mawar, above n 79.

83 Sather, above n 45, p xiii.

84 Ibid.

85 Barbara Harrisson, *Pusaka: Heirloom Jars of Borneo* (Singapore: Oxford University Press, 1986); Tom Harrisson, "'Dusun' Jars: from Mayfair and Friesland through Cairo to Sabah,' *Sarawak Museum Journal* 12, no. 25–6 (July-December 1965): 69–74; Daniel Chew, *Chinese Pioneers on the Sarawak Frontier 1841–1941*, 2nd edn (Oxford: Oxford University Press, 1990), p 53.

86 Crisswell, above n 4, p 9; see also Chew, ibid, p 52; Sandin, *Sea Dayaks*, above n 8, p 9.

87 Sandin, *Adat and Augury*, above n 45, p 4.

88 Jensen, above n 15, p 114.

adat fine, the wronged person was entitled to seize their property by force in a process called *ngerampas,* which could be preliminary to negotiating a settlement in which the seizer might keep some or all of the property. In the ordinary course, the would-be seizer would seek support from his kin and would have to 'pledge jars to compensate any supporters killed or injured in carrying out the seizure,' since it was 'done openly and with force'.[89] Other mechanisms for redress recognised in *adat* included ordeals of endurance such as diving contests; *batempoh,* a public contest using wooden weapons in case of boundary disputes between neighbouring communities, and *bepalu,* a retaliatory beating with a wooden club, such as by the wronged husband in case of adultery.[90] In addition, many breaches of *adat* required 'ritual propitiation.'[91] Doing so avoided *kudi,* a 'state of sterility where the natural order cease[d] to function,' which flowed from 'particularly blatant offences' including incest and murder. For example, 'One area in the Lemanak was considered "sterile land" (*tanah kudi*) because it had at one time been the site of bloodshed at a head-hunting encounter.'[92] To make good *kudi,* a sacrifice was required so that the blood might 'purify the land and water against the sin committed.'[93]

The '*adat* community' depended on its members behaving in accordance with custom, including the principle of *minta adat,* meaning 'to ask for *adat.*' That is, a wronged person was 'expected to insist upon compensation,' while longhouse leaders were responsible to ensure 'correct fines and ritual sanctions' were applied to restore 'social harmony and spiritual health.'[94] The dispute resolution process itself was based on 'a "court" of longhouse members,' and, 'if found guilty by consensus' the person was fined or otherwise directed to make good the harm caused.[95] The kinship connections of the longhouse were an important foundation for this process.[96] If consensus could not be reached, one party might resort to *bepalu* or *ngerampas*, risking an escalation of violence. To avoid this, leaders would work 'to restrain the parties involved and press them to accept negotiation or submit to ritualized conventions such as diving ordeals (*kelam ai*) or contests with wooden clubs (*batempoh*).'[97]

89 Sather, above n 45, p xxii.
90 Ibid, pp xxii-xxiii.
91 Ibid, p xiii; see also Jensen, above n 15, p 113.
92 Jensen, ibid, p 113.
93 Sandin, *Adat and Augury,* above n 45, p 4.
94 Sather, above n 45, p xiv.
95 Jensen, above n 15, p 114.
96 Gregory Nyanggau Mawar, 'Adat Iban: the Origin of Iban Adat,' *Iban Cultural Heritage,* https://gnmawar.wordpress.com/adat-iban/, 7 September 2022.
97 Ibid.

These methods to control disputes and the threat of violence existed at longhouse level, but there was no formal comparable mechanism between longhouses, which allowed 'a state of intermittent warfare' to prevail.[98] Some specific groups did develop de-escalatory customs. For example, in the Saribas, individuals might be tasked as *penunggu* or 'go-betweens.' The *penunggu* would travel to the longhouse where the person suspected of breaching *adat* lived, and, once there, 'typically constructed a shelter (*langkau penunggu*) some distance away made of materials supplied by the culprit's kinsmen. Here they received unarmed emissaries from the latter's longhouse,' with a view to negotiating a settlement. The value of the go-between process for a people who 'traditionally placed a high value on masculine aggressiveness,' was that 'it allowed the principals to submit to negotiation without direct confrontation and made it possible to make and accept reparation without suffering loss of face.'[99]

Adat on raiding, headtaking, and even negotiations, played an important part during the Iban confrontation with James Brooke and the Royal Navy. For the latter, Iban raiding was piracy and headhunting a barbaric tradition; their response was to suppress both. At the same time, in forming alliances with some Iban groups against the Saribas and Skrang 'pirates,' Brooke increased their opportunity to raid and take heads, even as he outlawed the practice.

6 Iban Warfare and Colonial Confrontation

As a maritime zone, the Borneo region engendered an essentially maritime response by European powers seeking influence and engagement, if not territorial acquisition, there. Thus, an 1846 magazine piece regarding Brooke in Borneo contended that, prior to Brooke's arrival in Kuching in 1839, the island had been the centre of

> a corsair system ... which has been so formidable as to have scared away all trade, and so fatal, so satanic in its influence, as to have rendered islands remarkable for their beauty and resources, the abode of misery and want.[100]

98 Ibid.

99 Sather, above n 45, p xxiv.

100 'Borneo – Captain Keppel and Mr Brooke,' *The Dublin University Magazine* 27, no. 160 (April 1846): 387–405, p 387.

In general terms, 'piracy' has been described 'as a means to control seaborne trade and to expand [European] influence and domains.'[101] Its operative meaning centred on the way in which the term divided users of the sea into the legitimate, to be protected from interference and encouraged freely to engage in trade or navigation, and the illegitimate, who were to be suppressed by force. In this way, the maritime discourse of 'piracy' could be used be a means of defining legitimate access to the sea, in order to justify attempts to control its use. In direct contrast to the Royal Navy's suppression of the African slave trade as an exercise in moral legitimacy,[102] the need to suppress Bornean piracy was not argued on explicitly moral grounds, even though south east Asian 'piracy' was directly associated with an Asian slave trade.[103] Instead it was the inherent legitimacy of law which was called upon – albeit in a strongly positivist sense when compared to modern approaches to lawful use of force, given that British legislation provided from 1825 that 'head money' could be paid to the Royal Navy or 'hired armed ships' for each pirate killed or ship taken, following judgment by a prize court.[104]

The Brooke period in Sarawak began when James Brooke, a former officer of the Indian army turned self-funded adventurer, arrived in Kuching and was drawn into the rebellion against the ruling Rajah Muda Hassim, uncle of the Sultan of Brunei. Between 1839 and 1842, according to Brooke,[105] the Rajah Muda invited Brooke to support him against rebels led by the Iban chief Datu Patinggi Ali. The rebels were objecting to practices such as forced trade and corruption, especially by the Pangeran (Prince) Indra Mahkota, part of Hassim's court. Brooke agreed, and, as part of supporting the Rajah Muda, soon allied

101 Xu Ke, 'Piracy, Seaborne Trade and the Rivalries of Foreign Sea Powers in East and Southeast Asia, 1511 to 1839: A Chinese Perspective,' in Graham Gerard Ong-Webb (ed), *Piracy, Maritime Terrorism and Securing the Malacca Straits* (Singapore: International Institute for Asian Studies, 2006), pp 221–2.

102 Although the extent of the claim that suppressing the slave trade was intended to achieve moral good has been contested: see, for example, Paul Michael Kielstra, *The Politics of Slave Trade Suppression in Britain and France, 1814–48: Diplomacy, Morality and Economics* (Basingstoke: Palgrave MacMillan EBook, 2000), eg pp 2–6.

103 See further Warren, *Sulu Zone*, above n 1, especially Part II.

104 *An Act for Encouraging the Capture and Destruction of Piratical Ships and Vessels 1825*, 6 Geo 4, c 49, s 1.

105 Brooke journal, 15 August 1839, in Captain the Hon Henry Keppel, *The Expedition to Borneo of HMS Dido for the Suppression of Piracy: With Extracts from the Journal of James Brooke, Esq, of Sarāwak,* 3rd edn (London: Chapman and Hall, 1847, first published 1846), vol 1, p 30. See also Robert Payne, *The White Rajahs of Sarawak* (Singapore: Oxford University Press, 1986), p 32.

himself with the Sebuyau Iban in Lundu, recently raided by the Saribas Iban (and who had themselves recently raided Paku, on the Saribas).[106]

In supporting the Rajah Muda, Brooke's desire for adventure was disappointed. Joining an armed expedition against the Siniawan Malays in October 1840, he was surprised to find engagement by both sides was often by 'vociferous shouts' rather than actual battle. In fact, the greatest risk to the Rajah's force was the possibility of renewed intertribal hostilities among his own Iban force.[107] Later, he engaged more directly in negotiations with the rebel leaders, who surrendered their last stronghold at Balidah on Brooke's promise that he would be 'responsible for their safety until the orders of their sovereign arrived.' This he did by immediately closing the river to traffic and declaring that he would fire on any attacker.[108] Having in his own mind succeeded in his task, Brooke returned to Kuching to await his quid pro quo from Hassim: the grant of Sarawak to rule in his own right. This eventually occurred in September 1841, in return for an annual payment to the Sultan of Brunei, and Brooke's promise to 'respect the laws and customs' in force in the country.[109] However, Hassim and his court, including Pangeran Mahkota, remained in Kuching alongside him.

Brooke took immediate steps to reform the political organisation of Sarawak, and issued a body of laws on 2 February 1842, under his own authority. The Code provided that 'heinous crimes' were to be dealt with according to local laws after a 'fair enquiry;' that trade would generally be free; and that piracy, headhunting and debt-slavery were outlawed.[110] These prohibitions provided a domestic legal basis for Brooke's subsequent campaigns against the Iban and others, and in so doing Brooke gained the support of certain Iban groups against their Iban 'enemies' in Skrang and Saribas.[111] Indeed, within days of

106 Sandin, *Sea Dayaks*, above n 8, p 70.

107 St John, *Life of Sir James Brooke*, above n 67, pp 36–8.

108 Brooke journal, 8 January 1841 in Keppel, above n105, vol 1, p 185.

109 James Brooke, *A Letter from Borneo: with notices of the country and its inhabitants: addressed to James Gardner, Esq*, ed. John C. Templer (London: L and G Seeley, 1842), pp 29–30; Brooke to Templer, 25 September 1841, in John C. Templer (ed), *The Private Letters of Sir James Brooke* KCB, *Rajah of Sarawak, Narrating the Events of his Life from 1838 to the Present Time* (London: Richard Bentley, 1853), vol 1, p 117.

110 Brooke journal, 10 January 1842, in Keppel, above n105, vol 1, pp 267–9; Payne, above n 105, p 47. The outlawing of headhunting at around this time was confirmed in the case of *HH the Rajah v Dunggaw and Unjar* (1934) SCR 37, paragraph 11, reported in The Hon Tan Sri Datuk Lee Hun Hoe, *Cases on Native Customary Law in Sarawak* (Kuching: National Printing Department, 1976), p 4. The case, however, described it as an offence *sui generis* against the common law, rather than an offence against the *Code*, implying some doubt as to the legal status of the code under the then-existing grant of Sarawak.

111 Crisswell, above n 4, pp 11–12.

receiving his grant, Brooke sent an expedition against the Singé Iban, whom he believed were allied with Mahkota against him. As Brooke had 'positively forbidden' the Iban in Sarawak warring upon each other,[112] the captured leaders from Singé, Parimban and Pa Tumno, were tried and then executed behind Brooke's own house in Kuching.

Yet Brooke's Code was not to be confused with a strict application of British law, for Brooke saw himself as the arbiter of justice according to his own rules and sense of justice; there could be no juries in place of his personal judgment, for example, as he considered them an opportunity for inefficiency and corruption.[113] Moreover, his policies disturbed traditional practices and relationships, especially in restricting Iban migrations and outlawing raiding and head-hunting – these changes 'evoked bitter resentment' among many Iban communities,[114] even as others supported him. An important reason for this was that the overlay of central Brooke government and his suppression of 'piracy' and headhunting disturbed the primary means by which Iban tradition allowed the restoration of the cosmic balance, and therefore the nature of *adat* itself.[115] Brooke's approach to raiding and headhunting was also at odds with the requirement in his grant of authority that he respect local custom, and the implication in his Code that *adat* would continue as indigenous customary law along with the recognition of the Malay *Undang-Undang*. Other elements of *adat* were not proscribed but substituted. For example, under Brooke there was a move away from property seizure (*ngerampas*) to a greater use of fines.[116] At the same time, in cultivating Iban alliances and pursuing other Iban sub-groups as illegitimate pirates, Brooke in fact provided many Iban with an *increased* opportunity for head-taking and raiding. For example, following Brooke's early clash with the Lingga Iban, he secured their support against Syarif Abu Bakr. In supporting Brooke, the Lingga people gained the opportunity to take heads, and therefore to re-establish social and ritual organisation disrupted by the original clash.[117]

The two years from 1843 to 1844 were defined by the building of Brooke's close friendship with Captain Sir Henry Keppel, Royal Navy, which allowed him to 'mature' plans for the suppression of Skrang and Saribas piracy.[118] Together,

112 Brooke journal, 20 June 1842, in Keppel, above n 105, vol 1, p 300.
113 Brooke journal, 5 November 1841, ibid, p 258.
114 Sutlive, above n 10, p 17.
115 Mawar, 'Adat Iban: the Origin of Iban Adat,' above n 96.
116 Sather, above n 45, p xvi.
117 Walker, above n 71, p 79.
118 A.B. Ward, *Outlines of Sarawak History 1839–1917* (Kuching: Government Printing Office, 1927), p 3.

Brooke and Keppel conducted expeditions using a joint force of Naval vessels, Brooke's own yacht and boats, and the warboats of his Iban allies in both river systems, destroying many boats and burning longhouses. Following the Saribas campaign in 1843, Keppel concluded a formal agreement with Hassim, on behalf of the British government, for the suppression of piracy.[119] When settling the Skrang campaign at an 1844 peace conference with the tribes, Brooke spoke to them of the British government's determination to suppress the horrors of piracy, as well as 'the blessings arising from peace and trade.'[120] After this defeat, Gassing, a leader controlling parts of the lower Skrang, declared 'that he would with his own hand kill the first who committed piracy on the ocean, or in any way departed from the wishes of Mr Brooke.'[121]

The destruction of 1843–44, while it did not significantly impact political or maritime control in the Saribas and Skrang river systems, did have a 'profound, non-material' effect on the Iban there through the destruction of longhouses and ritual objects such as ceramic jars.[122] Efforts to restore the spiritual balance had to follow. As a result of this damage to Iban spirituality, Walker argued, some Skrang and Saribas Iban reacted to Brooke by seeking to restore their power and prowess through association with Brooke or, conversely, by opposing him, through opportunities for taking heads, mounting expeditions and renewing pioneer migration to new river systems to the north.[123]

Brooke's own objectives, as he had clarified them by the end of 1844, were official recognition by the British government and the commercial development of the island of Borneo, which he believed would lead to its civilisation. The suppression of piracy with Naval support remained, in his mind, a precondition for this. During the years 1845 to 1846, Brooke secured the support of the acting commander in chief on the China and East Indies station, Rear Admiral Sir Thomas Cochrane, to suppress an expanded conception of Bornean piracy,

119 See St John, *Life of Sir James Brooke*, above n 67, p 168.

120 Captain Sir Edward Belcher, *Narrative of the Voyage of H.M.S. Samarang during the Years 1843 46, Employed Surveying the Islands of the Eastern Archipelago* (London: Reeve, Benham and Reeve, 1848), vol 2, p 154; Keppel, above n 10, vol 2, p 120.

121 Hugh Low, *Sarawak, its inhabitants and productions: being notes during a residence in that country with His Excellency Mr. Brooke* (London: Bentley, 1848), pp 183–5; and see Walker, above n 71, p 80.

122 Walker, ibid, p 75.

123 Walker, ibid, pp 76, 80. Walker noted at p 78 that 'Saribas Iban leaders tried to enlist Brooke's help in resolving their conundrum, increasingly trying to get him to identify enemies whom they might attack,' to which Brooke responded 'I always tell them to go to Singapore and kill the English' (citing, Brooke to Templer, 21 October 1845, in Templer, above n 109, vol 2, p 94).

which extended to the defeat of a Malay settlement under Syarif Osman at Marudu Bay and then bombardment of Brunei itself.

Brooke's focus returned to Saribas and Skrang piracy later in the 1840s, culminating in a heavy Iban defeat at a sandy promontory known as Beting Marau, in the mouth of the Kaluka river, in 1849. After the initial battle, Brooke and his force pursued the Iban upriver and burnt a number of key settlements, including Paku. On 19 August, they reached Kanowit town, at the headwaters of the Kanowit river, where British Parliamentary reports indicate that Brooke imposed a fine of £150 on the local Iban 'in preference to more violent measures.'[124] The battle at Beting Marau and subsequent upriver campaigning came to be seen by Brooke's opponents in Britain as a massacre; it is thought that 1000 Iban of a force of 3000 were killed or died of wounds in the initial engagement, whereas British losses were two dead and six wounded.[125] The outrage was such that, eventually, an 1854 Parliamentary Commission of Inquiry was established to consider, among other things, the propriety of Brooke's actions against the Saribas and Skrang Iban. Royal Navy support, while not formally withdrawn from him, was nonetheless no longer made available. A key reason for the redeployment of Naval support was new orders from the Admiralty, limiting 'piracy,' for the purposes of Naval intervention, to attacks on British-flagged vessels.[126]

After Beting Marau, and no doubt influenced by the withdrawal of Naval support, Brooke changed largely to a fort-based strategy against Iban 'pirates.' His forts were constructed in key rivers, intended permanently to prevent the egress of raiding parties.[127] Controlling the raiding parties also had the effect of controlling riverine trade, and especially the movement of salt upriver, a measure previously employed by the coastal Malay rulers.[128] This reinforced and consolidated Brooke rule more effectively even than the Naval campaigns,[129] but also generated conflict between Iban living up and downriver of the forts

124 Parliamentary Papers (UK), House of Commons Papers, 1852–3 LXI.281 [4], *Despatches from Naval Officers on China Station Relative to Attacks on Natives of Borneo, 1842–49*, Farquhar to Collier, 25 August 1849, p 13.

125 See Walker, p 71, and the references he cites.

126 Brooke received this news as a 'public despatch,' not personally: Brooke to Templer, 22 July 1853, above n 109, vol 3, p 264.

127 Parl Papers, *Despatches from Naval Officers*, above n 124, Farquhar to Collier, 25 August 1849, p 13.

128 Wagner, above n 4, p 52.

129 Nicholas Tarling, 'The Superintendence of British Interests in Southeast Asia in the Nineteenth Century' *Journal of Southeast Asian History* 7, no. 1 (March 1966): 97–110, at 104–5; and see Tarling, *Britain, The Brookes and Brunei*, above n 24, p 69.

as the power relationships between them and with the powerful Malay class changed.[130] Brooke did continue some direct operations using his allied Iban forces against a varied 'pirates' in the region; in 1853, for example, he led his own expedition against in the Sambas area.[131]

At the same time as the forts impacted riverine control in Iban areas, there was a strong resurgence of Iban opposition to Brooke.[132] It manifested as renewed inter-Iban warfare, as well as ongoing fighting with Brooke's own forces. A warleader from upriver Skrang, Rentap, attacked downriver in January 1853. Following his raid, Gassing, the chief of a downriver group of Skrang Iban allied with Brooke since Keppel's campaigns, attacked and defeated Rentap, burning many longhouses. Rentap withdrew and fortified his position at Sungei Lang. A number of Brooke-led or organised expeditions, including overland efforts, followed to dislodge Rentap from Sungei Lang and later from Bukit Sadong between 1853 to 1861.[133] Eventually Rentap and his fighters withdrew north into the Kanowit and Julau rivers.

Rentap's campaign was the last major Iban resistance to Brooke rule, and also confirmed the decline in the central Iban practices of raiding and headhunting. Late reports of headhunting raids persisted into the early twentieth century, when both practices appear to have fallen into disuse for *adat* purposes.[134] Other practices began to take on high significance instead. For example, into the twentieth century the 'custom of *bejalai*' (going on a journey, or, often, an expedition) came to be 'interpreted in many respects as the equivalent of the headhunting expeditions in the past. Other trophies have taken the place of heads: valuable jars and gongs, and even outboard engines.'[135]

130 Pringle, above n 14, pp 122–3.

131 Steven Runciman, *The White Rajahs* (Cambridge: Cambridge University Press, 1960; republished Kuala Lumpur: S.A. Majeed and Co, 2007), p 138.

132 Bob Reece, *The White Rajahs of Sarawak: A Borneo Dynasty* (Singapore: Archipelago Press, 2004), p 42; Crisswell, above n 4, p 31. See also Pringle, above n 14, p 90.

133 Crisswell, ibid, pp 33–4.

134 In 1903, an Iban leader from the Baleh, Koh anak Jubang, led a raid on a group of Madang, part of the Kenyah people, in the Rejang, in retaliation for the murder of his uncle – 'According to Kohn, forty-four Madang heads were taken – six of them by Koh himself' as well as some captives; Jensen, above n 15, p 51, see also p 5.

135 Jensen, ibid, p 51.

7 Conclusion

It has been suggested that Brooke's fort strategy from the 1850s, by limiting Iban raiding and therefore the opportunity to take heads outside a group's home river, actually encouraged up and downriver groups to make enemies of each other, as happened in the Skrang in the 1850s.[136] As more generally during the early Brooke period, this exemplifies Wagner's 'double paradox': that is, 'Brooke policy stimulated head-taking and was also responsible for its ending.'[137] A key stimulation factor was the 'legal outlet' provided for continued headtaking in support of Brooke expeditions,[138] and therefore the maintenance of *adat* for Iban allies, but Wagner qualifies this with the interesting observation that in many Brooke era accounts of expeditions against Iban 'there is information of burning, plundering and uprooting of *padi* but no "enemies" seem to have been killed.'[139] That is, the opportunities may have been stimulated, but actual evidence of a similar increase in the prevalence of headtaking is missing.

During the nineteenth century, Iban *adat* was a system that, among its fundamental spiritual purposes, reduced and regulated conflict between Iban to that which was 'right,' including by regulating key means and methods of warfare such as raiding and headtaking, between Iban and against others. *Adat* began a process of codification from oral traditions into written rules from 1915, revised through a series of conferences with Iban leaders from the 1930s,[140] and its methods of restoring the cosmic balance also developed over time. Thus, even though raiding and headtaking declined during the nineteenth century, *adat* has continued to evolve as a living non-Western system of social organisation and sanction among the Iban people of Borneo.

136 Walker, above n 71, p 85.
137 Wagner, above n 4, pp 1, 50–51.
138 Ibid, p 74.
139 Ibid, p 56.
140 See Sather, above n 45, p xviii.

CHAPTER 7

South Sudanese Laws of War

Marco Chol Ayat, Ruben SP Valfredo and Justin Monyping Ater

This chapter is written in the authors' personal and private capacities. The opinions expressed, and assumptions made in this chapter are the authors' own. They do not reflect the views or opinions of any of the institutions or individuals referred to or mentioned herein.

1 Introduction

Spats of violence and conflict have been experienced by human beings, and were a common recourse amongst them, since immemorial times and as long as humans existed on planet Earth.[1] At some times and in some instances, these sporadic events of violence degenerated into sorts of warfare between groups of organised individuals and/or in other instances between communities or nations.[2] Groups and communities within the current South Sudan have not been an exception to this reality; as it could be observed from history that since the existence of human beings in this geographic area, numerous groups engaged in a sort of warfare for the sake of advancing their competing interests.[3]

However, as humanity and civilisation advanced through various eras, warfare has also evolved to become more intense, brutal and catastrophic.[4] As a result, attempts and suggestions were made in order to set principles and rules aiming to regulate warfare and its conduct.[5] These attempts steadily evolved and led to a set of regulations and rules which regulate

1 Steven LeBlanc, "The Origins of Warfare and Violence" in Garrett Fagan, Linda Fibiger, Mark Hudson, and Matthew Trundle (eds), *The Cambridge World History of Violence,* Cambridge University Press, Cambridge, 2020, p. 39.

2 Ibid, p. 41.

3 Stephanie Beswick, 'Nilotic Chaos: Dinka, Nuer, Atwot, and Anyuak; Sudan's Blood Memory: The Legacy of War, Ethnicity, and Slavery in South Sudan' Boydell and Brewer, Suffolk, 2004, pp. 164–174.

4 Steven LeBlanc, Above note 4, p. 52.

5 Amanda Alexander, "A Short History of International Humanitarian Law", *The European Journal of International Law,* Vol. 26, No. 1, 2015, P. 111.

 | DOI:10.1163/9789004512566_009

warfare.[6] The aforesaid rules and regulations have set the foundation and led to the formation of international humanitarian law.[7] These set of regulations and rules on the conduct of hostilities are currently deemed to comprise of international treaties and conventions;[8] and also as rules of international customary law.[9]

Notwithstanding the fact that the rules on the conduct of warfare are considered as both treaty and customary, rules of warfare within what is today's South Sudan communities appear to have some sort of set or rules on the conduct of warfare,[10] which are distinct and unique in their own rights in some aspects; and similar and in correlation with the existing international legal framework for humanitarian law in other aspects.[11] Furthermore, aspect(s) of correlation are attributed to the in-depth belief within these traditions of their moral convictions and cultural beliefs.[12] Conversely, it is not informed by the international obligations of the Republic of South Sudan as the sovereign state in which these traditions exist and rules apply.[13]

6 Mohammad Islam, "The Historical Evolution of International Humanitarian Law from Earliest Societies to Modern Age", *Beijing Law Review*, Vol 9, 2018, p. 294.

7 Ibid, p. 299.

8 The First Geneva Convention for the Amelioration of the Condition of the Wounded and Sick in Armed Forces in the Field, The Second Geneva Convention for the Amelioration of the Condition of the Wounded, Sick, and Shipwrecked Members of Armed Forces at Sea, The Third Geneva Convention Relative to the Treatment of Prisoners of War, and the Fourth Geneva Convention Relative to the Protection of Civilian Persons in Time of War (all adopted on 12 August 1949 and entered into force on 21 October 1950); the First Protocol relating to the Protection of Victims of International Armed Conflicts, the Second Protocol relating to the Protection of Victims of Non-International Armed Conflicts (both adopted on 8 June 1977) and entered into force on 7 December 1978); and the Third Protocol relating to the Adoption of an Additional Distinctive Emblem (adopted on 8 December 2005 and entered into force on 14 January 2007).

9 Nils Melzer and Etienne Kuster, *International Humanitarian Law: A Comprehensive Introduction,* International Review of the Red Cross, Geneva, 2022, p. 22.

10 This assertion is supported and evidenced from empirical research which this chapter has conducted and analysed.

11 Ibid.

12 Wendy James, "Religious Practice and Belief" in John Ryle, Jusitn Willis, Suliman Baldo and Jok Madut (eds), *The Sudan Handbook,* The Rift Valley Institute, London, 2012, p. 88.

13 The Republic of South Sudan acceded to the Four Geneva Conventions and its three additional Protocols on 16 July 2012; it has also enacted the Geneva Conventions Act 2012 to give domestic effect to these conventions.

This chapter examines the existing customary warfare rules of some of the communities in South Sudan,[14] and then assesses whether these rules are reproducing and/or complementing the core principles of international humanitarian law,[15] namely the principles of distinction, necessity and humanity, proportionality, and precautions. As it stands, it seems that there is limited research pertaining to the legal jurisprudence on the nexus between the customary rules of warfare in South Sudan and international humanitarian law principles; and this chapter aspires to fill in that vacuum.

The chapter relies, in its examination and assessment, on relevant available literature and empirical research in the form of qualitative interviews with key individuals comprising chiefs and former fighters in communal warfare in South Sudan. Qualitative interviews have been conducted with twelve Chiefs and former fighters from the Dinka, Nuer, Mundari and Lotuka ethinic groups of South Sudan. Additionally, doctrinal research of the relevant treaties and conventions of international humanitarian law in addition to the vast scholarly writings on these principles are utilised to showcase comparative analysis and presentation.[16]

The chapter is structured into the following parts: methods and means of warfare, the application of the traditional warfare rules and regulations, the types of prohibited conduct, defences to and consequences of breaches of these rules and regulations. The chapter concludes by summing up its findings and recommendations.

2 Customary Methods and Means of Warfare

Generally, it is easy to trace the time of recognition of the methods and means of warfare to the development of, and the adoption of, the Geneva Conventions and its Additional Protocols and the Hague Regulations in Europe. However, in South Sudan, empirical research suggests that the methods and means of warfare are as old as the existence of the communities studied in this chapter. Therefore, there existed methods and means even before, during, and after

14 Six communities originating in South Sudan have been considered with two from each of the three historic regions, namely Upper Nile, Bahr El Ghazal, and Equatoria. The Commnuities included Dinka, Nuer, Mundari and Lotuka.

15 Nils Melzer and Etienne Kuster, Above note 12, p. 17.

16 This chapter focuses entirely and limits itself to the study of the mentioned principles, and its research has not aimed to expand its study to other principles or rules of international humanitarian law.

other communities in the world. However, it is important to note that the methods and means of warfare have evolved over time.[17] This may be because of the influence of Western methods and means of warfare. Today, some communities use European tactics and weapons. This practice can be attributed to the Western colonisation and their methods and means of warfare that came with it.[18] However, this study is only concerned with presentation of the customary methods and means of warfare of South Sudanese communities and therefore does not interrogate the Western influence.

The methods and means of warfare differ from one community to the other in South Sudan. This is because South Sudan has diverse communities with different beliefs and traditions that guide their way of life including in situations of warfare.[19] Because of the diversity of the communities in South Sudan, some communities' practices in relation to warfare align with the rules of international humanitarian law.

In the Nuer community, traditions of warfare dictate that women, children, and the elderly should always be alerted during warfare to evacuate the areas where confrontations would take place.[20] This is because in these areas use of methods that can result in disproportionate incidental loss to civilians is most likely to happen. To avoid excessive loss from happening, the above categories of people are informed through the traditional hitting of drums.[21] The drum hitting does not only serve as a way of informing children, women and the elderly to leave but also to inform warriors to turn up and also to design the tactics and then engage in fight.[22] The way of hitting the drum and the sound the drum makes is normally different and indicates that there is an imminent battle to take place and that those who do not qualify should evacuate as soon as possible.[23] Additionally, in the Nuer communities' traditions of warfare, women play a crucial role in taking part in warning measures. Instantly, they take part in a practice referred to as 'wewe'.[24] This is a traditional practice of warfare where women blow whistles to alarm people of the imminent warfare. While undertaking this warning practice, warriors take their weapons and

17 Zahra Zahbea, 'Means and methods of warfare: An evolving reality'.
18 M.A. Mohammed Salih, 'The Europeanisation of war in Africa: From traditional to modern warfare'. Vol.12, No.1(1989), pp.27–37.
19 South Sudan has sixty-four tribes. These ethnic groups constitute the communities in South Sudan.
20 Interview with a chief and a former fighter of the Nuer community.
21 Ibid.
22 Ibid.
23 Ibid.
24 Ibid.

join the frontline whereas children, women, and the elderly remain at home. However, interestingly, when the measures above are not followed and war reaches the locations where children, women and the elderly are hiding, the winning side calls off the attacks immediately to avoid harm being done to these groups.

These methods are also reflected in the traditions of warfare of the Dinka Community of Bahr El Ghazal. When the warfare reaches the location of children, the fighters will shout 'kong koc tong aci lu meetheich'.[25] This translates to 'stop, the confrontation has reached the children's location'. Notably, women in the traditional warfare of the Dinka communities of Bahr El Ghazal are important actors in situations of conflict. Apparently, the first woman who will be aware of the indicators of attacks must start informing people immediately by shouting 'lala'.[26]

Similarly, in the Dinka Upper Nile, traditions of warfare provide that people such as children, women, and the elderly are always alarmed to leave the battleground.[27] These communities also use drums as a measure of warning non-combatants and at the same time informing combatants.[28] However, in situations where sporadic confrontations have taken place and are ongoing, individuals who have become aware immediately run and reach out to everyone informing them of the ongoing confrontation and the possibility of its escalation. This way, non-combatants will be informed to remain in safe locations and warn them of the consequences of random movement.[29]

In the same vein, when there is an anticipated confrontation among or between Mundari communities and other communities, the Mundari traditions of the methods of warfare indicate that the first step is to call people using 'Dugi kira'.[30] The Dugi Kira is a traditional tool for warfare used to alarm the people of the presence of an enemy. Following the call using dugi kira, the warriors are identified and selected to design the tactics and attack or defend whichever relevant. Non-combatants are fully informed to leave the war zone. It is crucial to note that women play a role in warning both warriors and non-warriors using the 'luluju' voice.[31] As a matter of traditions of warfare of the Mundari communities in Terkeka, residential areas are at all times avoided as

25 Interview with a chief and a former fighter of the Dinka Community of Bahr El Ghazal.

26 Ibid.

27 Interview with a former fighter of the Dinka Bor Community.

28 Ibid.

29 Ibid.

30 Interview with a chief and a former fighter of the Mundari community.

31 ibid

battlegrounds for war. Furthermore, as required by their traditions, the warriors call off attacks against the enemy if it becomes apparent that children, women, and the elderly are in the midst of the adversary.[32]

Meanwhile, Lotuka Community traditions of warfare, just like the Dinka traditions, hit drums in a style that indicates there is an imminent war.[33] Following this act, every warrior would join the fight and in the case of non-combatants they stay indoors. The traditions also provide that fighting should take place as far as possible away from the residential areas.[34] However, in circumstances where fighting has reached where non-combatants are, warriors must cease to engage in the conflict.[35]

Generally, these communities combinedly fight their wars with strict adherence to the traditional rules of warfare. Common to the rules of these communities is the prohibition of perfidious acts and such those who invite the confidence of their enemies and end up killing them are treated as cowards.[36]

A closer look at the same communities indicates that their tactics are all the same. For example, they all hit drums in order to inform both warriors and non-warriors about a fight. Following this practice, the warriors design, form lines for attack or defence whereas non-warriors leave fighting locations. However, for the Dinka community of Bahr El Ghazal, the warriors go further through intelligence in identifying the warriors on the enemy side. This information is useful when selecting warriors who will individually face warriors from the adversary side in an individual confrontation within the collective confrontation. An illustration is when for example the means of warfare is the use of traditional sticks. Normally, the warriors in these communities of Bahr El Ghazal would not engage in confrontations where warriors on the enemy side are not mature or in their own volition are not their equals.

On a different note, about the traditional means of warfare; they are sort of limited similar to under the international humanitarian law regime. However, some communities do not limit their means at some points. In traditional settings, most of the weapons that are used in warfare do not have the capability of causing incidental loss to non-combatants who are often not close to fighting locations. Therefore, non-combatants are usually spared since the weapons do not have the magnitude to reach their locations.

32 Ibid.
33 Interview with a chief and a former fighter of the Lotuka Torit community.
34 Ibid.
35 Ibid.
36 Interview with all the selected communities.

The Dinka communities of Bahr El Ghazal use traditional fighting sticks and spears.[37] These weapons do not have the capacity to affect those not in combat locations. Similarly, the Nuer community of Upper Nile uses the same weapons employed by the Dinka community of Bahr El Ghazal.[38] However, there are situations where some of the Dinka communities of Bahr El Ghazal use fire in warfare. The empirical research, of this chapter, indicates that the losing warriors are normally frustrated by their loss and would sometimes resort to surprise attacks where in these surprise attacks they would burn down houses.[39] This indicates that there are situations where means such as the use of fire would cause excessive incidental loss to everyone including children, women, the elderly, and persons with disabilities.

Similar to the communities of Bahr El Ghazal, the Lotuka communities of Equatoria region use similar weapons such as spears and traditional fighting sticks.[40] Obviously as indicated above these weapons do not result in massive violation of any principle relevant to the conduct of hostilities under international humanitarian law. Beside the above weapons, the Mundari and the Lotuka community share some commonalities in relation to the use of a traditional air bow.[41] The air bow is also a weapon that does not have the magnitude of affecting non-combatants not close to the combat location.

As such, the observation of core international humanitarian law principles has been noted in the methods and means of warfare in the traditional rules of warfare of the communities studied in this chapter. The Nuer, Mundari, Lotuka and Dinka communities of the Upper Nile, Bahr El Ghazal and Equatoira, before confrontations ensure a practice which is similar to that of the principle of precaution is observed at all times. This is done by taking measures to inform the warriors and non-warriors of the imminent war. The non-warriors are told to remain indoors and not be close to the battlefields. Furthermore, even when the warriors who have been fighting in the war zone run close to the non-warriors, the winning side normally calls off the confrontations to avoid non-warriors being affected by the conflict.

As shown above, the means and methods of warfare under the traditional rules of warfare in the stated communities are very much similar to the core

37 Interview with a chief and a former fighter from the Dinka of Bahr El Ghazal from Aweil Community.

38 Interview with a chief and a former fighter of Nuer Community.

39 Interview with a former fighter of the Dinka community in Tonj.

40 Interviews with a chief of the Lotuka community; and with a former fighter and a chief of Mundari community.

41 Ibid.

principle of precautions of international humanitarian law. For example, Article 57 (1) of the Additional Protocol I 1977 which makes reference to the principle of precautions provides that in the event 'of military operations, constant care shall be taken to spare the civilian population, and civilian objects.

Furthermore, sub-article 1 of article 57 of Additional Protocol I also makes provision for the categories of people and objects to be 'spared' during hostilities. These categories and objects are clearly provided in other provisions such as articles 48, 50y, 51, and 52 of the abovementioned protocol. Notably, article 57(1) is in place to ensure that military commanders must take precautionary measures to distinguish these categories of people from 'combatants' and civilian objects from 'military objectives' in order to avoid any attack or 'incidental losses to them or their objects.

The following sub-articles to article 57 refer to situations of an 'attack' and 'choices' in the event of an armed conflict. Sub-article 2(a) (i) obliges state parties to undertake precautionary measures to 'verify' the persons or objects to be attacked. This is to ensure protection for those who are not lawful targets. Sub-article 2(a) (ii) obligates state parties to take practical measures by adopting tactics or using weapons that would prevent 'damage or incidental loss' to unlawful targets. Sub-article 2 (a) (iii) explicitly requires state parties to avoid making decisions related to 'attack' that would in any case result in 'incidental loss of lives or damage to civilian objects'. Sub-article 2(b) further stipulates that state parties to the armed conflict must revoke any decision related to the 'attack' or 'suspend' if determined that the object to be attacked is an unlawful object or that incidental loss or damage to the object would result 'which would be excessive in relation to the concrete and direct military advantage anticipated'. However, in situations where the actual attack has been decided, the provision of sub-article 2(c) requires state parties to give an 'effective advance warning' to prevent non-combatants or non-military objects from being targeted. However, this obligation is not absolute given the language of the provision.[42]

Article 57 (3) governs the 'choices' that military commanders are to make in relation to 'several military objectives for obtaining a similar military advantage'. This provision guides military commanders to undertake such attacks that would 'cause less danger to civilian lives and their objects'.

The previously mentioned guidelines in light of the observation of the principle of precaution apply in all situations and anywhere whether in the sea

42 Additional Protocol I, note 8 above, article 57(2) (c).

or in the air.[43] Furthermore, these guidelines are in place to ensure civilian's safety and their properties.[44]

The principle of precaution is reflected in treaty provisions relevant to international armed conflict and in international customary rules for both non-international and international armed conflict. Furthermore, there are various decisions that have affirmed the precautionary principle as a custom.[45]

3 Types of Prohibited Conduct

This part assesses the application of the traditional warfare rules and regulations of a number of the communities of South Sudan. It uses empirical research to scrutinise three approaches presented under international humanitarian law. First, it tests whether an attack is permissible towards all members of a community or not; second, the extent of protection of civilian properties against attack; and third, the circumstances that change the status of protected civilian properties into lawful targets.

The foundation of laws of war is based on a balance between the principle of military necessity and humanity. While IHL recognises that it is necessary for belligerents to cause death, injury, and destruction to an adversary during wartime, it does not however, allow taking measures that are contrary to IHL rules.[46] Empirical research suggests that most South Sudanese communities traditions of warfare share common values regarding observance of this balance. However, the legal requirement to make a balance between military actions and humanity reflect the essence of international law, placing the principle of military necessity and humanity at the core of IHL. This Principle underlies the entire regulating framework of IHL, it provides informative guidance on how its rules and other principles of distinction, precautions and proportionality must be interpreted.[47]

This principle was noted in the Hague Regulations of 1899 and 1907 respectively as: the right of belligerents to adopt means of injuring the enemy is not

43 ibid, article 57 (4).

44 ibid, article 57(5).

45 International Criminal Tribunal for the Former Yugoslavia, The Prosecutor v. Kupreskic et al (2000).

46 Knut Dormann, "The Legal Situation of Unlawful/Unprivileged combatants". IRRC March Vol. 85 No 849.

47 ICRC, Interpretive Guidance on the Notion of Direct Participation in Hostilities under International Humanitarian Law, 2009 (ICRC DPH Guidance), pp. 78–79

unlimited.[48] This principle underlies the development of many rules in IHL; and explains the prohibition of certain activities such as employment of poisons, armed projectiles and materials which cause unnecessary suffering. This inclination inspired expansion of this notion in numerous international treaties, including the four Geneva Conventions of 1949.[49]

This was confirmed by the military trials in the aftermath of world war II, The American Military Tribunal asserted that:

> Military necessity permits a belligerent, subject to the laws of war, to apply any amount and kind of force to compel the complete submission of the enemy with the least possible expenditure of time, life, and money. ... It permits the destruction of life of armed enemies and other persons whose destruction is incidentally unavoidable by the armed conflicts of the war ... but it does not permit the killing of innocent inhabitants for purposes of revenge or the satisfaction of a lust to kill. The destruction of property to be lawful must be imperatively demanded by the necessities of war. Destruction as an end in itself is a violation of international law. There must be some reasonable connection between the destruction of property and the overcoming of the enemy forces.[50]

3.1 *Prohibition of Attack Against Certain People*

In the traditional rules of warfare in South Sudan, there is an implicit consensus on a rule which provides for the prohibition of attack or harm against certain categories of people perceived to be non-combatant.[51] Before engaging in a fight with an adversary group, it is imperative to detect and identify who is an opponent group. This is usually done through short conversation with groups according to the traditional rules of the Dinka communities of Bahr El

48 Hague Regulations, Article 22.

49 Geneva Convention Relative to the Protection of Civilian Persons in Time of War art. 53, Aug. 12, 1949. By the convention, extensive destruction or seizure of property is a grave breach when "not justified by military necessity and carried out unlawfully and wantonly." Id. art. 147. It further permits limits on relief for internees based on military necessity, albeit only under strict conditions. Id. art. 108; see also id. art. 143 (regarding visits by representatives of Protecting Powers); Geneva Convention Relative to the Treatment of Prisoners of War art. 126, Aug. 12, 1949, [hereinafter GC III] (regarding visits to prisoners of war).

50 United States v. List (The Hostage Case), Case No. 7 (Feb. 19, 1948), reprinted in 11 TRIALS OF WAR CRIMINALS BEFORE THE NUREMBERG MILITARY TRIBUNALS UNDER CONTROL COUNCIL LAW NO. 10, at 1230 (1950)

51 This was reflected in all twelve interviews.

Ghazal.[52] Furthermore, empirical data from the three regions of South Sudan, indicates that children, elderly people, and women including young girls are not subject to an attack during fighting between communities. Apparently, there is no peculiarity to this general rule, children according to Dinka communities of Bahar El Gazal are perceived to belong to the Community, an ancient proverb says: '*meth ye ken jang bin*' which literally means 'child belongs to everyone'.[53] Similarly, women and elderly are perceived weak, and they lack necessary physical strength to take part in fighting. However, in some irregular situations, some women in the community appear to have considerable physical strength and could sometimes be stronger than men. When a woman chooses to become a warrior and participate in warfare, she certainly loses her protective status and becomes a lawful target.[54]

In the IHL analogy, rules of the principle of distinction are the fabric of IHL according to ICJ "The rule of principle of distinction was established as a norm of state's practice under Rules of International Customary Law, military attack must only be directed against combatant".[55]

Correspondingly, Mundari communities of Equatoria region believe that children are angels of God,[56] and attacking them can inflict curse to the attacker and his or her close family. The lack of equal power in attacking women and elderly people prevents a Mundari fighter from that community from attacking these groups. This is considered an unjustified attack, which is labelled as a cowardice tactic of warfare, as no warrior would like to be described as a coward. Similarly, the Lotuka community perceive women as weak and should not be always subject to an attack. A former fighter from the community narrated that 'Even if a warrior decides to attack a woman, the victim will swiftly expose her breasts to the attacker and he will immediately stop.[57] This is a durable defensive tactic women use to push-back an imminent attack, empirical data from former fighters shows no single violation to this practical rule.

52 Interviews were conducted with two chiefs and two former fighters from the Dinka communities of Bahr El Ghazal Region.

53 Ibid.

54 A former fighter from the Tonj Community of Bahar El Gazal indicated that his aunt used to fight alongside them, and she was even given a warrior nickname similar to that of men.

55 ICJ, Legality of the Threat or Use of nuclear weapons, Advisory Opinion, 1996, paras 78–79

56 This was indicated during interviews with two former fighters from the community.

57 Interviews with two former fighters from the Lotuka community indicate that women use showing of breasts to remind the attacker that he is about to attack a woman or a mother which is protected by traditional rules of fighting. It is also reminding attackers of their mothers' breasts.

Consistently, the Nuer community of Upper Nile region differentiate between warriors and other categories of people namely, women, elderly people, and children.[58] While it is easy to make a distinction between women and elderly people on one hand and warriors on the other hand; it is hard sometimes to draw that line concerning children between the ages of ten and fifteen years old. However, an adult from Nuer community is identified through marks on their foreheads[59]. Interestingly, unmarked males from the Nuer community are considered as children even if their ages exceed twenty years old. An unmarked male is possibly considered a child while his younger brother is perceived to be an adult due to marks. Attacks on unmarked males is in violation of traditional rules related to protection of children.[60] Another reason which prevents warriors from launching attacks against children is the fear of reprisal. Warriors believe whatever action they take against children of an adverse group will result in a similar fate to their own children. Accordingly, adherence to this rule ensures safety of children from counterattacks. Towards this end, it is clear that traditional rules of fighting in South Sudan provide a protection rule to certain categories of people amongst the community populations.

Worthy of note, is that different communities in South Sudan share similar rules on the application of traditional fighting related to protected persons. It is well aligned with the principle of distinction, which is a central notion under International Humanitarian Law. Its generic essence is to allow military attack on certain people and objects which belong to armed forces participating in an armed conflict, while civilian populations and their objects should always remain spared and protected against the effects of the warfare. The rule of the principle of distinction was established as a norm of state's practice under the rules of international customary law, military attack must only be directed against combatants.[61] Notably, the principle of distinction as such is viewed under two main concepts namely, men in uniform are different from their fellow civilians even when all of them are citizens of an enemy state. The second concept sets a justification for attacking military personnel only, while there is never any justification for attacking the rest of the civilians.[62] Thus, an attack

58 An interview with a chief and a former fighter from the Nuer community.

59 Each community has their own unique identification marks; for instance, Nuer uses six lines around the head; Mundari's marks take the shape of V at the forehead, Dinka use marks similar to Nuer with slight differences.

60 An interview with a former fighter from the Nuer community.

61 The International Committee of the Red Cross, Customary International Humanitarian Law, Rule 1.

62 Asa Kasher. The Principle of Distinction. Journal of Military Ethics. (2017) 6. 152–167.

which is not directed against a lawful target 'military objectives' is therefore a violation of the principle of distinction and consequently constitute an 'indiscriminate attack'. This includes employment of means or methods of combat which cannot be directed to specific objectives, or its effect is uncontrollable.[63]

Article 48 of Additional Protocol I requires parties to a conflict to "at all times distinguish between the civilian population and combatant and between civilian objects and military objectives".[64]

Significantly, this chapter asserts that it is crucial to understand whether the effect of war could extend to properties belonging to civilians. It is worthy to note that the notion of military property in traditional warfare applies only to fighting tools, while other properties are considered civilian according to traditional rules of fighting.[65] A former fighter from Mundari community attested that destruction of properties, burning of houses and destruction of farms are not permitted in their community in the course of warfare.[66]

As outlined above, South Sudanese traditional rules of warfare share core values relating to dispersing of children, women, and elderly people from the effects of war. In the Dinka Aweil community rules of warfare, elders among warriors play commander's role in guiding conduct of hostilities. They usually take position behind warriors, to closely monitor their actions, and to control their movement.[67] One of the significant roles of those commanders is to stop an about-to-happen attack against protected persons. Orders of ceasefire fall under their responsibility as well.[68]

As per South Sudanese warfare traditions, women by their nature do not participate in war and therefore are not subject to an attack. According to the Equatoria ancient communities, the proliferation of humankind relies on women, hence, it is prohibited to cause any sort of harm to them.[69] One of the outstanding examples relate to the prohibition of attack against women was narrated by a former fighter as follows:

> If a fighter finds himself in an area surrounded by an opponent group, he must enter any nearby tokole [70] for his safety. Also, if a fighter gets injured

63 Article 51 (4) of Additional Protocol I to the Four Geneva Convention of 1949.

64 Protocol I Additional to the Geneva Conventions of 12 August 1949, and relating to the Protection of Victims of International Armed Conflicts, adopted on 8 June 1977, article 48.

65 An interview with a former fighter from the Nuer community.

66 Interviews conducted with former fighters from these communities.

67 An interview with a former fighter from the Dinka Aweil community.

68 Ibid.

69 Interviews with a former fighter from Mundari and Lotuka communities.

70 This is in rooms where women and children are probably sheltering during war.

> and about to be killed, women interfere and safeguard him with their bodies. In both scenarios, attackers would immediately stop to avoid possible harm to women.[71]

Conventionally, both IHL and South Sudan traditional rules of warfare of the selected communities prohibit attack, causing harm to children, women, and elderly people.

3.2 *Prohibition of Looting and Destruction of Properties*

In accordance with Article 51 of Additional Protocol I, civilian objects are protected against attack. Moreover, Article 53 of the same protocol,[72] prohibits attack or destruction of objects of indispensable nature for the survival of civilians during armed conflict.[73] Indispensable objects include water source, foodstuff, installations among others. In analogy to those IHL provisions, South Sudanese rules of warfare prohibit destruction of properties as a rule and allow fighters to solely ruin their fellow combatants and their fighting tools. According to Mundari practice of warfare, a battlefield is designated in distant areas from residents, to ensure safety of civilians and their properties from effects of war.[74] Similarly, fighters from the Dinka Bor community are not allowed to destroy or burn properties belonging to adversaries. A former fighter from the Dinka of Bahar El Gazal region specified that: "In our time, no burning of houses, no destruction of crops, no looting, all these behaviours are prohibited in our rules of fighting".[75]

Empirical data from the three historical regions of South Sudan signifies that rules of traditional warfare provide protection to civilian properties as a rule, with an exception of taking foodstuff for instant consumption purposes. However, in a rare situation, fighters may take an adversary's cattle in an intensifying war that has resulted in taking the lives of distinguished fighters.[76] This usually occurs when a leader fails to control angry fighters due to intense war. This is an exceptional situation reflected in one community and can not be generalised to all.[77]

71 An interview with a former fighter from the Dinka Tonj community.

72 Protocol Additional to the Geneva Conventions of 12 August 1949 and relating to the Protection of Victims of International Armed Conflicts, adopted on 8 June 1977, article 48.

73 Ibid.

74 An interview with a former fighter from Mundari community.

75 Interviews with two chiefs and two former fighters from the Dinka communities of Bahar El Gazal region.

76 An interview with a former fighter from the Tonj community of Bahar El Gazal region.

77 Ibid.

In the Equatoria region, it is prohibited to loot properties belonging to an opponent community according to both Mundari and Lotuka traditional rules of fighting.[78] Furthermore, property destruction is not permissible at all.[79] Community's civilian properties include cattle, goats, hens, crops, and other livelihood means. Depending on the level of intensity of fighting, warriors are allowed to take already made or cooked food which are subject to instant consumption if they feel hungry. A similar practice exists in the Dinka Aweil community of Bahar El Gazal region. However, when a warfare intensifies and results in many casualties, exhausted warriors[80] may decide to loot cattle of the enemy according to Tonj community (in accordance with military necessity). In the Upper Nile region, and for the Bentiu community in particular, looting cows is only permissible during inter-community hostilities, but prohibited in intra-community hostilities.

The research underpinning this chapter also explored situations whereby protected people and objects turn into lawful targets in the midst of a traditional warfare (direct participation in hostilities). Apparently, inputs from the three regions of South Sudan signify the non-existent of such scenarios in traditional rules of fighting,[81] in which attacks would be directed against protected people or against civilian properties. According to Mundari and Lotuka communities of the Equatoria region, traditional fighting rules are well set in a manner that could not allow the occurrence of such violations among communities. By a way of contrast, civilian objects in the international humanitarian law regime can turn into military objectives when it makes an effective contribution to military action, and their total capture or neutralisation, in the circumstances ruling at the time, would offer a definite military advantage.[82] A military attack is only justified if it is directed towards a lawful object being people or objects. Military objects are those which by its nature, location, purpose, or use make a positive contribution to enemy action and its neutralisation will make military advantage. While this notion does not exist in traditional rules of warfare, this presents evidence that traditional rules of fighting of communities in South Sudan is more protective and advanced to some extent compared to the same rule of IHL.

78 Ibid.

79 Interview with a chief and a former fighter from the Lotuka Community of Equatoria region.

80 Usually when a stronger fighter falls down in war.

81 This was reported in all of the empirical interviews.

82 Ibid.

The last assessment in this part is employed to check the level of protection of worship areas and materials with cultural importance. In the Upper Nile region, there is a general belief that those objects are not subject to an attack according to Nuer and Dinka Bor communities. The Mundari and Lotuka communities opinionated that destroying worship materials may bring bad luck to the community.[83] It is a curse according to the Dinka communities in Aweil and Tonj. This curse might stay longer and extend from generation to another.[84] In addition, the broader communities of South Sudan believe worship gods belong to all human beings and should be respected by all. At the same time, worship materials provide protection against 'Jack rech' which could literally be translated as devils according to the Dinka community.[85]

3.3 *Treatment of Prisoners of War*

In pursuant to the provisions of the Third Geneva Conventions, prisoners of war must be treated humanely and with dignity, endangering the life and health of prisoners of war is prohibited and amounts to a grave breach.[86] Correspondingly, relative rules for treatment of prisoners of war exist in South Sudan traditional warfare. For instance, causing harm to prisoners of war is prohibited according to the Dinka communities in Aweil, Tonj and Bor.[87] Moreover, if an eminent fighter falls at the hand of an opponent group, he is kept safe and treated humanely. Seemingly, strong fighters are treated with more respect than other fighters. In the Equatoria region, a captured enemy is subject to "*Abetu*" and is allowed to leave. This is a type of punishment which applies to children when they commit mistakes. *Abetu* could possibly be translated as caning, it is a process of lashing a person with a light whip which does not cause injury to the body. In the case of prisoners of war, *Abetu* applies in a more dramatic setting.[88] Application of *Abetu* does not necessarily indicate a maltreatment to a captured fighter.

Obviously and as a wider pretext, the general traditional rule concerning prisoners of war in South Sudan communities is to take them to the chief of

---

83 Interviews conducted with two chiefs and two former fighters from the Mundari and Lotuka Communities of the Equatoria region.

84 Interviews conducted with two chiefs and two former fighters from the Dinka communities of Bahar El Gazal region.

85 This was indicated by interviewees from the Dinka communities of Bahr El Ghazal and Upper Nile Regions.

86 The third Geneva Conventions relative to the treatment of prisoners of war adopted on 12 August 1949, article 13.

87 This was reflected in all interviews conducted at the three regions in South Sudan.

88 Application of Abetu which indicates the principle of respecting captured combatant.

the area who will treat them humanely before allowing them to leave. This indicates that the aim of community warfare is to defeat the enemy in a just and fair war rather than to kill them.

In summary, this part has presented empirical research evidence of the existence and application of traditional rules and regulations to spare civilians from combatants. Those rules are deeply integrated in the collective great belief of the communities that no violation was witnessed to these rules, exemplary, is the protection of worship places and the protection of children.[89]

4 Defences for Breaches of Customary Regulations and Rules of Warfare

Defences to apparent or perceived violations or contraventions of the customary regulations and rules of warfare of the selected communities in South Sudan appear to be centred on two notions. First, that an attack or a battle after mass is not exceeding or excessive when a comparison is drawn between the final outcome of the battle and the collateral damage. Second, it is argued that there have been, and, in most times, there is an important and eager-ing need and reason to attack an adversary despite all the reasons and the causes. It appears that within some of the traditional waring communities of South Sudan there is no determination done or conducted, prior to the launch of an attack, on the need to call-off or suspend an attack if such an attack would result into causalities to noncombatants, or even if a counterattack is targeting non-combatants in the adversary waring community.[90]

The first two traditional warfare regulations and rules of South Sudanese communities, based on the empirical research of this chapter, appears to be similar and relative to international humanitarian law principle of proportionality,[91] a core international treaty and customary law rule of international humanitarian law.[92] The third context of not calling off or cancelling an attack should it be directed towards noncombatants – in counter offences – or if it

89 Interviews with chiefs and former fighters from Equatoria, Upper Nile and Bahar El Gazal regions.

90 An Interview with a former fighters from the Dinka community of Tonj.

91 Jeroen van den Boogaard, Proportionality in International Humanitarian Law: Principle, Rule and Practice, Repro FBD, 2019, p. 117.

92 Nils Melzer and Etienne Kuster, International Humanitarian Law: A Comprehensive Introduction, International Review of the Red Cross, Geneva, 2022, p. 17.

would result in death or injury to civilians, is apparently divergent and distinct of international humanitarian law treaty and customary law provisions.[93]

In South Sudan, traditionally, when communities fight the first consideration is to be as proportionate and balanced as possible. Sparing or aiming not to attack those who are not part of the adversary's warring counterpart appeared to be a sacred determination.

In the Upper Nile Region of South Sudan, the Dinka Bor Community, in accordance with their traditional methods of warfare do not permit any attacks on anyone who is not directly participating as an adversarial party in a warfare.[94] Furthermore, the Dinka Bor community traditions dictate that they should spare non-combatants, and a planned attack on an adversary community, at all times, is considerate of not inflicting injuries nor death to the other warring community nonparticipating or civilian people.[95] Along the same line within the Upper Nile Region, the Nuer Community, asserts that in their communal warfare the weapons used to attack an adversary have no capability to reach and extend to the adversary's people who are not part or participating in the battlefield.[96]

Similarly, in the Equatoria Region of South Sudan, the Mundari Community simplify that, every time their community combat another adversary community, they do not aim to attack any other party, but only the adversary who is combating and counter attacking their community.[97] Along the same line, the Lotuka Community proclaim that the means and methods that they use to attack an adversely warring community targets the members of the warring community who are also combatants of the adversary party.[98]

Conversely, the studied communities in the Bahr El Ghazal Region of South Sudan, in accordance with their customary traditions of warfare, do only utilise means and methods of warfare that could only inflict injury or death on adversary fighters, and in doing that they only attack and direct their weapons towards an adversary.[99] Meanwhile, Dinka communities in Tonj, only used and continue to use unsophisticated weapons when combating an adversary

93 Georg Nolte, "Thin or Thick? The Principle of Proportionality and International Humanitarian Law", Law and Ethics of Human Rights, Vol. 4, No. 2, 2010, p. 245.

94 An Interview with two former fighters of traditional communal warfare.

95 Ibid, the interview referenced above.

96 An interview with a Chief and a former fighter of traditional warfare.

97 An interview with a Chief and a Former Fighter from Terekeka.

98 An interview with a Chief and former fighter from the Lotuka Community.

99 Interviews with a Chief and a former fighter of the Aweil Community.

community which is always similar and proportionate to the means an adversary has used while attacking.[100]

The aforementioned practices are similar to the treaties and customary law rules of international humanitarian law assertions pertaining to the principle of proportionality.[101] The First Additional Protocol to the Geneva Conventions asserts that:

> An attack which may be expected to cause incidental loss of civilian life, injury to civilians, damage to civilian objects, or a combination thereof, which would be excessive in relation to the concrete and direct military advantage anticipated.[102]

This is also evident in international customary rules of international humanitarian law, in which rule 14 states the following:

> Launching an attack which may be expected to cause incidental loss of civilian life, injury to civilians, damage to civilian objects, or a combination thereof, which would be excessive in relation to the concrete and direct military advantage anticipated, is prohibited.[103]

A second aspect used as one of the defences is that in each planned and actual warfare situation, non-combatants are given protection even if they, incidentally, become or appear in the battlefield ground. In the Upper Nile Region of South Sudan, the Dinka Bor Community assert that, as per their traditional warfare rules, adversary fighters are the only target in a battlefield, and nothing else.[104] It is suggested that attacking anything and anyone else violates their code of warfare.[105] Similarly, the Nuer Community in the Upper Nile Region of South Sudan have revealed that their warfare regulations aim to only attack an individual who is part of an adversary attacking force;[106] and if an adversary

100 An interview with a Chief and a former fighter from the Tonj Community.

101 Nils Melzer and Etienne Kuster, International Humanitarian Law: A Comprehensive Introduction, International Review of the Red Cross, Geneva, 2022, p. 17.

102 Protocol Additional to the Geneva Conventions of 12 August 1949, and relating to the Protection of Victims of International Armed Conflicts, adopted on 8 June 1977, article 51 (5) (b).

103 International Committee of the Red Cross, Customary International Humanitarian Law, 2005, Rule 14.

104 An Interview with two former fighters of traditional communal warfare of the Dinka Community in Bor.

105 Ibid.

106 An interview with a Chief and a former fighter of traditional warfare.

runs into or barricades themselves amongst noncombatants of their own folk and/or goes into the "tokols"[107] of his or her own people who are not part of the fight, they will not be pursued therein.[108]

Similarly, the Dinka Community of the Bahr El Ghazal Region of South Sudan have affirmed that in a fight none of their fighters is allowed to harm someone from an adversary group, but the ones who are fighting their community.[109] The Aweil community even confirmed that a fight is usually intermittently paused to allow those who are not part of the fighting to pass through, should such a situation presents itself.[110] However, in the Dinka Tonj community of the Bahr El Ghazal Region of South Sudan, the practice and rule appears to be uncertain and unsettled. According to a former fighter, the warfare practice does not limit an attack to an adversary combatant, rather it pursues an adversary even if they run into a heaven which accommodates members of their community who are not part of the fight.[111] Disputably, a Chief from the same Tonj Community has indicated that in warfare the rules do not allow any attack on someone who is not counter fighting.[112]

In the Equatoria Region of South Sudan, the warfare rules of the community of Mundari do not permit pursuing an adversary if they run into a civilian settlement, and the rules even dictate that the fight should be called off in order for the non-participating people to flee or pass through.[113] In a similar vein, communities of Lotuka observe a similar code of practice.[114]

These traditional considerations are reflective of the letter and spirit of article 57 of the First Additional Protocol to the Four Geneva Conventions, which states that:

> Those who plan or decide upon an attack shall: iii) refrain from deciding to launch any attack which may be expected to cause incidental loss of civilian life, injury to civilians, damage to civilian objects, or a

107 A tokol is a traditional housing structure of pastoral communities in South Sudan.
108 An interview with a Chief and a former fighter of traditional warfare.
109 Interviews with a Chief and a former fighter of the Dinka Aweil Community.
110 Ibid.
111 An Interview with a former fighter from the Dinka Tonj Community.
112 An Interview with a Chief from the Tonj Community.
113 An interview with a Chief and a Former Fighter from Mundari.
114 An interview with a Chief and former fighter from the Community.

> combination thereof, which would be excessive in relation to the concrete and direct military advantage anticipated.[115]

Conversely also, rule 18 of the rules of Customary international Humanitarian Law stipulates that adversaries in whichever type of conflict are required to assess the "excessiveness" of an attack before they launch it in view of the situation if such attack might cause incidental loss to those who are not an adversary.[116]

On a separate note, a conclusive matter which appears not to be accommodated as per the traditional customary warfare rules is the condition to cancel or suspend an attack as required under the treaty provisions and customary rules of International Humanitarian Law. It is a well-known factor that article 57 (2) (b) of the First Additional Protocol to the Geneva Conventions and rule 19 of the Customary International Humanitarian Law Rules, requires that fighting adversaries are required to cancel or at least suspend a warfare if there would be no military objective achieved.[117]

In this regard, the interviews employed to assess the notion within the customary rules of warfare in South Sudan points out that it does not extend to this consideration. In the Dinka and Nuer Communities of Upper Nile Region, the research reveals that adversary fighters are the only target in a warfare;[118] and if the adversary fighters run into civilian areas the attack would be called off automatically.[119] This trend seems similar and replicated in the traditions of warfare of the Mundari and Lotuka communities in the Equatoria Region.[120] In contrast, as per the Dinka Community in the Bahr El Ghazal Region, two factors have come into play. The first is that an attack is suspended temporarily to permit those who are not part of the fight to pass through to whichever destination they are headed, and also in order not to harm them.[121] The second asserts that an attack is not called off nor suspended, even if it becomes

115 Protocol Additional to the Geneva Conventions of 12 August 1949, and relating to the Protection of Victims of International Armed Conflicts, adopted on 8 June 1977, article 57(2)(a)(iii) and (b).

116 International Committee of the Red Cross, Customary International Humanitarian Law, 2005, Rule 18.

117 Ibid, Rule 19; and note 25 above, article 57 (2) (b).

118 An Interview with two former fighters of traditional communal warfare.

119 An interview with a Chief and a former fighter of traditional warfare.

120 Interviews with a Chief and a Former Fighter from Terekeka, and also with a Chief and a Former Fighter from a community in Torit.

121 Interviews with a Chief and a former fighter of the Aweil Community.

apparent that there would be no military requirement and inconsiderate of any civilian casualties which might transpire.[122]

To sum up this part, it is clear that the defences to breaches within the traditions of warfare align with the requirements of military necessity, and that its excessiveness is considered with the need to spare civilian injuries or casualties. This is reflective of the same core fundamentals of the principle of proportionality in international humanitarian law.

5 Consequences for Breaches of the Traditional Rules of Warfare

The consequences for the breach of traditional rules of warfare in South Sudan are not uniform. The communities in Upper Nile and Bahr El Ghazal which practise the Dinka culture never entertained the death penalty as a consequence for any breach including breaches of the rules of warfare. It is argued that these communities equate the life of a cow to that of a human being.[123] Hence, compensation is offered for the life lost unjustly whether in individual fights or in communal confrontations. The compensation is normally in the form of cows. The life of one person who is unjustly murdered is worth thirty-one cows. However, this does not go for an individual who was unintentionally murdered. Notably, there are consequences for non-compliance with regard to the payment of cows as compensation. One of these consequences is continued revenge killing.[124]

Likewise, the communities of Upper Nile of the Nuer culture have the same rules deeply entrenched in the traditions of warfare. This could be because the Nuer and Dinka communities are historically traced to share the same ancestry.[125]

In addition to this, the general literature on African communities suggests that African societies treat 'murder as a civil wrong' and the concept of the death penalty has never been associated with African societies and that there were rare cases where the punishment of death would be invoked.[126] Consequently,

122 An Interview with a former fighter from the Tonj Community.

123 LB Deng 'Social capital and civil war: The Dinka communities in Sudan's civil war' (2010) 109 *African Affairs* 231.

124 W Bedigen 'Significance of Societal Customs in the South Sudan Civil War Resolution' (2020) 15 *Journal of Peacebuilding & Development* 3.

125 ibid.

126 T Nhlapo 'Homicide in traditional African societies: Customary law and the question of accountability' (2017) 17 *African Human Rights Law Journal* 1.

for most South Sudanese, the means of retribution as a result of committing a breach, which is against the traditional rules of war, is through cows.

Unlike the practices of the above communities in relation to how they handle breaches of the rules of war, international humanitarian law framework provides completely different methods of responding to breaches of the rule of armed conflicts.[127] The international humanitarian law framework expressly provides for the criminal punishment of those who have committed grave breaches of its norms. The punishments could be done either at the national level or at the international level.[128] South Sudan, besides having ratified the Four Geneva Conventions and their Additional Protocols, has also domesticated the Geneva Conventions treaty provisions. through the *South Sudan Geneva Conventions Act*. The *South Sudan Geneva Conventions Act of 2012* makes provisions for penalties for the breach of international humanitarian law. Section 6 provides that:

> Any person, of whatever nationality, who, in the Republic of South Sudan or elsewhere, commits, or aids, abets or procures any other person to commit, a grave breach of any of the Conventions and Protocols I and III is guilty of an indictable offence.

Section 6 provides for the punishment of breaches of the Conventions and Additional Protocol I. This indicates that the provision is not exhaustive, as it does not expressly reference other instruments such as Additional Protocol II. However, section 7 of the aforementioned Act enshrines punishment for breaches not covered in section 6 above.

Section 8 of the *South Sudan Geneva Conventions Act* stipulates the penalties and procedures. It provides that:

> A person found guilty and convicted of any offence under section 6 and 7 shall- (a) if the offence involves the willful killing of a person protected by the relevant Convention or by Protocol I be liable to imprisonment for life or any lesser term; and (b) in any other case – imprisonment for a term not exceeding 14 years. (2) No charge shall be preferred under sections 6 & 7 unless it is by or on behalf of a public prosecutor.

---

127 ICRC 'International criminal jurisdiction'. https://www.icrc.org/en/document/international-criminal-jurisdiction accessed on 8 November 2023.

128 American Red Cross Fact Sheet 'IHL_ProsecutionofViolations.pdf' <https://www.redcross.org/content/dam/redcross/atg/PDF_s/Family___Holocaust_Tracing/IHL_ProsecutionofViolations.pdf> accessed 8 November 2023.

Section 10 gives the High Court of the Republic of South Sudan exclusive powers to entertain matters of violations of international humanitarian law norms.

Of important notice is the fact that the traditional practices and international humanitarian law norms in relation to breaches are not in conformity. The former redresses breaches in a civil manner whereas the latter in a criminal form.

In addition to the above considerations from existing writings, empirical research hereunder supports and in other instances diverge on the consequences for violations and/or contraventions of the traditional and customary regulations and rules of warfare of the communities in South Sudan. It focuses on two matters. The first, there are consequences for fighters who launch attacks on noncombatants and which as a result cause harm and injuries to children, women, and elderly groups of an adversary. The second, provide for and reflect the consequences for burning and/or destroying the properties of the vulnerable groups of an adversary who are not part of an ongoing fight or warfare.

As per the qualitative interviews conducted to inform the proposition of this chapter about the customary traditions of warfare in South Sudan, it could be argued that the overall remedy for contraventions of traditional warfare rules appears to be restorative and compensatory for a victim rather than being punitive to the violator or the contravener, who would be a traditional fighter.

In the Upper Nile Region of South Sudan, in the first instance, the traditional rules of the Dinka Bor Community dictates that a fighter who kills or injures non-fighters, of an adversary waring community, to pay higher blood compensation. However, in comparison to the custom, traditions stipulate separate consequences for instances of killing or death which occur in ordinary domestic and non-warfare situations.[129] Also, a fighter who burns the property of vulnerable groups of an adversary would be "named and shamed" and the moral shame which associates with the culture would follow and hunt that fighter.[130] Add to that, if such burring results in damaging the crops of a non-fighting group which is part of an adversary populace, a compensation, as a requirement would be applied and to be offered to that victim.[131]

However, within the same region but to the contrast, the Bentiu Nuer Community traditional rules and regulations present that a more higher blood compensation in the form of additional cows would be rewarded to a noncombatant victim of an adversary, should the victim be from their same

129 An Interview with two former fighters of traditional communal warfare.

130 Ibid, same interview with the same personalities.

131 Ibid, same interview with the same personalities.

community, and in a fight within the same community.[132] This situation suggests that should a warring adversary be of a different traditional community then there could be no additional cows and bulls as a higher blood compensation, let alone no compensation at all.[133] Similarly, the Bentiu Community asserts that there is no remedy or consequences for the destruction of the property of an adversary noncombatants.[134]

In the Equatoria region of South Sudan, the two matters emanating from attacking nonfighters and/or destroying their properties are resolved with identical consequences. The Mundari Community Code of traditional warfare asserts that at the end of each fight, the Chief of the community, in their capacity as head of the warring party, identifies and singles out those fighters, from his/her community, who have violated the rules and attacked non-fighters of an adversary, and then the Chief will penalise these fighters by ordering them to pay cows/bulls or other goods to their victims.[135] In the same vein, fighters who damage any form of property belonging to the non-warriors of an adversary fighting community will be condemned to remedy the damage in a form of compensation to the adversary community members.[136]

While the Torit Community have identified that in situations of causing harm or any form of injury to an adversary's vulnerable populace, cows/bulls would be paid as a form of compensation to the victims of the opposing party.[137] Furthermore, the community has argued that, in their traditional fights, they have never encountered a situation in which fighters of their community damage the ownings of noncombatants at all, and if a fighter, exceptionally, deviates, then he or she would be immediately ordered to compensate the damaged belongings.[138]

More elaborately and detailed, traditional rules of warfare of the Dinka Aweil Community of the Bahr El Ghazal Region in South Sudan, expresses that a different and more peculiar blood compensation should be determined and then awarded to the members of the adversary party, when a fighter, from their community, kills or attacks children or women from an adversary.[139] The traditional rules of the Dinka Aweil Community, also, assert that a traditional

---

132 An interview with a Chief and a former fighter of traditional warfare from Bentiu.

133 Ibid, same interview with the same former fighters.

134 Ibid, same interview with the same former fighters.

135 An interview with a Chief and a Former Fighter from Terekeka.

136 Ibid, interviews with the same persona.

137 An interview with a Chief and former fighter from the Community.

138 Ibid, interviews with a Chief and former fighter from the Torit Community.

139 Interviews with a Chief and a former fighter of the Aweil Community.

tribunal will be set to try and adjudicate instances of a fighter from their own community, who is accused and suspected of burning the noncombatant items of an adversary.[140]

Another apparent and opposing practice, is from the Dinka Tonj Community of the Bahr El Ghazal Region of South Sudan. This Community's rules command that in a fight and warfare zone, between them and adversary power, any possible scenario to achieving victory, is possible and there would and should be no consequences or reparations to the defeated party.[141] However, if an incident is an exception from a wider trend, and is deemed as a personal occurrence by an individual fighter, it would necessitate an appropriate compensation.[142] Transparently, the Dinka Tonj Community have advised that their fights take place outside noncombatant settlements, casualties to the property of vulnerable people is not envisioned.[143]

6 Conclusion and Recommendations

This chapter provided an African perspective, from a Third World Approach to international Law (TWAIL) perspective, to debunk arguments that Africa did not have rules and regulations before the advent of European civilisation. As shown throughout this chapter the weapons employed in the traditional warfare of the South Sudanese selected communities do not have the capacity of causing excessive loss to non-combatants such as children, women, the elderly and persons with disabilities. However, some communities use fire as a means of warfare. Communities who undertake this practice do not spare children, women, the elderly and persons with disabilities. Furthermore, this research has uncovered shared commonalities of the communities studied in relation to the methods of warfare. For example, perfidy is prohibited and those who engage in it are regarded as cowards. As indicated throughout this chapter, the traditional rules and regulations of warfare of the South Sudanese communities largely conform with the core principles of international humanitarian law. For instance, under the traditions of warfare of the communities studied, attacks against non-combatants and their properties are not permissible. Non-combatants can only be attacked when they actively participate in hostilities.

140 Ibid, the two interviews with the two persons from Aweil.

141 An Interview with a former fighter and an interview with a Chief from the Tonj Community.

142 Ibid, interview with concerned people from the Tonj Community.

143 Ibid.

Also, before the start of confrontations, women, children, the elderly and persons with disabilities are normally warned in order to evacuate attack locations. However, in situations where confrontations have reached their hiding locations, attacks would be called off.

Additionally, this research has also unpacked that South Sudanese selected communities do not encourage the use of weapons such as fire that would disproportionately cause incidental loss. It has also uncovered that those who are unable to defend themselves should not be harmed. These findings indicate that international humanitarian law core principles of distinction, precaution, proportionality, humanity and necessity are largely observed in the traditions of warfare of the South Sudanese communities. Interestingly, the South Sudanese traditions of warfare recognise and accord the prisoner of war status to captured adversaries.

Although there is largely conformity between the traditions of warfare of the South Sudanese communities and the core principles of international humanitarian law, notable differences still remain. Firstly, The former prescribes or redresses breaches in a civil manner whereas the latter in a criminal form. Secondly, as shown above, some communities allow use of fire which may in most instances cause disproportionate harm to non-combatants and their properties. Therefore, in order to correctly and fully implement international humanitarian law norms, South Sudan must reconcile the local practices with the international humanitarian law norms. However, should it opt for the latter rules only, then massive education should be carried out to inform the societies of the changes in rules.

Finally, this chapter recommends that in order to understand the traditions of all communities in South Sudan, further research covering all communities be conducted. In this further research, consideration should also be given to principles of international humanitarian law that have not been studied.

CHAPTER 8

Maltese Laws of War

Samara J. Cassar

One should not ask whether Malta's history is significant, but rather, how history is significant because of Malta.[1] Indeed, the language itself provides a cheat's glimpse into Maltese history – it is a latinized variety of spoken historical Arabic. It was developed as a Maghrebi Arabic dialect, influenced by Italian and to a lesser extent French, and written in the Latin alphabet. Situated south of Sicily, and east of Tunisia, Malta figuratively and literally bridges the East and West. The main island is almost 27 kilometres long and 15 kilometres wide. It is adjoined by a handful of smaller islands: Gozo (which is about half its size) and Comino (which is even smaller). Perhaps this goes some way into explaining why – and how – the island has been a staging point since antiquity for invasions and, under the Knight's rule, conquests. One could justifiably speculate that Malta's history may not be as colourful as it is, but for its location. There was no mineral or resource that was under strong pursuit. Rather, Malta's strategic location made it so attractive. Malta is an acute example of Clausewitz's aphorism of war being the continuation of politics by other means.

Amidst this, no clear *codified* rules of warfare or custom can be distilled. Historians explain that at the end of each conquest, attempts were made to erase any documentary record of the prior conqueror.[2] Ths was not uncommon of the time. For instance, Rome's rise to prominence, brought its own version of laws of war that remained unwritten. It is therefore inaccurate to conclude that Malta was law-less. Song, maps and architecture make clear that a system of governance was in place at the turn of the sixteenth century.

Come 25 March 1530 a bargain was struck. In exchange for a falcon, Charles V – the King of Naples – perpetually enfeoffed the island of Malta to the Grand Master, the leader of the Knights Hospitallers of the Order of St John of

1 Samara Cassar is a Solicitor at Law (Bachelor of Laws (Hons I) and Bachelor of Arts (International Relations) at the University of Queensland). All views expressed herein are her own, and do not reflect the views of any organisation/s that Samara is associated with.

2 Brian Blouet, *The Story of Malta* (Faber and Faber, 1967) 11; Stephen Spiteri, 'The 'Castellu di la Chitati' the medieval castle of the walled town of Mdina' (2000) *Malta Archeoogical Review* 4, 3.

 | DOI:10.1163/9789004512566_010

Jerusalem, Knights of Malta (herein referred to as the Order). It is this moment of history that this chapter starts from. The case shall be made that even if there had not been 'laws' – as we now understand them – the Knights certainly cultivated a governance system within a sphere of recognised norms.

1 Temporal Scope

Between 1530 and 1798, Malta was the sole seat for the Order. In 1798, Napoleon invaded and implemented a new government. The British arrived in the 19th century and ruled for approximately 180 years. It is not until after the second World War, around 1964, that Malta became internally self-governed. Even then, colonial vestiges remained till 1979 when the United Kingdom formally concluded their use of Malta as a military base. Malta joined the European Union in 2004. This chapter will specifically focus on the way the Knights governed Malta between 1530 and 1798, because this period is the most informative. Indeed, the Order is now recognised as one of the oldest and most prestigious of its kind, and rather uniquely, is both a fighting force *and* recognised as a State (albeit arguably)[3] at international law.

2 Limitations

A limitation of this paper is that conclusions drawn are deductive because of the limited information available from the time. The Order lacked chroniclers, and tend to receive footnote treatment from historians concerned principally with the great powers who occupied the land during the Order's rule. Historian Brian Blout concludes that the 'history of Malta is marked by several periods in which our knowledge of the islands is extremely limited'.[4] A position confirmed by another historian who observes how many primary documents were lost, or purposefully destroyed, during the inquisition.[5] For instance, the French troops in 1798 were said to have purposefully burnt and destroyed documentation during their occupation. Similarly, others report that the Order distorted primary accounts to 'erase' the period of Muslim rule and present

3 See Section 5, below.

4 Brian Blouet, *The Story of Malta* (Faber and Faber, 1967) 11.

5 Frans Ciappara, 'The Roman Inquisition Revisited: The Maltese Tribunal in the Eighteenth Century' (2017) 103(3) *The Catholic Historical Review* 437.

history as a continuously Catholic one from the time of Saint Paul's shipwreck first discovering Malta in the first century AD.[6]

3 Locating Malta

The Maltese archipelago consists of two main islands – Malta and Gozo. The larger of the two, Malta, is only twenty-nine kilometres wide and fourteen kilometres long. The islands are divided by a small channel, in which lies the inlet of Comino – a smaller island no more than thirteen by six kilometres wide. Cominotto, is an even smaller rock adjacent to Comino. Fifla, is another rocky outcrop, a few miles south-west of Malta. Zooming further out, Malta is approximately eighty kilometres south of Sicily, and less than five hundred kilometres from Tunisia. It is sensibly referred to as a 'cross-roads island' between the East and West. It's 'cosmopolitan and polygot'[7] population reflects the 'ethnic and linguistics mixtures of Phoenician, Arab, Sicilian and British colonial influences'.[8]

4 System of Governance – Relationship between Church and State

The Order was first recognised by the Pope on 15 February 1113.[9] To this day it remains under the auspices of the Vatican, and is said to be the oldest surviving Order of chivalry. The collective noun, 'the Order' is misleading. Initially, they were two distinct groups with different modus operandi – the Religious Order of the Hospital of Saint John of Jerusalem, and later the Order of the Knights Templar. The former built hostels and provided medical aid, while the latter had a purely military function dedicated to fighting the Moslem infidel

6 Commendatore Fra Gian Francessco Abela, Della descrittione di Malta Isola nel mare Siciliano con le sue antichita, ed alter notizie (1647, Malta).

7 Godfrey Baldacchino, 'A Nationless State? Malta, National Identity and the EU' (2002) 25(4) *West European Politics* 191, 195.

8 Ibid; Bruce Ware Allen, *The Great Siege of Malta: the Epic Battle between the Ottoman Empire*, 22; John Scott, 'The Phoenicians and the Formation of the Western World' (2018) 78(1) *Comparative Civilization Review* 25, 29.

9 Karol Karski, 'The International Legal Status of the Sovereign Military Hospitaller Order of St John of Jerusalem of Rhodes and of Malta' (2012) 14(1) *International Community Law Review* 19, 20; Arthur Breycha-Vauthier Michael Potulicki, 'The Order of St John in International Law: A forerunner of the Red Cross' (1954) 48(4) *The American Journal of International Law* 554, 554; Ernle Bradford, 'Great Siege: Malta 1565' (*Wordworth Editions Ltd*, 1999) 27.

and protecting Christian pilgrims as they travelled to Jerusalem. In around 1145 to 1153, the Pope granted the Order full jurisdiction under canon law over its territories and its members.[10] At that time it was understood that the Order became a subject of international law, equal in its sovereignty to other States.

5 The Order

A live debate remains as to whether the Order has adopted the status of a State in its own right.[11] This is because as it currently stands, the status of the Order is unique and not shared by any other military faction annexed to a State. The Knights of Malta enjoy permanent observer status in the United Nations. And, while no longer enjoying a defined territory,[12] it possesses a population – but not exclusively – with its members also citizens of other nations. As an entity, it is also landless. Needless, as eminent publicist Sir Hersch Lauterpacht explains, it is not disentitling for 'bodies other than states ... [to be] made subjects of international rights and duties ... not inconsistent with the structure of international law'.[13] Accepting this, when the question is posed on what methods and means of warfare Malta used, the better enquiry is to focus on the conduct of the Order.

So, the balance of this chapter is focused on the way in which the Order assumed the exigencies of a central rule directing both those designated as part of the military arm (i.e. Knights) but also the citizenry,[14] to assist in the broader military defence of the Maltese State.

Touching upon a theme which shall be explored in greater detail below, one must pause to reflect on the fact that the Order's origins were rooted in religion which, in turn, constituted the raison d'etre for Malta's military campaign. After all, the Order is a military *religious* order, under its own papal charter, charged with the care and defence of the Holy Land. For instance, one of the entry requirements for those joining the Order was that they declare to

10 Noel Cox, 'The continuing question of sovereignty and the Sovereign Military Order of Jerusalem, of Rhodes and of Malta' (2006) 13 *Australian International Law Journal* 211, 214.

11 See, for example, Cox (n 10).

12 Hersch Lauterpacht, 'The Subjects of the Law of Nations' (1947) 63 *Law Quarterly Review* 444.

13 Lauterpacht (n 10).

14 George Cassar, 'The Role of the Maltese Inhabitants during the Great Siege', *The Great Siege 1565: Separating Fact from Fiction* (Sacra Militia Foundation 2005) 2; A F Cirni, *La Guerra ultima di francia, la celebration del Concilio Tridentino, il soccorso d'Orano, l'impresa del Pignone, e l'Historia dell'assedia di Malta* (Roma 1567) 102.

protect and defend the Christian faith. In fact, the Order was prohibited from fighting against another Christian force on the battlefield.[15] And, that before leaving the port, the corsair captain had to both swear not to attack Christians and provide a solvent surety to guarantee this obligation.

The Order's motto makes clear it had a strong spiritual foundation – *Tuitio fidei et obsequium pauperum* (defence of the faith and assistance to the poor). And, the Maltese Cross – as worn by the Order – is instructive in its symbolism. It features four v-shaped quadrilaterals, meeting at a single point in the centre. The outer edge exhibits eight points, with four arrows meeting in the middle. The four arms are said to symbolise the four cardinal virtues: prudence, justice, temperance and fortitude. While the eight points represents the Eight Beatitudes, recounted by Jesus in the Sermon on the Mount, as outlined the Gospel of Matthew. It was the symbol worn by the Order, and remains the symbol of Malta today.

Thisgoes to show how the authority of the Order blurred the lines between military regulation and social governance. Indeed records indicate that at one time, Maltese society were not organised by a central Maltese government, but by the Order.[16] Treaties were executed by the Grand Master of the Order, as *qua* head of Malta, and it was the Order that entered into negotiation and legal agreement on behalf of the State.[17] A contrarian would explain that the Order offered protection. Perhaps this was the compromise willing to be paid by the Maltese who had previously endured countless conquests. As one historian writes, '[t]ogether, the Templars and Hospitallers brought a desperately needed influx of manpower and martial expertise' to a nation 'starved of military resources'.[18] For instance, prior to the Order's efforts to fortify the archipelago a raid in 1551 saw five thousand Maltese enslaved, and Gozo completely depopulated.[19] Clearly, the Knights provided essential protection to the local inhabitants, and severely reduced the wretchedness brought upon by invading Muslim corsairs.

15 Arthur Breycha-Vauthier Michael Potulicki, 'The Order of St John in International Law: A forerunner of the Red Cross' (1954) 48(4) *The American Journal of International Law* 554, 554.

16 George Cassar, 'The Role of the Maltese Inhabitants during the Great Siege', *The Great Siege 1565: Separating Fact from Fiction*, 2.

17 Cox (n 10) 211.

18 Thomas Asbridge, The Crusaders, the Authoritative History of the War for the Holy Land (Harper Collins New York, 2010) 170.

19 Roger Crowley, *Empires of the Sea: the Final Battle for the Mediterranean, 1521–1580* (Faber & Faber 2009) 100; George Cassar (n 10) 2–3; Blouet (n 2) 62.

6 Setting Base in Malta

Guided by their religious values, fighting the 'Moslem infidel' was an underlying motive of the Order. After the Kingdom of Jerusalem fell around 1291, and having been conquered by the Sultan of Turkey, the Order moved to Cyprus.[20] They stayed till 1310[21] before moving to Rhodes. Here, the Order was established as its own State for the first time. Recapturing the island from the Turks, the Order took over the island, and the Pope concomitantly granted the Order the right to establish its own State. There they remained till 1523.[22] After an unsuccessful siege, the Order were forced to abandon Rhodes and seek temporary shelter in Italy.[23] They remained till around 1530.

In 1524 the Knights commissioned an investigation to determine the suitability of the Maltese archipelago.[24] Their assessment was gloomy: '[t]he island's defences, they said, were weak, the soil poor, resources few, well water scarce and brackish, and the people targets of frequent sea raids'.[25] Similarly, in a secondary text, it was said that Malta was a rocky island home to some twelve thousand 'impoverished natives who were a mixture of Sicilian and North Africa, speaking more Arab than Latin'.[26] Notwithstanding, there were stronger pull-factors. The harbours proved a critical drawcard and were considered essential to the Knight's fleet. Centrally located in the Mediterranean meant that it was favourably positioned in their ongoing contest against the Islamic Ottoman Empire for control in the Mediterranean.[27]

On 24 March 1530, in exchange for the promise of one falcon per year, the Order received the Maltese islands in a perpetual lease from Emperor Charles v.[28] The Order's mandate was three-fold. First, to protect Christian merchant ships, maintain a naval stronghold and suppress piracy in the Levant, particularly against the Ottoman-endorsed Barbary corsairs operating around the North African coastline. Second, to advance the Christian stronghold that had been seeded nearly three hundred years prior following the second Norman

20 Cox (n 10) 34; Bradford (n 9) 27.
21 Karski (n 9) 20–21.
22 Cox (n 10) 34.
23 Bradford (n 9) 26.
24 Alfred Cremaono, 2011 'In defence of Malta's military architecture' (Dissertation) page 11.
25 Allen (n 8) 21; Blouet (n 2) 61–62.
26 Crowley (n 20) 100.
27 Alison Hoppen, The Fortification of Malta by the Order of St John (Mireva Publications, 1999) 5.
28 C d'Olivier Farran, 'The Sovereign Order of Malta in International Law' (1954) 3(2) *The International and Comparative Law Quarterly* 217, 223; Allen (n 8) 21.

conquest.[29] Third, and finally, to fortify Malta. Absent the funds and skill, the Order relied upon the fortification of the city as a method of war. Historian Spiteri argues that '[w]ithout their fortified bases, the Knights would not have been able to take the war to their enemies, nor defend themselves'.[30] Indeed, prior to arriving in Malta, the Order had developed a fortress-building tradition. Their administration and organisational mechanism prior to 1523 was geared towards perpetual warfare, which had developed over centuries. Naturally then, the Order's settlement in Malta set off a process of militarisation which resulted in the widespread fortification of the island.

7 Methods of Warfare

The cultural impact of the Order was profound. In furtherance of the goal - to protect against Ottoman conquest – the Order set about fortifying the State. Historians point out that the Knights were 'great builders. They gradually built an enormous military base, but also many palaces and churches. There were ceaseless building. Malta was made into a centre of trade'.[31] Perhaps this is why the Maltese were receptive to the rule of the Knights: they had more to lose than to gain in resisting their direction.

8 Architecture

Prior to the Order's occupation, the island's fortifications were incapable of withstanding gunpowder artillery attacks in the new era of warfare.[32] Contemporary fortifications were essential. Historian Spiteri argues that '[w]ithout their fortified bases, the Knights would not have been able to take the war to their enemies, nor defend themselves'.[38]

Aspects of the Maltese archipelago were used as a natural defence system. Historians note that the 'stone-built fortifications of Malta make up a rare ensemble of defensive forms'.[33] Malta had a natural harbour, big enough to

---

29 Miller, *Malta* (Miller Distributers Limited 2007) 25; Allen (n 8) 5.

30 Stephen Spiteri, 'The Art of Fortress Building in Hospitaller Malta' (*BDL Publshing*, 2007) 3.

31 Hoegen Dijkhof, 'The Legitimacy of Orders of St John: a historical and legal analysis and case study of a para-religious phenomenon' (2006) 127.

32 Stephen Spiteri, 'The 'Castellu di la Chitati' the medieval castle of the walled town of Mdina' (Online Journal of Military Architecture) 1, 10.

33 Spiteri (n 31).

accommodate any size of fleet, and the abundant supply of stone was ideal for realising extensive and large-scale fortress-building programmes.[34] The Order mobilised and instructed the Maltese constructing fortresses and watch towers. [35] The ancient capital city of Mdina was fortified, and became a village composite of a labyrinth of narrow streets that only the locals knew how to expertly navigate.

> Il-fortifikazzjonijiet tal-Krucjati, kemm jekk kienu bli-
> et imdawra bis-swar kif ukoll jekk kienu kastelli, saru arma
>
> krucjali ghall-invaijoni u element indispensabbli ghad-difiia
> tal-fruntieri u 1-imkejjen ta' refugju ghal dawk il-Franki,
> ighar fil-ghadd, Ii kienu marru joqoghdu f'dawk 1-artijiet.

Which translates:
Crusader fortifications, whether walled towns or castles, became both *crucial* weapons of invasion and *indispensable* elements of frontier defence and places of refuge'.[36] In fact it has been said that had the Order not arrived in Malta, it would have likely been conquered by neighbouring States.[37] Upon its arrival, the Order set out to fortify the city. And, thirty years later, in the Great Siege (detailed further below) the Order secured victory despite being vastly undermanned and outnumbered. The fortifications were instrumental to the Order's success.[38] This is made clear when you consider how Malta was conquered prior to the fortifications, and how they succeeded following. In July 1551 a small Turkish fleet of 10,000 men landed in Marsamxett Harbour. The defence line consisted of only 800 Maltese men. The raid saw five thousand Maltese enslaved and Gozo completely depopulated.[39] This is in stark contrast to the victory achieved by the Maltese in the Great Siege in 1565.

Aqueducts are another example of how the Maltese architecture was part of a broader military campaign. The issue was the lack of a reliable and constant water supply to the capital city, Valetta. The solution was the construction of the *L-Akwedott ta'Wignacourt* (the Wignacourt Aqueduct), a 17th century

34 Spiteri (n 31) 5.
35 ibid 3–4.
36 Spiteri (n 31) (emphasis added).
37 Blouet (n 2) 61 (emphasis added).
38 Tony Bunting, 'Siege of Malta: European History 1565' (Brittanica Encyclopedia).
39 Crowley (n 20) 100; George Cassar, 'The Role of the Maltese Inhabitants during the Great Siege' *The Great Siege 1565: Separating Fact from Fiction*, 2–3; Blouet (n 2) 62.

aqueduct in Malta which was built by the Order to carry water from springs between Dingli and Rabat (districts in Malta), to the newly built capital city Valetta. The aqueduct was named after Grand Master Alof de Wignacourt, who partially financed its construction. It allowed for the Maltese to remain a stronghold behind the fortified city, in turn, resulting in a prolonged siege and (hopefully) a starved (and thirsty) invading force who would have to invariably retreat from a lack of supplies.

Rock-hewn mortars is yet another example of the way in which architecture was used. These mortars were designed to fire large quantiites of stone onto approaching ships.[40] This weapon was a unique adaptation of the fougasses-pierrier (the pierrer being a stone-firing cannon), 'particularly in its method of construction and unorthodox application in a coastal defence role'. It was powerful. It constituted three types of weapons: the fougasses, the explosive mine and the mortar. Indeed, this weapon is uniquely situated to the topography of Malta. Spiteri recalls that '[t]he local method of construction gave the weapon a permanence, solidity, and form *not enjoyed elsewhere*, especially since most fougasses were generally employed in field defences and earthworks thus earning in the process an ephemeral quality'.[41] In conclusion, this section has hoped to show how non-traditional methods of warfare were used by the Maltese.

9 Operationalising Weapons of War, during War

9.1 *Great Siege*

The Great Siege has been described as 'one of the most vaunted military confrontations of the early modern era, between the Ottoman Empire and Western Europe'.[42] On 18 May, contemporary estimates that there were between 20,000 to 40,000 Turkish troops that arrived,[43] as against a defending Maltese force of fewer than 6,000 composed of 500 Knights, 1,200 mercenaries and 4,000 (comparably unskilled) locals.[44] Maier writes how 'hastily printed maps … documented the siege's every triumph and reversal'.[45] It is crucial, therefore, to note that maps of the time depict Malta being surrounded by the Ottoman fleet.[46]

40 Spiteri (n 31) 45.
41 Ibid (emphasis added).
42 Jessica Maier, 'Cartography and Breaking News: Mapping the Great Siege of Malta' (2022) 75(1) *Renaissance Quarterly* 459, 461.
43 ibid 472; Francesco Balibi di Corregio, *The Siege of Malta 1565*, page 36.
44 Maier (n 42) 472.
45 Ibid 462–3.
46 Maier (n 42) 473.

This siege was not unexpected. Indeed, prior to the Turkish assault efforts were made to augment existing fortifications.[47] Come 1551, Ottoman fleet commander Sinan Pash raided the island but was unable to take control in Birgu or Mdina, so diverted to Gozo, and then ultimately beyond, to Tripoli.[48] A narrow escape. But, a for-warning. In response, the Order set about fortifying the island. In 1558, there was another close call when Malta was bypassed by Ottoman forces en route to Italy.[49] In response, de Valette commissioned engineers to draw up the design to fortify and protect Malta's harbour. Tensions escalated following pirate attacks by the Order, around June 1564. The Order were attributed to both capturing a large Turkish vessel, the *Sultana*, that appropriated merchandise worth 80,000 ducat (the trade coin used at the time) and influential Turkish personalities too.[50] In response, Suleiman the Magnificent – Sultan of the Ottoman said:

> I intend to conquer the island of Malta … The island of Malta is a headquarters for infidels. The Maltese have already blocked the route utilised by Muslim pilgrims and merchants in the eastern part of the White Sea, on their way to Egypt.[51]

Two observations. First, the fact that identical iterations of this statement have been referenced in multiple secondary sources vindicates the credibility of the same. Second, in speaking to the need to conquer Malta, implicitly affirms that the Order were achieving their stated aim: namely, to prevent Ottoman expansion and secure Christendom in the Levant.

---

47 ibid 470; Albert Ganado and Joseph Schiro, *The Pre-Siege Maps of Malta: Second Century AD – 1564* (BDL Publishing 2016) 89, 92.

48 Edgar Erskine Hume, 'A Proposed Alliance between the Order of Malta and the United States, 1794: Suggestions Made to James Monroe as American Minister in Paris' (1936) 16(2) *The William and Mary Quarterly* 222, 223.

49 Maier (n 42) 471; Allen (n 8) 71, 74.

50 David Abulafia, 'Akedniz – the Battle for the White Sea, 1550–1571' in David Abulafia, *The Great Sea: A Human History of the Mediterranean* (Penguin Press 2014) 429; Kevin Brown, 'The Siege of Malta, 1565' (2019) 8(2) *American International Journal of Social Science* 18, 19.

51 Ibid; Allen (n 8) 78–79.

10 Governance of Malta

The rules that applied during the Knight's rule were not concordant with those widely accepted by the European community at the time.[52]

One Historian writes that the 'Maltese islands at the time of Bonaparte's arrival were still slumbering in a benign despotic State under the Knights of Malta, who were fast approaching their last chivalric days'.[53] Chief Commissioner Regnaud de St Jean d'Angely remarked 'Priests are in charge'.[54] These observations are further corroborated by the records of Francois Bernoyer, the head official tailor of the French Army who mused at the time of France's occupation in Malta:

> All the inhabitants of the island have become French citizens and form part of the Republic. Outside the city walls, one could see sporadic miserable peasant habitations amid dry, arid land, badly cultivated. One does not see the beautiful villas usually found outside European cities; only convents, numerous chapels and wayside crosses at every corner. *It gives you a clear idea of the people's faith.*[55]

Accepting Bernoyer's description as truth, allows one to understand the depth of the Maltese faith and why – despite how 'despotic' Malta was at the time – there are scant writings on socio-political unrest during the time the Order ruled Malta.

Another way to reach this same conclusion is to consider the civil unrest that *did* occur when the Order was not the ruling force. For instance, one could look to the revolts that occurred when the French arrived in the eighteenth century. Around September 1798, a mob of Maltese looted items that were intended to

---

52 The *Del Dritto municipal di Malta* – otherwise referred to as the Codice de Rohan – was commissioned in 1776 by Grand Master, Emanuel de Rohan Polduc, the last Grand Master of the Order. Part of de Rohan's reforms included restructuring the courts and revising the Constitution. The Constitutional Charter and Code of the Order was first promulgated 27 June 1961, with later revisions (See, Order of Malta, 'Constitutional Charter and Code of the Sovereign Military Hospitaller Order of St John of Jerusalem and of Rhodes and of Malta Promulgated 27 June 1961 revised by the Extraordinary Chapter General 28–30 April 1997 (Web Page, 28 April 1987)<https://www.orderofmalta.int/wp-content/uploads/2022/02/Sovereign-Order-of-Malta-Constitutional-Charter-and-code-EN.pdf>).

53 Charles Xureb, 'Celebrating 1,000 years of Franco-Malta connections' (*Times of Malta*, 3 April 2022) <https://timesofmalta.com/articles/view/celebrating-1000-years-of-franco-maltese-connections-charles-xuereb.945351>.

54 ibid.

55 Ibid; See generally, Crowley (n 20) who provides a similar description of Malta.

raise capital for the French authorities. When the Commander of Mdina – a local village in Malta – attempted to seek order, he was murdered on the spot, his corpse allegedly thrown out a window. The Maltese insurgents then captured the neighbouring villages and within two days the French forces in Malta were corralled by the rebels. This demonstrates that the local Maltese certainly had the capacity to create social upheaval, if desired. The fact that such disorder is not documented during the time of the Order, allows the inference that the overall the system of governance introduced by the Order was – on some level – welcomed.

One could explain this by pointing to the ideological similarities between Maltese society, and the military Order. Bonaparte, by contrast, was said to introduce a substantial corpus of new domestic Orders (not rooted in religions) that promoted equality, justice, administration to wrench Malta out of the feudal niche. But, as Aquinas explained, the rise of feudalism also resulted in the division of strict class ranks, where:

> Human law may be divided according to the categories of men who perform specific tasks for the common good, as priests who pray on behalf of the people, and knights who fight for their protection.[56]

Spiteri corroborates this view finding that there 'is no denying the fact that the fortifications did provide the inhabitants with an increasing sense of security, especially from 1566 onwards'.[57] Yet, over time, a concordance in ideological beliefs between the Order and the Maltese was not enough. The numerous and ongoing fortifications schemes were costly, and the increased taxes imposed on the Maltese led to 'a growing sense of resentment among the inhabitants which, coupled with other long-standing grievances, eventually resulted in the downfall of the Order'.[58]

11 Defences to Breaches

Piracy was an intentional form of naval wafare deployed by the Order.[59] Indeed, there were regulations in place, specific to cosairing. So, to answer

56 RC Van Caenegem, *Legal History: A European Perspective* (Hambledon 1991) 118.

57 ibid.

58 Spiteria (n 31).

59 Choice Higham 'The Maltese Cross: a strategic history of Malta' (2006) 44(3) *Praeger Security International;* Cox (n 10) 211.

the question, what was permissible, one must understand the necessities at the time. Simply put, the Order needed money (the cost of fortifying Malta was expensive). A core supply of the Order's income was sourced from the cargo – both chattels and humans alike – obtained from infidel ships seized by the Knights.[60] For instance, influential figures were known to be ransomed. Historians go so far as to suggest that the capture of influential figure was a 'decisive factor' that led to the Siege of Malta. [61] Moreover, the Order sold captives into the island's burgeoning slave market. Upon the corsairs application, licences were granted by the Grand Master (which makes clear that this conduct was endorsed by the State). If granted, the Knights were entitled to keep a portion of the proceeds obtained from goods seized.[62] Critically, this 'method' of warfare was in flagrant disregard of the norm against slavery, which was crystallising at the time. At this point, we draw the conclusion that causes of action that would 'ordinarily' constitute a breach of international laws of war, did not apply in Malta.

12 Consequences that followed

So, we know that the sixteenth-century Mediterranean was not a safe place to sail; it was infested with corsairs and pirates, both Muslim and Christian, who preyed on merchant ships and coastal towns. Yet, little is known about the consequences that followed. If religion was used to justify typically non-Christian practices, one is left questioning whether breaches *did* indeed flow? Absent evidence to suggest so, only strengthens the conclusion that such practices were justified. The below anaysis occurs within the realm of speculation.

This is clearly seen in Malta's tolerance of slavery. Crowley suggests that the Order swept 'the seas for Islamic plunder and slaves in the name of religion ... [t]he line between crusading and lucrative piracy was *wafer-thin*'.[63] Historians have noted how'the Knights institutionalised debt slaves'.[64] 'Buonavoglia' referred to an individual who could discharge their debts by rowing a galley for several years. This practice was plainly at odds with the prohibition on slavery which was crystalising at the time (for instance, the Declaration against the

60 Allen (n 8) 74.

61 Roger Crowley, Empires of the Sea: the Final Battle for the Mediterranean, 1521–1580 (Faber & Faber 2009) 95.

62 Dijkhof (n 32) 79.

63 Ibid, p. 84 (emphasis added).

64 Dijkhof (n 32) 43.

slave trade was made a part of the Congress of Vienna in 1815).[65] Historians further observe that there was an established practice of exchanging slaves with Christian prisoners captured in Berber States.[66] In 1798, when Napoleon occupied Malta, approximately 525 Turkish slaves were found.[67] Indeed, slavery in Malta was only abolished on 16 June 1798 when Napoleon abolished debt slavery and annulled the Buonavoglia contracts. These examples allow the inference that under the Knight's rule, much was rendered permissible.

13 Breaches of Laws (?) of War

Handicapped by the lack of historical writings on questions of law at the time (and enforcement of the same) it is difficult to postulate with any surety what consequences flowed from breaches. The Knights Code of Chivalry was a moral system that stated all Knights should protect others who cannot protect themselves. What transpired is the acceptance of some un-Christian behaviour, paradoxically, in pursuit of this value. Religion was used to mask and legitimise conduct that would otherwise be considered contrary to accepted practice. Indeed, academics write how corsairs achieved a 'level of brutality to warfare not seen since Roman times, particularly towards Muslims', driven by what was called 'sheer [religious] fanaticism'.[68]

The method of warfare utilised by the Knights was not uniquely Maltese. Historical accounts report that in the latter half of the sixteenth century, there was an 'explosion of piratical violence' in the eastern half of the Mediterranean in the decades following the Ottoman conquest of Cyprus.[69] The Maltese cosairs shared many of the forms and practices of violence as their Ottoman and Venetian cosairs.[70] Whether Muslim or Christian these individuals were collectively referred to as '*korsan*'. The collective noun demonstrates that the conduct carried no specific ethnic or geographic association, but was instead reflective of a common experience and accepted practice at sea. Further, a fundamental tenant of both Muslim and Christian corsairs was that religion

65 Ian Clark, *International Legitimacy and World Society* (Oxford University Press 2007) 43.
66 Dijkhof (n 32) 43.
67 Dijkhof (n 32) 43.
68 David Crowe, 'War Crimes and Genocide in History, and the Evolution of Responsive International Law' 37(6) *Nationalities Papers* 757, 758.
69 Joshua White, 'Holy Warriors, Rebels and Thieves: Defining Maritime Violence in the Ottoman Mediterranean' in *Piracy in World History*, 151.
70 ibid 155.

was used to legitimise seaborne violence and plundering. In turn, one could postulate how customs were created around seaborne practice of warfare. Indeed, the fact that historical sources do not have much to say with respect to breaches of law at the hands of the Knights (who mostly carried out siege warfare) may be viewed that it was accepted practice, and thus did not merit any comment.

14 Case Study – Corsaring in Malta

Corsairing in Malta has been categorised under three banners:

(a) *First,* corsairing as practiced by private corsairs who received a license to fly the flag of the Order; or

(b) *Second,* corsairing as organised by rich private Knights, including General Masters; or

(c) *Third,* the Order's galley squadron which, accompanied by other vessels of the Order, organised its yearly corsairing captains against Muslim ships and towns.

At first blush, there is an argument to be made that the classification of acceptable types of corsairing indicates that prescribing such conduct not only came without consequence, but that it was a recognised and accepted mode of warfare.

Academics note how the thuggery of piracy was cloaked in a legitimate form of warfare if it was sufficiently proximate to sovereign power and instruction.[71] The Grand Master of the Knights had the right to receive ten percent of the sale of captured Moslem slaves, shipping and merchandise that were carried on Christian ships.[72] Further, Maltese corsairs were bound to observe the strictest neutrality between other Christian nations, but could freely plunder others. Raids were a backbone of the Knights' economic military system. They were labelled as 'commerce raids' and seen as nothing more than a way for the Order to increase its economy might. In fact, there was a parasistic relationship between the cosairs and the slave trade. Slaves were used to maintain the military fleets which facilitated cosair. It is perhaps unsurprising then that Malta

---

71 Andrew Opitz, 'Agents of Chaos and Unlawful Combatants: Piracy in Philosophy and Law' (2011) 7(1) *Cultural Politics* 157, 159.

72 Thomas Freller, 'Aversus Infidels': Some notes on the Cavallier's Tour, and Fleet of the Order of St John, and the Maltese Corsairs' (Koninklijke Brill 2000) 405, 409.

is said to have become the hub of slavery in Christian Europe.[73] Bonello writes about the way slaves were relegated as rowers on the galleys:

> they lived the duration of a sea journey chained to benches, not being released for any reason. They usually relieved themselves on their immediate workplace, in an ambiance of unbearable stench. An *agozzino* enforced discipline.[74]

The 'agozzino' as referred to by Bonello, relates to the policing system that was in place to regulate the conduct of both the cosairs and the slaves. The 'agozzino' were tasked with general security, and were directly responsible for the slaves and buonavoglia (volunteer rowers on the galleys), ensuring that none of them escaped.[75] Interestingly, in modern day the word 'argużin' in Maltese refers to a heartless person who can only dish out cruelty. It therefore comes to no surprise that it is reported that '[s]ome slaves self-mutilated grievously, just to avoid galley service'.[76] From this, one can conclude that under the Order, slaves lacked agency. One historian states that on 4 October 1535, one agozzino of the Order's galleon received instructions to accept any slaves aged from twenty to twenty-six who had been procured for the Order by another Knight.[77] The Agozzino's operated under the State command. Pointedly, no consequences flowed from their conduct.

For instance, Judge Guilio Cumbo was appointed by the Grand Master Perollos in 1698. Yet, this Judge enforced a rule of law that was plainly at odds with international law. An instrument referred to as the 'Spanish donkey' – its original Italian name 'cavelletto squarciapalle' became known in Malta as 'iż-żiemel ta' Cumbo' from the constant use made of it by Judge Guilio Cumbo. His Honour was said to have condemned to death 123 individuals on the apparatus.

In offering a religious licence, the foundations were laid for the Order to conduct itself in an otherwise unaccepted manner.[78] In fact, some Ottoman Christians who were captured by the Knights were said to receive more lenient

73 Russell Palmer, Slavery, captivity and galley rowing in early modern Malta (Cambridge University Press 2021).

74 Giovanni Bonello, 'Tragic Tales of Slaves in Malta' (16 July 2022, *Times of Malta*).

75 Godfrey Wettinger, 'The Galley-Convicts and Buonavoglia in Malta during the rule of the Order' 29, 29.

76 Ibid.

77 Ibid 29–30.

78 Salzmann (n 87), 411.

treatment.[79] Salzmann argues how Malta made confessional identity a zero-sum game, finding that:

> [w]ithin the Mediterranean, there is no little doubt that faith played a determining role in the forced transfer of populations. Some states, notably the Knights of St John at Malta, made confessional identity a zero-sum game. All non-Catholics – Orthodox Christians, Muslims and Jews alike – found aboard Muslim ships could be seized … Maltese captains would routinely … [confiscate] the cargo of Jews and Muslims. Even Jews with the requisite permits and passports would be sent to the slave auctions in La Valetta.[80]

So, while there is a lacuna as to the law that applied, clearly there was a consistency in the kind of conduct that was allowed at the time. The best explanation available, is that religion was used to justify the Knight's conduct. Efforts to anchor Christendom in Malta permitted the use of un-Christian practices to create a cordon sanitaire between the competing advance of Islam and non-monotheistic populations. Indeed, slavery was accepted in some readings of Roman Catholicism. John Chrysostom, who is regarded as a Saint in Roman Catholicism argued that slaves should be resigned to their fate, because by 'obeying his master, he is obeying God'.[81] At this point, we conclude that methods of warfare adopted by the Order were rooted in religious justifications, even if contrary to accepted rules of warfare.

15 Systems of Governance

In time, systems were put in place to regulate the burgeoning pirating industry. Once a corsair received the appropriate licences from the Grand Master, there conduct was legitimate, distinct from an infidel or a thief.

On 17 June 1605, the Grand Master established a court called the *Magistrato degli Armamenti*, a court of first instance, where any cause concerning the

79 Molly Greene, Catholic Pirates and Greek Merchants: A Maritime History of the Mediterranean (Princeton University Press 2010) 115.

80 Ariel Salzmann, 'Migrants in Chains: On the Enslavement of Muslims in Renaissance and Enlightenment Europe' 4(3) *Religions* 391; Wettinger (n 82) 40.

81 Henri Daniel-Rops, *Cathedral and Crusade* (1957) 263. Further, Augustine of Hippo explained that slavery was part of the mechanism to preserve the natural order of things. See, Elaine Pagels, *Adam, Eve and the Serpent* (1988) 114.

Maltese corsairs was heard. All corsairs who were licensed to sail with the flag of the Order were subjected to the Magistrato. It was comprised of five Commissioners, all of which were nominated personally by the Grand Master with a two-year tenure.[82] Their main role was to settle disputes between individual amateurs and their captains and to sort out the division of booty.[83] Later, in 1697, a second tribunal known as the *Consolato del Mare* was set up in response to the increased case load. Privateering was regulated, breaches of which were punishable by prison or hard labour aboard the galleys. Caveliero writes: '[t]he rules were simple: any Turkish or Infidel vessel was legitimate gain, and any Christian vessel was not'.[84] Needless, the establishment of these admiralty courts demonstrate an attempt to create a system of governance. Mark Hanna notes that a:

> primary reason for the rise of vice-admiralty courts in the fourteenth and fifteenth centuries as the attempt to regulate and restrain some of the outrages that inevitably stemmed from private warfare, distinguishing between legitimate acts of war and overt piracy.[85]

16 Adjudication and Division of Loot

Historians note that aggression was a characteristic of seaborne trade. Accordingly, violence was not an unfamiliar feature of early-modern period sea going merchants.[86]

Authorised plunders may have looked like Christian corsairs from the West venturing eastward to plunder Turkish ships and possessions in the Levant; while Moslem sea robbers from the Barbary coast attacked European ships and ports.[87] If successful, the corsair would return to its home port. At the time, Malta was said to serve as a market for the spoils of war that could be disposed of quickly. Indeed, historical accounts speak to the 'business' of piracy. In this way, the corso was an instrument for the dispossession and appropriation of

82 Paul Caruna Curran, 'The Maltese Corsairs' page 1.

83 Roderic Caveliero, 'The Decline of the Maltese Corso in the XVIIth Century: A Study of Maritime History' (Paper read at St Albert the Great College, Valetta on 29 May 1956) 225.

84 Caveliero (n 91) 225.

85 MG Hanna, Pirate Nests and the Rise of the British Empire, 1570–1750 (2015) 40.

86 NAM Rodger, 'The Law and Language of Private Naval Warfare' (2014) 100(1) *The Mariner's Mirror* 5, 6.

87 Paul Cassar, 'The Maltese Corsairs and the Order of St John of Jerusalem' (1960) 46(2) *The Catholic Historical Review* 137, 137.

revenue on the opposing shores of the Mediterranean in an atmosphere of rivalry between competing nationalities. A core supply of income was sourced from the cargo seized by the corsairs – both chattels and humans alike. On this lens, piracy was an intentional form of warfare deployed by the Order. Needless, at its highest, the abstention from crystallising norms against such conduct – or at minimum, acquiescence of the same – goes towards demonstrating that the conduct was endorsed. Benefiting from the spoils of the corsairs meant that Malta's position was one of general disregard of conventional international law.

17 Defences – Implied Immunity and Sovereign Orders

This behaviour is at paradox with the Knights guiding principles of chivalry. So, how was it accepted? Siege warfare – the type of warfare monopolised by the Knights – was uniquely designed to 'distress the enemy more by famine than the sword'.[88] In monopolising non-traditional methods and means of warfare, corsairing was viewed as a 'staple industry'[89] of the island: a way to amass wealth and resources for the Order. Needless, Maltese corsairs enjoyed religious sanction. And, in turn, separated them from mere pirates engaging in unlawful banditry.

Further, in many instances of Roman history, actions by individuals could be absolved if they were *remotion criminis* or *metastasis* or as modern translations called it, the defence of superior orders. The position was posited by Justinian as:

> He who causes loss who orders it to be caused; but he is without blame *culpa,* who is under the necessity of obeying.[90]

The corsairs flew the Grand Master's flag, and in turn were subject to the Grand Court.[91] Raids conducted under the cover of law were considered lawful, and

88 Vegetius, *The Military Institutions of the Romans* (Greenwood Press Westport, Westport) 11.

89 Roderic Caveliero, 'The Decline of the Maltese Corso in the XVIIIth Century: A Study of Maritime History' (Paper read at St Albert the Great College, Valletta on 29 May 1956). Thomas Freller, 'Aversus Infidels': Some Notes on the Cavalier's Tour, the Fleet of the Order of St John, and the Maltese Corsairs' (Koninklijke Brill 2000) 405, 409.

90 Lenel, Palisgenesia Juris Civilis 1889, I 1150.

91 Andrew Opitz, 'Agents of Chaos and Unlawful Combatants: Pirates in Philosophy and Law' (2011) 7(1) *Cultural Politics* 157, 159.

their accumulated booty all but the recompense of heroes. Unauthorised plunders, by contrast, were seen to be governed by the laws of nature rather than the laws of the State. The Knights could rely upon patronage from the Grand Master, which afforded them the capacity to pursue piratical warfare without consequence. For instance, before leaving port, the corsair captain had to swear an oath that it would not attack Christians, and to concomitantly provide a solvent surety (*pleggio di bandiera*) to guarantee this obligation. Furthermore, this idea that otherwise unlawful conduct could be legitimated by a grand sovereign (in this instance, the Grand Master) concords with Cicero's theorem of sovereign orders. Cicero explains that by pleading *remotion criminis*, an agent disassociated themselves from the entire affair.

Predictably, historians reflect that the administration of justice was severely undermined in such a paradigm. The sovereign had a vested interest in piracy. That said, it *did* amass wealth and power for Malta, and created the illusion of strength and military fortitude, which in turn, increased Malta's security in the Mediterranean.

18 Conclusion

This chapter has hoped to demonstrate that under the Knight's rule, much was rendered permissible. It was explained how religion was used to excuse practices that were in flagrant disregard of international norms that were crystallising at the time. Indeed, religion was used to demarcate the line between lawful practices of warfare and piracy. It is hoped that this chapter provided a unique perspective into the way in which non-traditional methods and means of warfare were monopolised to fight mightier powers.

Conclusion

> If you have no more to tell us than that one barbarian succeeded another on the banks of the Oxus or Ixartes, what use are you to the public?[1]
>
> VOLTAIRE

Jean Pictet, one of most famous scholars and practitioners of the laws of war addressed the universality of what he titled 'international humanitarian law'. He held that:

> humanitarian principles are common to all human communities wherever they may be. When different customs, ethics and philosophies are gathered for comparison, and when they are melted down, their particularities eliminated and only what is general extracted, one is left with a pure substance which is the heritage of all mankind.[2]

What this work has sought to address is this 'pure substance'. Every chapter, in every volume, to me is a 'dataset'. The secondary research questions emerge then from having wider 'datasets' to find patterns in. Whilst approaching a critical mass of comparative case studies, we can begin to use *The Laws of Yesterday's Wars* as a resource to try address some of the more difficult questions in international humanitarian law through a truly international lens: who should be considered directly participating in hostiles? Is there a historical argument for 'sharp war'? Have the laws of war sought to protect non-combatants, or empower combatants? When does the principle of military necessity find a limit?

These questions – and more – go to the heart of the issue raised in the introduction: what is the inter-relationship of the laws of war, and customs of war? The earlier is understood to be codified, in a tradition that the ICRC harks back

1 I. Berlin, *The Crooked Timbre of Humanity* (New York, 1991) 52–3.

2 Jean Pictet, "Humanitarian Ideas Shared by Different Schools of Thought and Cultural Traditions", in Jean Pictet (ed.) *International Dimensions of Humanitarian Law* (Henry Dunant Institute, M. Nijhoff, 1988) 3, 4.

 | DOI:10.1163/9789004512566_011

to the Lieber Code,[3] but clearly pre-dates the European tradition of Medieval Europe. It is an important point to stress. Studies that claim to reflect customary international humanitarian law (CIHL), whilst commendable, can be questioned as to methodology and datasets. The *Laws of Yesterday's Wars* provides a wider authority that can be relied upon to critically engage with issues of IHL – such as the contentious issue of when a civilian is directly participating in hostilities, that the conclusion of Volume 2 analysed.[4]

To that end, in the conclusion to Volume 3, I wanted to reflect upon some customs that are supported by the International Committee of the Red Cross' CIHL study and others that are not. In doing so, it methodically works through the series volume by volume, chapter by chapter. It has deliberately not engaged with the European chapters (Medieval Europe, Renaissance period, Lieber Code, pirates & privateers) as these are reflected in wider discussions about the Eurocentricity of IHL. Whilst many more principles of IHL could be discussed – the concepts of reprisals; prohibited weapons; precautions in an attack; or mutilation – it focuses upon four rules which are most contentious, and most fundamental, to modern IHL.

1 Customs of War Supported

Rule 1 – Distinction of Combatant/Non-combatant

It is fitting that the first rule that the *Laws of Yesterday's Wars* supports is, indeed, Rule 1 of the CIHL. That Rule reads:

> The parties to the conflict must at all times distinguish between civilians and combatants. Attacks may only be directed against combatants. Attacks must not be directed against civilians.

Although the principle of distinction was first codified in the laws of war in the *St. Petersburg Declaration*, which states that "the only legitimate object which States should endeavour to accomplish during war is to weaken the military forces of the enemy"[5] it is clear that the concept existed prior to that. These studies have shown that almost all cultures analysed have demonstrated a

3 Jean-Marie Henckaerts & Louise Doswald-Beck, 'Introduction' in *Customary International Humanitarian Law Study* (Cambridge University Press, 2003) ('CIHL Study').

4 Rule 6 – CIHL Study.

5 St. Petersburg Declaration, preamble (cited in Vol. II, Ch. 1, § 83).

divide between combatant and non-combatant; those that are in the fight and those that are not.

Volume 1 highlighted that First Nation Australians were a society that divided itself into distinct groups: initiated and uninitiated; male and female; Elders and not. Warfare itself reflected these distinctions, and there were clear customs that regulated who was targetable, by who, in armed conflict.[6] Oral records, and colonial observations, makes clear that it was considered a blatant breach of the customs of warfare if one category of people (uninitiated) were to target another (initiated, women & children, or Elders).[7] Within the Maori Wars, Profession Gillespie highlighted four categories of non-combatants recognised by Maori chieftains and codified in their conflict against the British: those *hors de combat,* soldiers unarmed, soldiers who flee the battlefield into a church, as well as women & children.[8] The Mexica exhibited a society where one's military ranking – denoted by explicit rights to clothing and hairstyles – dictated roles both on and off the battlefield. Warfare itself revolved around the seeking, engagement and hopeful capture of, similar ranked individuals on the battlefield.[9] Warfare, with the exception of one's first season of fighting, was a solitary endeavour. To that end, those not of a similar rank were viewed as non-combatants and it was viewed as a gregarious breach of custom to target someone of a lower rank.[10] Vikings too exhibited a clear distinction between combatants and non-combatants. This was, however, an internal divide. Externally, there were limited distinctions made between those who could be targeted and those who could not, which reflected a pragmatic approach to raiding. Internally, society recognised distinctions between *haulds* (multi-generational farmers), *thralls* (slaves) and freedmen, as well as those who went *Vikingr* – pillaging. True heroes (*kappar*) could ascend to Valhalla, whilst those who went *berserkirs* could not, as they lacked honour.[11]

Volume 2 reinforces support of the principle of distinction's customary status. Zuzana Spicova, in an excellent piece of work, shows warfare to be the 'duty of adult male *ksatriyas,* (where) everyone else is theoretically excluded

6 Ray Kerkhove & Samuel White, 'Indigenous Australian Laws of War' in Samuel White (ed.) *The Laws of Yesterday's Wars* 3–44.

7 Ibid, 31.

8 Alexander Gillepsie, 'Maori Laws of War' in Samuel White (ed.) *The Laws of Yesterday's Wars* 45–68.

9 Samuel White & Ray Kerkhove, 'The Aztecs' in Samuel White (ed.) *Laws of Yesterday's Wars Volume* (Brill Nijhoff, 2021) 69–101.

10 Ibid, 75.

11 Andrew Butler, 'Viking Laws of War' in Samuel White (ed.) *The Laws of Yesterday's Wars* (Brill Nijhoff, 2021) 150–171.

from it'.[12] The *Mahabharata* shows that 'an old man and a young boy should not be killed, nor a woman and a twice-born [holy person], one with a mouth full of grass, and one who says: "I am yours"'.[13] The concept of *ksatriyas* moreover extended to not fighting against someone who was crippled, or even ugly.[14] Hellenic laws of war – exemplified through the city-state of Carthage – did not prohibit targeting those who were beauty-challenged, but did prohibit the targeting of sacred locations, sacred individuals (such as envoys and heralds) and prohibitions on mutilating bodies.[15] These rules, relevantly, did not apply in siege warfare – a principle carried through to Roman laws of war. This is perhaps were the similarities end; the Roman concept of *guerre mortelle* was famously known as the Roman way of war.[16] Siege warfare was particularly brutal, and deliberately so. Yet the nuances of Roman law are perhaps lost on a modern audience. Roman laws of war divided combatants into those legally accepted (the *hostius justus*) and those incompatible – pirates, slaves, rebels.[17] Cicero held that:

> reason has taught to the wise: necessity to the barbarians, custom to the *gentes* and nature to brute beasts that they should repulse on every occasion by every means all violence to their bodies, their heads and their lives.[18]

The Qur'an, and several *hadiths*, command combatants to 'fight in the way of God those who fight against you and do not transgress'.[19] Dr Al-Dawoody expands on this, showing that women, children, the aged, the clergy and the *usafa* (combat service supporters) should remain outside of hostilities.[20] Limiting warfare was integral to North-Eastern Native American Nations, although the principle of distinction as about the *nature* of warfare (big wars

12 Zuzana Spicova, 'Ancient Indian Laws of War' in Samuel White (ed.) *The Laws of Yesterday's Wars Volume II* (Brill Nijhoff, 2022) 5–45.

13 Having grass in one's mouth is apparently a signifier of surrender, being analogous to being a cow.

14 David Feeny, 'Carthaginian Laws of War' in Samuel White (ed.) *The Laws of Yesterday's Wars Volume II* (Brill Nijhoff, 2022) 45–110.

15 Ibid.

16 Samuel White, 'Roman Laws of War' in Samuel White (ed.) *Laws of Yesterday's Wars Volume II* (Brill Nijhoff, 2022) 110–126.

17 Ibid, 115.

18 *Pro Milone*, XI, 30.

19 Qu'ran, 2:190.

20 Ahmed Al-Dawoody, 'Islamic Laws of War' in Samuel White (ed.) *The Laws of Yesterday's Wars Volume II* (Brill Nijhoff, 2022) 126–146.

or little wars) rather than those in it.[21] Scalps could be taken from women, children, Elders or military-aged males.[22] Women, however, were more generally protected as their capture formed the basis for marriage.[23] Anna Kretowitz makes the point, when reflecting on *bushido* or the customs of Japanese samurai warfare, that treatment of non-combatants was entirely circumstantial.[24] These circumstances however were rather definite – whether individuals were on the battlefield (armed or unarmed) or whether they were not. Convention – *kirisute gomen* – allowed for samurai to kill those below them in the social hierarchy, but there is little documentary evidence to suggest this occurred, and the *Kujikata Osadamegaki* – a compendium of criminal laws in 1742 AD – suggests that unnecessary violence was to be abstained.[25] Volume 2 concluded with a discussion on the large socio-ethnic bloc of East Africa, including Kenya, Uganda, and Ethiopia. Mutama and Massingham highlight that women, children, envoys, priests and rainmakers were all excluded from targeting by the Maasai: 'it was thus a spectacle to see Maasai women walking with impunity in a battlefield'[26] completely unmolested. Indeed, "Maasai warriors in East Africa wore distinctive armbands to distinguish themselves from the civilian population."[27] Amongst the Somali, they recount that the general principle of 'those oblivious to the war' should be excluded.

This Volume has challenged, however, the consistency of the principle of distinction. It started with a discussion of Highland Papua New Guinean warfare, reflected in modern practice. Macdonald and Kirami explained that Highland warfare has historical been seen throughout the highlands as a strictly male domain.[28] Wars were "men's affairs" and a woman's place was to ensure that warriors were fed and the domestic sphere was maintained.[29] However, Emily Defina contended that "whether or not a woman could be considered a legitimate target depended on consideration as to whether injury to her would be

21 Wayne E. Lee, 'Eastern Native American Laws of War' in Samuel White (ed.) *The Laws of Yesterday's Wars Volume II* (Brill Nijhoff, 2022) 146–183.

22 Ibid.

23 Wayne E. Lee, 'Eastern Native American Laws of War' in Samuel White (ed.) *The Laws of Yesterday's Wars Volume II* (Brill Nijhoff, 2022) 146, 177.

24 Japanese Laws of War' in Samuel White (ed.) *The Laws of Yesterday's Wars Volume II* (Brill Nijhoff, 2022) 183–214.

25 Ibid, 202.

26 Kenneth Mutuma and Eve Massingham, 'East African Laws of War' in Samuel White (ed.) *The Laws of Yesterday's Wars Volume II* (Brill Nijhoff, 2022) 214–241.

27 Sarah Jean Mabeza, 'Changing the Narrative: A Tool on African Traditions' (2022) 104 *International Review of the Red Cross* 1638–1649.

28 See p. 16.

29 See p. 16.

advantageous or disadvantageous to the group as a whole, in terms of the retribution it would attract."[30] Sanoj Rajan and Sheena Sivadasan however showed the principle of distinction in the highly regulated and ritualised Keralite tradition of *ankam* (duel) – a type of battle or combat, frequently employed in feudal mediaeval Kerala as a means of resolving conflicts that could not be resolved by local political assemblies. There was also a form of ankam known as *poithu*, which involved two people engaging in a duel. To ensure that all participants in *ankam* or *poithu* could acquire the utmost degree of competence with kalaripayattu's traditional weaponry, the participants had up to 12 years of training and preparation before the ankam was actually fought.[31] Professional mercenaries with *kalaripayattu* training were occasionally paid to perform *ankam* on behalf of others.[32] Those without training – being a majority of the population – were therefore non-combatants. The Mongol tradition was such that there was a clear distinction – contrary to popular opinion – between combatant and non-combatant. Whilst those in *mo balya* – bad cities – were punished *en masse*, the experiences of the Mongols dealing with the Tartars highlighted that when the ultimate punishment of dispersing a tribe was enforced, it was limited still to men taller than the linchpin on the wheels of a cart.[33] Steppe women & children (male and female, with some exceptions for blood enemies) were still viewed as non-combatants; this was found within the nomadic cultures of the Cossacks. Another culture that has been re-constructed by popular opinion was that of the head-hunting Iban. Dr Angeline Lewis outlined expertly the concept of *adat*, and recounted the instructions given after the submission of the Kantu tribe by Rukok instructed Sampar. Guiltless tribes were non-combatants, as were surrendered enemies.[34] This reflected a wider practice that '[a]ny mature man who had occasion to mount an attack ... could become a *pun ngayau* (originator of war),' whom others could choose to join if they wished.[35] Those who wished to stay out of the fight could, and were intended to remain protected – a cardinal principle found within the various ethnic groups in South Sudan (such as within the Nuer community, where non-combatants were to be alerted to hostilies as soon as possible and would warn others through the 'wewe'). Samara J. Cassar offers a unique contrast of Christian values, shaped by environmental factors of the

30 See p. 17
31 See p. 126.
32 See p. 133.
33 See p. 41.
34 See p. 155.
35 See p. 156.

Middle Sea. Piracy was key to the economy of Malta, and national security in creating a *cordon sanitaire*. Yet distinctions were still made about who could be targeted: fellow Christians were forbidden, but all others were allowed.[36] This provides for an interesting contrast to the Elizabethan piracy covered in Volume 1.[37]

This is to say that whilst the principle of distinction is now codified in Articles 48, 51(2) and 52(2) of Additional Protocol I, it is clearly a customary principle that pre-exists the laws of Geneva and the laws of the Hague. The principle of distinction is a strongly supported, resilient concept of international humanitarian law. It is not necessarily matched by a definition of what a civilian is, which Rule 5 outlines as:

> Civilians are persons who are not members of the armed forces. The civilian population comprises all persons who are civilians

Custom, for the most part, probably supports a wider definition of the male, fighting-age population. For the most part however, these Volumes have demonstrated that women (Rule 134) and children (135) seem to have been historically protected across time and space – albeit for various reasons. So too have the elderly, disabled and infirm (Rule 138).

Rule 6: Direct Participation in Hostilities

Another rule, relating to the principle of distinction, is that protection is lost when civilians directly participate in hostilities. Rule 6 reads:

> civilians are protected against attack, unless and for such time as they take a direct part in hostilities.

A precise definition of the term "direct participation in hostilities" does not exist, and it remains a vexed issue in modern IHL today. The topic was discussed passingly in the conclusion to Volume 2; but merits further analysis.

The Inter-American Commission on Human Rights has stated that the term "direct participation in hostilities" is generally understood to mean "acts which, by their nature or purpose, are intended to cause actual harm to enemy

36 See p. 170.

37 Andrew Read, 'Pirates and Privateers' in Samuel White (ed.) *Laws of Yesterday's Wars Volume* (Brill Nijhoff, 2021) 171–187.

personnel and matériel".[38] There is little or no guidance however on the interpretation of the term "direct participation". The military manuals of Ecuador and the United States give several examples of acts constituting direct participation in hostilities, such as serving as guards, intelligence agents or lookouts on behalf of military forces.[39] The Report on the Practice of the Philippines similarly considers that civilians acting as spies, couriers or lookouts lose their protection against attack.[40]

What do wider historical practices show? The First Nations of Australia distinguished between combatants and non-combatants in warfare. First Nation tribes, in most battles, employed the use of women, children and sometimes elders to recover spears and other thrown implements. Great care was taken to ensure that 'a picker-up of spears' was not targeted – even though this seems, at first brush, some level of direct participation.[41] Additionally, there was a general protection for Elders protecting them from violence in regulated battles.[42] However, they continued to take part in duels against rival peers, and would provide command and control in regulated battles.[43] The threshold for direct participation seems rather high. During the conflict of the Far North, Heike, one of the leaders of the Nga Puhi tribe, tried to avoid the killing of 400 civilians.[44] However, during the Dirty War, Te Kooti and his followers killed 56 Ngati Pahauwere man, women and children, and committed atrocities against settler families.[45] While these atrocities occurred, he was punished by the Crown for these actions.[46] In addition to these sanctions, on 28 March 1864, Henare Taratoa drafted a code to provide to the enemy with respect to the rules regulating the conflict. Rule 4 stated that '[t]he unarmed Pakehas, women, and children, will be spared'.[47] Those armed fell under the concept of directly participating.

38 Inter-American Commission on Human Rights, *Third report on human rights in Colombia* (§ 811).

39 Ecuador, *Naval Manual* (§ 822); United States, *Naval Handbook* (§ 829).

40 Report on the Practice of the Philippines (*ibid.*, § 849).

41 Ray Kerkhove & Samuel White, 'Indigenous Australian Laws of War' in Samuel White (ed.) *The Laws of Yesterday's Wars* 3, 39.

42 Ibid, 38.

43 Ray Kerkhove, *How They Fought* (Boonalong Press, 2023).

44 Alexander Gillepsie, 'Maori Laws of War' in Samuel White (ed.) *The Laws of Yesterday's Wars* 45, 46.

45 Ibid, 65.

46 Ibid, 65.

47 Ibid, 58.

Outside of a siege construct,[48] Mexica practice highlighted that direct participation was for those of the same rank; participation and distinction thus went hand-in-hand. To that end, porters (*tlamemeh*) were sacrosanct, and considered indirectly participating even if they were actively engaged in hostilities. Dr Zuzana recounted that war was the duty of adult males; theoretically, everybody else was excluded from harm in ancient Indian warfare.[49] This meant, young boys, old men and women were protected from harm.[50] Members of non-combatant staff in battle were never killed – this included, charioteers, horses, those who bring weapons, drummers or conch-blowers.[51] However, if they engaged in battle, it was fair to strike them.[52]

Consistent with the exceptionalism of siege warfare, Carthaginians practice would be to offer terms for surrender (including freedom and giving quarter). However, if they did not accept, a siege would begin.[53] There were no protections.[54] Accordingly, the Carthaginians were permitted to slaughter or enslave an entire city that had to be taken by force.[55] During the raid of Selinute, only the women and children that took refuge in the city's temples were spared.[56] Similarly to their Carthaginian neighbours, if the Romans were required to take a city by force, there was no mercy for non-combatants.[57] They debauched and killed without hesitation.[58] During the capture of Cremonia in 69 AD, it was a free for all – the Romans indulged in lust and cruelty, killing whoever they pleased. However, non-combatants were to be spared by the Roman's in other circumstances – although, this was discretionary.[59]

As noted in the conclusion to Volume 2, Islamic law requires that fighting be directed solely against enemy combatants.[60] Accordingly, the *usafā* – those

48 Samuel White & Ray Kerkhove, 'The Aztecs' in Samuel White (ed.) *Laws of Yesterday's Wars Volume* (Brill Nijhoff, 2021) 69, 81.

49 Zuzana Spicova, 'Ancient Indian Laws of War' in Samuel White (ed.) *The Laws of Yesterday's Wars Volume II* (Brill Nijhoff, 2022) 5, 18.

50 Ibid, 19.

51 Ibid, 19.

52 Ibid, 19.

53 David Feeny, 'Carthaginian Laws of War' in Samuel White (ed.) *The Laws of Yesterday's Wars Volume II* (Brill Nijhoff, 2022) 45–103.

54 Ibid, 103.

55 Ibid, 103.

56 Ibid, 103.

57 Samuel White, 'Roman Laws of War' in Samuel White (ed.) *Laws of Yesterday's Wars Volume II* (Brill Nijhoff, 2022) 110–115.

58 Ibid, 116.

59 Ibid, 118.

60 Ahmed Al-Dawoody, 'Islamic Laws of War' in Samuel White (ed.) *The Laws of Yesterday's Wars Volume II* (Brill Nijhoff, 2022) 126, 136.

hired by the enemy to provide supporting services to the battlefield, but did not engage in the fighting – were viewed as not participating. Civilians and non-combatants were protected from deliberate attacks during the course of hostilities, a practice adopted and maintained by the Ottomans (as noted in this Volume).[61] However, if they engaged in hostilities, they lost their protection.[62]

There is substantial evidence that Native Americans engaged in indiscriminate destruction.[63] The Pequots informed the English settling in Connecticut that they would 'kill men, women, and children, and … will take away the horses, cows and hogs'.[64] The killing of children and women occasionally occurred, although adoption was often preferred.[65] The code of *bushido* did not provide a strict rule for the treatment of non-combatants in military attacks or battles.[66] For the most part, non-combatants in battle would be killed alongside combatants.[67] Outside of a battle, samurai had the right to kill civilians.[68] Disrespect or rudeness justified death, as it was seen as disrespecting the social hierarchy.[69] East African customs of war protected specific persons, and the environment, in times of armed conflict.[70] Non-combatants enjoyed protection from direct attacks. Non-combatants included, mediators, envoys, priests, medicine men, the elderly, the disabled, children, diviners, women and the rainmakers.[71] A man who killed a woman would be 'highly despised'.[72]

This Volume has highlighted that customary practice can help interpret the meaning of direct participation, a reoccurring issue in international law. Emily Defina's original and novel research into the on-going warfare in Papua New Guinea shows how customary practice can evolve into modern urban centres.

---

61 Ibid, 136.

62 Ibid, 137.

63 Wayne E. Lee, 'Eastern Native American Laws of War' in Samuel White (ed.) *The Laws of Yesterday's Wars Volume II* (Brill Nijhoff, 2022) 146–173.

64 Ibid, 172.

65 Ibid, 175.

66 Anna Kretowicz, 'Japanese Laws of War' in Samuel White (ed.) *The Laws of Yesterday's Wars Volume II* (Brill Nijhoff, 2022) 183, 208.

67 Ibid, 208.

68 Ibid, 208.

69 Ibid, 208.

70 Kenneth Mutuma and Eve Massingham, 'East African Laws of War' in Samuel White (ed.) *The Laws of Yesterday's Wars Volume II* (Brill Nijhoff, 2022) 214, 217.

71 Ibid, 217.

72 Ibid, 218.

She notes that

> Two communities mentioned that killing in cities and towns is permissible since these are public places. In general, people who do not belong to warring parties are not targeted. However, consistent with the approach taken to women and children from fighting communities, the expectation is that *they will leave the battlefield.*

Being on the battlefield therefore is sufficient to being directly participatory. This was expanded from further research, where it was held that:

> Schools, health centres and churches did not exist in the pre-colonial era when such traditional beliefs developed. The data gathered by the 2019–2020 ICRC interviews shows that opinions as to whether they can be attacked were sometime divided within communities, but the majority opinion was that they are protected as neutral services that benefit the whole community … *In general, the people that work in these institutions have less protection than the buildings themselves, repeating the pattern of presence on the battlefield legitimating attack.* Teachers or health workers from neutral clans are not usually targeted, but they are expected to leave the battlefield when fighting begins. If they are from the enemy's community, they can be attacked like any other member of that clan; just two communities said they would give them a warning and the opportunity to leave before attacking them. Pastors and priests have a more protected position, with most communities agreeing that they cannot be attacked.

The customs of Papua New Guinea would suggest then that direct participation can be from both status (being part of an enemy's community) or location. This mirrored the practice of the Mongols, and in particular their treatment of enemies: *The Secret History* is littered with examples of enemy tribes being turned to ash, including all men and children.[73] So too amongst the Iban, participation in hostilities was expected for all except where explicity carved out. Lewis recounts that

> Unggang (an Iban chief) … reached agreement with Chinese traders in the Sarawak river around the start of the nineteenth century, for example: the Chinese could trade pots, shells and beads for *padi*, provided they flew a white flag from their vessels at all times. However, anyone who

73 See p. 38.

> ventured into the river without such a flag, and who was not a Saribas Malay, would be killed and their head taken.[74]

Conversely, the role of the *ankam* for the Malabar coast was to heavily restrict those who were deemed directly participating in hostilities. The *Mamankam* arose to control conflict over appointment of Perumals, who governed on a cycle of twelve years, after which they were expected to stand down for a newly elected monarch. This event was celebrated for 28 days, and on the 28th day, the monarch put down the state sword, and the assembly declared the throne vacant and chose a new king.[75] As Sanoj & Sheena note, direct participation in the *manankam* was open to all but controlled through strict geographic and temporal limitations: contestants would make their way through the monarch's guards and challenge the king on a *Manithara*. As Sanoj & Sheena note, "according to records, as many as 55 Chaver Pada members died in vain attempts in a single day, and this continued until the final day of the Mamankam." Such a conflict resolution made clear who was participating in hostilities, and reduced civilan casualties to nil by conducting the military conflict in a planned location under strict control.

This is all to say that the concept of 'direct participation' shifts according to geography and environment. In cultures with highly stratified warrior cultures – such as the the ethnic groups of now South Sudan, the Mexica, the Ottomans, the knights of chivalry, followers of *bushido*, or participants of the *manakam* – the concept of 'direct participation' was quite narrow. In cultures which were more egalitarian – such as First Nation Australians, the Iban, or the Vikings – the concept was widened. Finally, in environments where there was no strict distinction between citizen and warrior – such as with the Mongols, or in the Highlands of Papua New Guinea – it suffices that being on the battlefield or one's status as an enemy tribe would suffice for 'direct participation'.

In a report on human rights in Colombia, the Inter-American Commission on Human Rights sought to distinguish "direct" from "indirect" participation:

> Civilians whose activities merely support the adverse party's war or military effort or otherwise only indirectly participate in hostilities cannot on these grounds alone be considered combatants. This is because indirect participation, such as selling goods to one or more of the armed parties, expressing sympathy for the cause of one of the parties or, even more

74 See p. 153.

75 Jonathan Duncan, *Transactions of the Literary Society of Bombay* (London: Longman, Hurst et al, 1819), 4–5.

> clearly, failing to act to prevent an incursion by one of the armed parties, does not involve acts of violence which pose an immediate threat of actual harm to the adverse party.[76]

For the most part, this finding is supported by the datasets of the *Laws of Yesterday's Wars* – particularly with stratified societies. What seems less based in cultural practices is retaining protected status whilst providing logistical support.[77]

2 Customs of War Not Supported

It is necessary then to turn to some customary principles of international humanitarian law, that are not supported by the datasets of *The Laws of Yesterday's Wars*. The first is the conflicting prohibition on pillaging (Rule 52) and the acceptance of taking war booty (Rule 49). Specifically, these two rules read:

Rule 49
The parties to the conflict may seize military equipment belonging to an adverse party as war booty.

Rule 52
Pillage is prohibited.

The distinction between the two can be summarised as looting having a military purpose, and pillaging being focused upon private property (or being inherently destructive in nature).[78] This is by no means the only definition – in *Al-Nawar* before Israel's High Court in 1985, Judge Shamgar held that:

> All movable State property captured on the battlefield may be appropriated by the capturing belligerent State as booty of war, this includes arms and ammunition, depots of merchandise, machines, instruments and even cash.

---

76 Inter-American Commission on Human Rights, Third report on human rights in Colombia (*ibid.*, § 811).

77 See generally the *Commentaries* to Rule 6 of the CIHL; see in particular the Rwanda submissions, as well as US targeting rules.

78 *Black's Law Dictionary*, Fifth Edition, West Publishing, St. Paul, Minnesota, 1979, p. 1033.

> All private property actually used for hostile purposes found on the battlefield or in a combat zone may be appropriated by a belligerent State as booty of war.[79]

This definition is therefore wider than just military equipment; it can include 'all moveable property'. It is a particularly wide interpretation of Rule 49, compared to a wide reading of Rule 52 promoted by the ICRC, who in the *Commentaries* define pillage as:

> ... "the forcible taking of private property by an invading or conquering army from the enemy's subjects".[80] The Elements of Crimes of the Statute of the International Criminal Court specifies that the appropriation must be done "for private or personal use".[81] As such, the prohibition of pillage is a specific application of the general principle of law prohibiting theft.

Seizing booty is therefore 'public' and pillage is 'private'. The customary prohibition on the latter is particularly weak from a historical lens, as it fails to accept that pillage was how combatants were often paid for their campaigning. The discussion below revolves around pillaging, of which the customs of diverse cultures does not support its prohibition.

Most early accounts agree that the majority of First Nations conflicts erupted as disputes concerning women. Often conflict arose due to the theft of women (on account of local shortages, when elders accrued a large number). For instance, a man called Waipuldanya recalled that around 1910 there was a surprise raid in which many women were taken:

> The *malanugga-nugga* came in from the coast to raid the Alawa, carrying off our women and killing our men (...) The raiding parties were known as *gulgar*. No more terrifying word existed in the Waliburu language. They descended upon us in hundreds, throwing spears and boomerangs indiscriminately and thrashing about them with nulla-nullas with cracked skulls and limbs.[82]

---

79 *Al Nawar v Minister of Defence et. al.* (Israeli High Court, 574/82) § 39.

80 *Black's Law Dictionary*, Fifth Edition, West Publishing, St. Paul, Minnesota, 1979, p. 1033.

81 Elements of Crimes for the ICC, Pillage as a war crime (ICC Statute, Article 8(2)(b)(xvi) and (e)(v)).

82 Douglas Lockwood, *I, the Aboriginal*, Rigby, Adelaide,1962, pp. 43–44.

The latter incident needs to be understood as part of retribution for past infringements of social etiquettes and law. It should be emphasised that abduction of women in Indigenous Australian society was 'regarded as a crime equivalent to a murder,'[83] meaning relationships between groups needed to be extremely strained for such raids to occur at all. In fact, the unjustified stealing of women was a common reason for full-scale war. So too did trespass often result in pillaging – as certain natural resources occurred in greater abundance within certain tribal territories, prompting jealousies and economic inequality.[84] For instance, conflict arose due to interlopers 'in defiance of the national law, audaciously hunted Emus within the territories' of their neighbours and the 'latter came to demand reparation for the insult offered.'[85] In another instance, relations between the Kukabrak and the Lower Kaurna peoples of South Australia were often strained because "the Kukabrak believed them to monopolise the red ochre deposits."[86] Alfred Howitt witnessed the Dieri people near Lake Eyre make secret, long-distance expeditions to raid red ochre mines, suffering "dangers" and "battles" as they passed through many hostile territories to bring back large "cakes" of the material. Such expeditions comprised "companies of picked men, (who) came prepared to fight their way."[87]

The Mexica were recorded looting slaves, gold, jewels, shields and insignia of rich feathers, clothing and many other things of great value.[88] The creation of wealth through enforcing tribute was the fundamental aspect of Mexica foreign policy – to the extent that the pillaging and plunder of enemy territory would end upon surrender. Should the Carthaginians be required to storm a city, they would not resist the temptation to pillage a city.[89] Accordingly, in the raid of Selinunte, Hannibal permitted his mercenaries to pillage the city. The Roman way of war was only contrasted due to its discipline in pillaging

83 Darmangeat, *Justice and Warfare in Aboriginal Australia*, p. 1570.

84 Lester Hiatt, "Aboriginal Political Life" in *Traditional Aboriginal Society* (Macmillan Publishing, Melbourne, 2nd ed., 1987).

85 Henry Reynolds, *Aboriginal Sovereignty* (Allen & Unwin, 1996) 26.

86 Ronald Berndt & Catherine Berndt, *A World that Was: The Yaraldi of the Murray River and the lakes, South Australia*, (Melbourne University Press/Miegunya Press, Melbourne, 1993), p. 20.

87 Robert Bruce, *Reminiscences of an Old Squatter*, (WK Thomas & Co., Adelaide, 1902), p. 15; T A Masey, "The Red Ochre caves of the Blacks," *Port Augusta Dispatch and Flinders' Advertiser*, 9 June 1882, 3.

88 Samuel White & Ray Kerkhove, 'The Aztecs' in Samuel White (ed.) *Laws of Yesterday's Wars Volume* (Brill Nijhoff, 2021) 69, 81.

89 David Feeny, 'Carthaginian Laws of War' in Samuel White (ed.) *The Laws of Yesterday's Wars Volume II* (Brill Nijhoff, 2022) 45–103.

and looting; leading to the defined term of *urbs direpta*.[90] There was no divide between valid war booty, and invalid pillaging. All property – private or public – was lawfully taken.[91] This was mirrored in the nomadic customs of the steppe (indeed, the confederation of the Mongols was for the purposes of wealth generation)[92] and even off the steppe: see the customs and practices of the Ottomans.[93] So too during the war of the Far North, the Maori forces burnt and looted Kororareka.[94]

This is a customary prohibition on which there is some discrepancies. The first Caliph, Abu Bakr, gave instructions to his army commanders: 'do not cut down fruit-bearing trees or destroy buildings; do no slaughter a sheep or a camel except for food; do not burn or drown palm trees; do not loot; and do not be cowardly'.[95] There was a general prohibition against looting.[96] Accordingly, Muslim soldiers were precluded from stealing an item of war booty before it was divided up.[97] Within the East African context, there were clearly rules to protect certain classes of property – sacred forces, shrines, burial groups, and resources including crops, animals and water sources.[98] This was on 'the premise that people and property fulfilled a social role of prime importance … (for) the survival and continuity of the community'.[99]

Sanoj & Sheena note in their chapter that the "Malabar kingdoms, like other kingdoms of the period, practised pillage, destruction, death of civilians, and targeted sexual violence. During conflicts, it was common practise to destroy captured areas by burning and plundering everything found there."[100] This catalysed the *ankam* and *Mamankam* conflict resolution system which sought to resolve looting and pillage, and promote trade. It can be implied that looting and pillaging, inconsistent with the *ankam,* would have been a breach of

90 Samuel White, 'Roman Laws of War' in Samuel White (ed.) *Laws of Yesterday's Wars Volume II* (Brill Nijhoff, 2022) 110, 115.

91 Ibid.

92 See p. 36.

93 See p. 97.

94 Alexander Gillepsie, 'Maori Laws of War' in Samuel White (ed.) *The Laws of Yesterday's Wars* 45, 46.

95 Ahmed Al-Dawoody, 'Islamic Laws of War' in Samuel White (ed.) *The Laws of Yesterday's Wars Volume II* (Brill Nijhoff, 2022) 126, 138.

96 Ibid, 140.

97 Ibid, 140.

98 Kenneth Mutuma and Eve Massingham, 'East African Laws of War' in Samuel White (ed.) *The Laws of Yesterday's Wars Volume II* (Brill Nijhoff, 2022) 214, 220.

99 Ibid.

100 See p. 133.

custom during the Chera rule.[101] So too in the Highlands of Papua, the groundbreaking study by Emily Defina noted that:

> Interestingly, the property of an outsider may be afforded more protection than their own person, because while a person can leave the battlefield their possessions sometimes cannot. The leaders of one community emphasised that the premises of a timber and plumbing business next to the battlefield of their 2018 fight was not touched by either side. … Similarly, the neutral status of other clans also contributed to protecting some community services, because attacking shared facilities would risk conflict with the neutral party. A tribe from the Southern Highlands province described how a neutral clan set up barriers of logs and branches to protect schools and churches close to the battlefield.[102]

Pragmatism would seem to have kept looting and pillaging in check during tribal warfare in the Highlands. This same pragmatism can be seen behind the Ordinances of the Renaissance period,[103] as well as underpinning the lawfare of the Lieber Code.[104]

However, even from a Eurocentric perspective, the alleged prohibition under customary law is weak. Within Medieval Europe, there were common cries to inform the soldiers of the extent to which they may acquire spoils. The cry of *butin* meant that all spoil was in according to rank; the cry of *prix d'une esguillette* meant strictly equal shares; or the rare *a bonne usance* meant the spoil was each to their own.[105] This mirrored the experience of Scandianavian raiders, whose private and public warfare was driven by wealth generation, with distinct rules governing the distribution of loot and wealth acquired through raids. Loot was distributed by the chiefs of each warband and was distributed according to wealth and rank.[106]

---

101 Reigned between 3rd century BC and 12th century AD, ruling over an area corresponding to modern-day western Tamil Nadu and central Kerala.

102 See p. 23.

103 Kyle Walker, 'The Renaissance' in Samuel White (ed.) *Laws of Yesterday's Wars* (Brill Nijhoff, 2021) 127–150.

104 Christopher Bailey, 'Code of Necessity – Lawfare During the United States Civil War' in Samuel White (ed.) *The Laws of Yesterday's Wars* (Brill Njihoff, 2021) 187–209.

105 Samuel White 'The Late Middle Ages' in Samuel White (ed.) *Laws of Yesterday's Wars* (Brill Nijhoff, 2021) 101, 118.

106 Andrew Butler, 'Viking Laws of War' in Samuel White (ed.) *The Laws of Yesterday's Wars* (Brill Nijhoff, 2021) 150, 166.

As Angeline Lewis notes in discussing *adat* for the Iban, headtaking (being a form of looting) was both a foundation for warfare and part of it.[107] For example, taking a new head was required to end the mourning period for a deceased person, as instructed by the 'spirit-hero *Puntang Raga*.'[108] It also played a role in key parts of the agricultural cycle,[109] and was essential for the status of *raja berani* (wealthy and brave)[110] – the latter an important step in securing a high value bride. The return from a raid with a head was the start of an important ritual process. The returning warriors, if successful, were met with the 'traditional festival of Enchaboh Arong to celebrate the enemies they killed and the loot they had brought home.'

This is all to say that the modern delineation between lawful taking of war booty, and prohibition on pillage/plunder seems to be unfounded in customary international humanitarian law. Whilst some basis for the divide may be found in the rise of professional, paid armed forces it is a stretch of legal history to claim that "the prohibition of pillage is a long-standing rule of customary international law already recognized in the Lieber Code, the Brussels Declaration and the Oxford Manual".[111] That it has been prohibited under the laws of Geneva[112] and the *Rome Statute*[113] is to be applauded; yet its customary status can be questioned.

Sexual Violence (Rule 93)

The final (and most unfortunate) customary principle of the laws of war to be interrogated is the prohibition on sexual violence. Rule 93 states

> Rape and other forms of sexual violence are prohibited.

This includes forced prostitution, sexual assault, and forced. With the exception of forced pregnancy, it is a gender-neutral concept; a crime that breaches human rights law; and one that is characterised by aggression.

Yet it is clear that for a majority of recorded human history, sexual violence has been a tool of warfare. Two-thirds of known First Nations' conflicts

107 See p. 154.
108 'Headhunting,' Vinson and Joanne Sutlive (eds), *Encyclopaedia of Iban Studies,* Vol 2 (Kuching: Tun Jugah Foundation, 2001), p 679.
109 Ibid.
110 See p. 151.
111 Lieber Code, Article 44 (cited in Vol. II, Ch. 16, § 470); Brussels Declaration, Article 18 (*ibid.*, § 471) and Article 39 (*ibid.*, § 472); Oxford Manual, Article 32 (*ibid.*, § 473).
112 Geneva Convention IV, Article 33.
113 ICC Statute, Art 8(2)(b)(xvi).

occurred over women.[114] From this, some cases involved the deliberate taking of women – on account of local shortages, when other elders had accrued significant amounts.[115] While this occurred, taking women was 'regarded as a crime equivalent to murder', and often justified reason for full-scale war.[116] However, during raids, women would be taken captive.[117] Taylor, in providing a series of rules of old custom and Murri law along the Edward River area of North Queensland, found that verbal abuse towards a sister, mother or mother's brother often was a catalyst for conflict.[118] As observed of the Tiwi Peoples of Melville Island, in the Northern Territory, this was due to a couple eloping, after which the husband and his friends would declare war on the group to which the eloping couple had fled, or otherwise attempt a "recovery raid."[119] Wife taking was the principle cause of conflict in Mongol society, until conferedation occurred: indeed, the primary source on steppe life – *The Secret History of the Mongols* – starts with a wife-stealing scene. Modern Highland Papuan conflict is concerned around sexual rights and wife-stealing. So too did the Vikings few their raids as a way to secure sexual access to women.[120]

Sexual violence moreover followed as an implied punishment within European (and wider) siege warfare. The Carthaginians would offer a city to surrender, if they did not accept, a siege would begin.[121] There were no protections for defeated soldiers or non-combatants, following the end of a siege.[122] Accordingly, the Carthaginians were permitted to slaughter or enslave an entire city that had to be taken by force.[123] Similarly, to their Carthaginian neighbours, if the Romans were required to take a city by force, there was no mercy for non-combatants. If terms were not accepted, and the siege was eventually successful, then the specific act of *diripio* would begin. This reflected the practice of spoil distribution: 'when a city was stormed, its booty fell to

114 Ray Kerkhove & Samuel White, 'Indigenous Australian Laws of War' in Samuel White (ed.) *The Laws of Yesterday's Wars* 3, 10.

115 Ibid, 11.

116 Ibid.

117 Ibid, 26.

118 Taylor, J. *Law and Order and Social Control* (1993, unpublished paper held at the Australian Institute of Aboriginal Studies Library, Canberra).

119 Charles William Merton Hart & Arnold Pilling, *The Tiwi of North Australia*, Holt, Rinehart and Winston, New York, 1959, p. 79.

120 Andrew Butler, 'Viking Laws of War' in Samuel White (ed.) *The Laws of Yesterday's Wars* (Brill Nijhoff, 2021) 150–171.

121 David Feeny, 'Carthaginian Laws of War' in Samuel White (ed.) *The Laws of Yesterday's Wars Volume II* (Brill Nijhoff, 2022) 45–103.

122 Ibid, 103.

123 Ibid, 103.

the troops; when surrendered, to the commanders.'[124] To merely translate the term as a Latin concept of systematic sacking of a city fails to capture the brutality intended: Ziolkowski notes that the term originally referred to the act 'to tear apart, to mangle, to rip to pieces'[125] but came later to mean 'to deprive, to take away or to divest, with an emphasis on the unruly and violent part of the act.'[126] Livy highlights this, noting that in 204 BC a Roman garrison treated the inhabitants of a captured town as such:

> They all rob, plunder, beat, wound, slay; they defile matrons, maidens and freeborn boys, dragged from the embrace of parents. Every day our city is captured, ever day it is being plundered (*cotidie capitur urbs nostra, cotidie diripitur*).[127]

This followed wider Islamic, Ottoman, Medieval and Renaissance practices. Sexual violence also characterised colonial expansion, from New Spain to New Holland.

Yet, it is clear that consideration of 'honour' of women was at the forefront of some cultures canvassed in *The Laws of Yesterday's Wars*. For ancient Indian combatants, women were considered a protected class of people.[128] Daughters were not heirs, but only intended for others, so they could not be tortured.[129] Whether torture includes sexual acts is not made clear. However, even when they took up arms, it was considered possible that women could still retain their protection.[130] Accordingly, sexual acts seem unlikely to be permitted. One of the purity expectations of Eastern Native American Warfare precluded the rape of enemy women.[131] Thereby, there appeared to be no equivalent with European soldiers who engaged in rape as a benefit of war. However, adoption was a common function for prisoners, and it is quite settled that adoption was used as a means to replenish tribes' populations.[132] African customs of war

124 Tacitus, *The Histories* (trans K. Wellesley, Lodon, Penguin, 1975) 156.
125 Adam Ziolkowski, '*Urbs Direptia,* Or How the Romans Sacked Cities' in John Rich and Graham Shipley (eds.) *War and Society in the Roman World* (Routledge, 1993) 70.
126 Ibid.
127 Livy, *The History of Rome*, 29.17.15–16.
128 Zuzana Spicova, 'Ancient Indian Laws of War' in Samuel White (ed.) *The Laws of Yesterday's Wars Volume II* (Brill Nijhoff, 2022) 5, 23.
129 Ibid, 23.
130 Ibid, 25.
131 Wayne E. Lee, 'Eastern Native American Laws of War' in Samuel White (ed.) *The Laws of Yesterday's Wars Volume II* (Brill Nijhoff, 2022) 146, 166.
132 Ibid, 174.

protected specific persons, and the environment, in times of armed conflict.[133] Non-combatants enjoyed protection from direct attacks. Non-combatants included, mediators, envoys, priests, medicine men, the elderly, the disabled, children, diviners, women and the rainmakers.[134] A man who killed a woman would be 'highly despised'.[135] Women would not be targeted and were crucial to peace processes,[136] and fell under the adoption framework of kin.

Again, it is to be applauded that even in living memory the explicit prohibition under treaty law of sexual violence in armed conflict has been successfully agitated for. However, its customary status remains opaque. It is an area complicated by quickly evolving treaty law. As recently as 1993, Yugoslavia acknowledged in its report to the Committee on the Elimination of Discrimination Against Women that abuses of women in war zones were crimes contrary to international humanitarian law and apologized for an earlier statement giving the false impression that rape was considered normal behaviour in times of war.[137]

3 The Fundamental Custom

These datasets highlight the folly of the 'straight line history of eternal progression',[138] where a Great White Man (Grotius, Vitoria, Augustine) discovered international law and it was developed progressively into the modern era. For many parts of *European* law, this is without a doubt correct – read the Chapters spread across *The Laws of Yesterday's Wars* on the progression of Roman,[139] Medieval,[140] and Renaissance[141] laws of war and how they shaped

133 Kenneth Mutuma and Eve Massingham, 'East African Laws of War' in Samuel White (ed.) *The Laws of Yesterday's Wars Volume II* (Brill Nijhoff, 2022) 214, 217.

134 Ibid, 217.

135 Ibid, 218.

136 Ibid, 218.

137 Yugoslavia, Statement before the Committee on the Elimination of Discrimination Against Women (*ibid.*, § 1677).

138 Alonso Dunkelberg, 'It's a Trap! Re-Thinking Samuel Moyn's *Humane* Beyond the North Atlantic' (2021) 12 *Journal of International Humanitarian Legal Studies* 345–360.

139 Samuel White, 'Roman Laws of War' in in Samuel White (ed.) *Laws of Yesterday's Wars: Volume II* (Brill Nijhoff, 2021).

140 Samuel White 'The Late Middle Ages' in Samuel White (ed.) *Laws of Yesterday's Wars* (Brill Nijhoff, 2021) 101–127.

141 Kyle Walker, 'The Renaissance' in Samuel White (ed.) *Laws of Yesterday's Wars* (Brill Nijhoff, 2021) 127–150.

the framework of the American Civil War.[142] This 'straight line' can be extrapolated, and explains many of the findings in the CIHL of the ICRC. The risk of this methodology was championed in 1795 by Robert War, when he wrote:

> We expected too much when we contended for the *universality* of the duties laid down by the Codes of the Laws of Nations ... however desirable such universality might be ... what is commonly called the Law of Nations ... is not the Law of *all* Nations but only of particular classes of them; and thus there may be a *different* Law of Nations for *different* parts of the globe.[143]

Ensuring respect for IHL – which Common Article 1 commands, and the ICRC obligates – does not mean we are exempt from critical judgment. Universality does not mean unanimity. It is too far to claim, as some have, that:

> the foundations of international humanitarian law, or at least their equivalents, are thus found in the major cultural systems on our planet: the right to life, the right to physical integrity, the prohibition on slavery, and the right to fair legal treatment.[144]

It is hard to argue that Mongol culture – one of the largest Empires in history – somehow guaranteed the right to life, physical integrity, freedom of body and fair legal treatment. It was characterised by pillaging, summary executions, denial of quarter, sexual violence, hostage taking, and environmental destruction.[145] Yet it did not exist in a legal desert; as Chapter 3 highlighted, underpinning all Mongol conduct was a fundamental custom: the great principle.

The ICRC's *Roots of Restraint* found that the law can play a crucial standard-setting role, but "that encouraging individuals to internalise the values the law represents through socialization is a more durable way of promoting restraint".[146] A continuous cycle of violations of the law appears less likely if the legal norms of IHL are central to an individual's identity and honour. Against this background, identifying the historical and contemporary reference

142 Christopher Bailey, 'Code of Necessity – Lawfare During the United States Civil War' in Samuel White (ed.) *The Laws of Yesterday's Wars* (Brill Njihoff, 2021) 187–209.

143 *Enquiry into the Foundation and History of the Law of Nations in Europe* (London, 1795) 1, xiii – xiv and 169.

144 Marco Sassoli, Atonie Bouvier and Anne Quintin, *How Does Law Protect in War? Vol 1* (ICRC, 3rd edn.) P 6.

145 See p. 33–57.

146 Fiona Terry and Brian McQuinn, *Roots of Restraint in War* (Report, 2018, ICRC), 65.

points for values equivalent to IHL can increase the influence of arguments for restraint.[147]

Across nearly every culture, the fundamental & foundational custom of keeping one's word is apparent. It is the 'pure substance' Pictet was hinting at – the heritage of all mankind. Breaking rules resulted in payback within First Nation Australians; the concept legitimacy and justice – *junkarti* ('straight' in Lardil); *dalgi giban* ('to make even' in Wiradyuri); makaratta ('coming together after a struggle' in Yolngu); *yorrp-ba* ('to fall out and rejoin' in Wagiman); or *warnmala* ('to seek balance' in Pitjantjatjara). Payback provided an exact, tit-for-tat reciprocity for past actions,[148] ensuring equity and helping curb the violence and brutality of warfare. Within New Zealand, the Treaty of Waitangi provided a clear legal framework for humane treatment. The repeated breaches of it during the Maori Wars was recgonised both at the time, and in subsequent formal apologies from the Crown, as being 'unwarranted' and 'unjust'.[149] Maintaining honour upon capture was so fundamental to Mexica warriors that upon their release by Spanish *conquistadors,* the *maltin* (captured foes) 'indignantly rejected the offer of release and demanded to be sacrificed'.[150] For those Scandinavian raiders known to history as Vikings, trickery and deception added to, rather than subtracted from, honour.[151] Yet honour still was core to warfare. The poem *Hávamál,* containing Odin's wisdom, demonstrates this:

> Cattle die, | and kinsmen die,
> And so one dies one's self;
> But a noble name | will never die,
> If good renown one gets.
>
> Cattle die, | and kinsmen die,
> And so one dies one's self;
> One thing now | that never dies,
> The fame of a dead man's deeds.[152]

147 Ibid.

148 Ray Kerkhove & Samuel White, 'Indigenous Australian Laws of War' in Samuel White (ed.) *The Laws of Yesterday's Wars* 3–44.

149 *Ngai Tāmanuhiri Claims Settlement Act 2012*, s 7(2)(g).

150 Diaz, *The True History of the Conquest of New Spain* (Penguin, 2009) 15.

151 Andrew Butler, 'Viking Laws of War' in Samuel White (ed.) *The Laws of Yesterday's Wars* (Brill Nijhoff, 2021) 150–171.

152 *Hávamál*, Verses 77–78 in Henry Adams Bellows, *The Poetic Edda: Translated from the Icelandic with an introduction and notes by Henry Adams Bellows* (The American-Scandinavian Foundation, 1923), 44.

Good renown was fundamental to warfare in the *Mahābhārata,* and as Zuzana notes in Chapter 1, Volume 2, "A just war, *dharmayuddha,* is more about the means of warfare than about the causes of a battle. The most important underlying rule of ancient Indian warfare is the idea of fairness."[153] So too did Carthaginian and Hellenic custom elevate honor in warfare. *Timē* is one manifestation of the fundamental custom. The idea signals a need to retain a certain reputation – for effectiveness, ruthlessness, vengefulness but above all trustworthiness.[154] *Timē* is the idea of credibility; it is the act of generating a reputation, through a strong record, of being credible. For the Romans, it is the concept of *fides publica*; the breach of which was the grievous crime that Julius Caesar was to be recalled and punished for.[155] Qur'anic revelations ensure that conduct in war is not unlimited; it must be fought with credibility and to protect *al-mustaḍʿafīn.*[156] Divine approval, and operating within a framework of rules, is fundamental to those of the Book. Although endemic within the North American continent, Professor Wayne Lee highlights that the blood revenge system (similar to First Nations Australians) curbed violence. This was done through structure (such as the divide between peace and war chiefs) as well as spiritual means.[157] Remaining spiritually pure required abiding by the great principle of honour, and acted as a check against sexual excesses.[158] *Bushido* – the all-encompassing code of conduct for a specific class of warriors in Japan – sought to induce compliance with the great principle across all areas of life.[159] Wider research into African customs of warfare, subsequent to the publication of Dr Mutuma's and Dr Massingham's chapter, has focused on the principle of *Ubuntu* – polylinguistic term that can be roughly translated as "the belief in a universal bond of sharing that connects all humanity", underlying African traditions.[160]

---

153 Zuzana Spicova, 'Ancient Indian Laws of War' in Samuel White (ed.) *The Laws of Yesterday's Wars Volume II* (Brill Nijhoff, 2022) 5–45.

154 David Feeny, 'Carthaginian Laws of War' in Samuel White (ed.) *The Laws of Yesterday's Wars Volume II* (Brill Nijhoff, 2022) 45–110.

155 Samuel White, 'Roman Laws of War' in Samuel White (ed.) *Laws of Yesterday's Wars Volume II* (Brill Nijhoff, 2022) 110, 117.

156 Qur'ān 4:75–76.

157 Wayne E. Lee, 'Eastern Native American Laws of War' in Samuel White (ed.) *The Laws of Yesterday's Wars Volume II* (Brill Nijhoff, 2022) 146–183.

158 Ibid, 166.

159 Anna Kretowicz, 'Japanese Laws of War' in Samuel White (ed.) *The Laws of Yesterday's Wars Volume II* (Brill Nijhoff, 2022) 183–214.

160 Kenneth Mutuma and Eve Massingham, 'East African Laws of War' in Samuel White (ed.) *The Laws of Yesterday's Wars Volume II* (Brill Nijhoff, 2022) 214, 214–220.

Within the Highlands of Papua New Guinea, proverbs governing conflict highlight the underlying humanity laws of war sought to achieve: "you live long if you plan the death of a pig, but not if you plan the death of a man".[161] Humans are recognised for the thing that makes them special – their humanity. This is in stark contrast to the Abrahamic concept of de-humanising one's foe. As Jonathan Shay, classicist and combat trauma psychologist notes:

> Twentieth-century nationalism has taken over the biblical tendency to measure loyalty by how vehemently one dehumanizes the enemy. When American soldiers and their commanders in Vietnam debased the enemy, they echoed very ancient proofs of their faith in God and of their own religious merit. … The Judeo-Christian (and Islamic) world view has triumphed … that dishonouring the enemy now seems natural, virtuous, patriotic, pious.[162]

This was expanded upon in the conclusion to Volume 2; however, its Eurocentricity is reinforced through this Volume. Chenggis' *anda,* Jamugha compare his breach of faith as that of an animal:

> What good would I be as your ally?
> I'd only invade your thoughts,
> Like a louse on your collar,
> Like a thorn under your shirt
> I went wrong when I strove to be a better man than my anda,
> It is I whose reached the end of his days.

Honour underpinned the *ankam*, and respect for the 12 year cycle brought a unique form of conflict-resolution along the Malabar coast. Dr Angeline Lewis outlined expertly the concept of *adat,* the importance of which cannot be understanded. The Malay idiom '*biar mati anak, jangan mati* adat' [better your children die than your *adat*] shows the extent to which *adat* is important to Malay people.[163] To this end, Rule 144 of the ICRC CIHL study seems clearly based in custom:

---

161 See p. 15.

162 Jonathan Shay, *Achilles in Vietnam* (Simon & Schuster, 1995) 115.

163 Salihahs Razak and Arba'ie Sujud, 'Penerapan Undang-Undang Adat Terhadap Kesalahan Sahsiah pada Zaman Kesultanan Melayu' [The Application of Customary Laws against Negative Personality Traits during the Malay Sultanate Era] (2016) 2 *EDUCATUM Journal of Social Science* 16, 17.

> States may not encourage violations of international humanitarian law by parties to an armed conflict. They must exert their influence, to the degree possible, to stop violations of international humanitarian law.

Such a customary principle is based upon Common Article 1, highlighted in the Introduction to this Volume. Modern international humanitarian law demonstrates a constant, consistent desire to regulate warfare in increasingly humane ways. There has been a fusion of the laws of Geneva (to protect wounded) and the laws of the Hague (to regulate weapons). History shows, both through individual case studies and clashes of cultures, that rules will always be created to regulate warfare. Fundamental to this is the idea of *pacta sunt servanda*: agreements must be kept. Yet as Stanley Baldwin captured, these conventions will often break down in the test of warfare:

> If a man has a potential weapon and has his back to the wall and is going to be killed, he will use that weapon whatever it is and whatever undertaking he has given about it. Experience has shown us that the stern test of war will break down all conventions.[164]

This philosophical underpinning is core to the idea of sharp war, discussed in Volume 2.[165] Yet what these additional chapters have demonstrated is that the existence of rules, seeking to regulate warfare, is a resilient concept. Whilst intended to challenge the laws of war, this work find itself legitimising their existence through a historical lens; indeed, the very *existence* of rules was core to the concept of warfare. It supports the final proposition then that man indeed "is not a 'wolf to his fellow men' – *homo homini lupus* – as the comedian [Plautus] says, but a fellow."[166]

---

164 Prime Minister Stanley Baldwin, United Kingdom, House of Commons, *Debates* (November 10, 1932) Cols 631–38.

165 Samuel White, 'Conclusion' in Samuel White (ed.) *The Laws of Yesterday's Wars Volume II* (Brill Nijhoff, 2022) 242–255.

166 Vitoria, *Political Writings* (Cambridge University Press, 2012) 278.

General Index

www.ingramcontent.com/pod-product-compliance
Lightning Source LLC
Chambersburg PA
CBHW071227230926
51849CB00001B/44
* 9 7 8 9 0 0 4 5 1 2 5 5 9 *